MARKETPLACE OF THE GODS

MARKETPLACE OF THE GODS

How Economics Explains Religion

LARRY WITHAM

OXFORD

UNIVERSITY PRESS

2010

OXFORD

UNIVERSITY PRESS

Oxford University Press, Inc., publishes works that further
Oxford University's objective of excellence
in research, scholarship, and education.

Oxford   New York
Auckland   Cape Town   Dar es Salaam   Hong Kong   Karachi
Kuala Lumpur   Madrid   Melbourne   Mexico City   Nairobi
New Delhi   Shanghai   Taipei   Toronto

With offices in
Argentina   Austria   Brazil   Chile   Czech Republic   France   Greece
Guatemala   Hungary   Italy   Japan Poland   Portugal   Singapore
South Korea   Switzerland   Thailand   Turkey   Ukraine   Vietnam

Published by Oxford University Press, Inc.
198 Madison Avenue, New York, NY 10016

www.oup.com

Oxford is a registered trademark of Oxford University Press

Library of Congress Cataloging-in-Publication Data
Witham, Larry, 1952–
Marketplace of the gods : how economics explains religion / Larry Witham.
p. cm.
Includes bibliographical references and index.
ISBN 978-0-19-539475-7
1. Economics—Religious aspects.
2. Economics—Religious aspects—Christianity.
3. Economics—Moral and ethical aspects.
4. Religion—Economic aspects. I. Title.
HB72.W585 2010
210—dc22
2009027524

CONTENTS

PREFACE

From first to last, this book will use economic images to talk about religion. Religion will be portrayed as a matter of choosing, consuming, marketing, and competing. In this form of expression, when we see temples or churches on street corners, they are "going concerns." Religious beliefs, by the same token, are goods and services, or they are matters that people invest their lives in, as if valuable stocks.

This is surely not the first time readers have heard religion talked about this way. It is part of our common language, and indeed, economic metaphors are pervasive in sacred scriptures, especially the Bible. But in this narrative, the purpose is very different: it is neither to be cynical about religion nor to be pious about it. This book is the story of a new project in the human sciences. It is being called the "economic view of life," and both economists and sociologists are applying it to all human behavior. This approach is also making new sense of the puzzles and mysteries of religion. Obviously, religion is not exactly like shopping or investing. It is a unique and serious pursuit of beliefs and values. But religion is also a behavior; a way of choosing and acting that says something universal about how human beings have always behaved—and will behave in the future. The economic approach to religion looks for these universal patterns.

Applying an economic approach to religion is not as narrow as it may at first sound. It brings together a variety of viewpoints, from the cool calculations of social science to the warm appreciation of human creativity and foibles. It also takes a respectful look at people and their faiths. This joining of the profane and the sacred, the economic and the religious, is never easy. The attempt to squeeze all human behavior into economic models has been called "economic imperialism," and perhaps rightly so. But over the past thirty years, the "imperialism" has developed enough finesse, good humor, and insight into the study of religion to make a general-interest book such as this possible.

This project has been made easier still by the efforts of some economists and sociologists to come down from the ivory tower and translate their technical words into a language and narrative for the common people. That narrative goes something like this: All people make choices. They calculate cost and benefit, usually seeking the latter. They live under various constraints and conditions in making these choices, including the culture they are born into and the one life they have to live. Despite the diverse nature of these constraints, also called a state of scarcity in life, some of the limits are universal. Everyone faces limits of time—think of train schedules and the grave—and typically of money as well. Finally, human beings live to consume. We do it in the present and make plans to do it in the future.

These principles are so simple that they may seem merely part of the background. But when used to probe life consistently, the economic approach can offer explanations of every behavioral and institutional side of religion, and some belief systems as well. Many economists and sociologists are applying this approach to the puzzles of religion, and these are the puzzles that this book will try to illuminate. They are puzzles about why religions form in human history, and how religious behaviors develop. Some religions thrive and others falter or fail; why is that so? And why do people change—or keep—particular religions? All religions share common organizational elements, yet some are strict and others lenient. In religion, we have certain kinds of behaviors, rituals, and belief systems, but why these and not others? Is the world becoming more or less religious? Since the terrorist attacks of 2001, we are also asking why it is that religion can do such good things but such bad things as well.

Economic philosophers from Adam Smith to Karl Marx have tried to explain religion before. Only since the end of World War II, however, has the economic approach equipped the behavioral sciences with a unique focus, typified since the 1950s by the use of the term *rational choice*. While that term has become a lightning rod, it shares a general approach with other sciences that view human behavior as a question of decisions, exchanges, opportunities, and even games. It is helpful to remember that the Nobel Prize in economics was established only in 1969. Since then, it has been a showcase of attempts by economists to explain human life in general. Prize winners are just as likely to talk about how people plot their relationships, households, risks, and pastimes as to talk about world markets, labor data, and eye-glazing statistical tables on the price of tea in China.

It is easy to make fun of statistical tables, as this book may often seem to do. However, the main character in this drama will unavoidably be "the data." The data—typically numbers or trends, but also facts of history and types of beliefs—are what give flesh and bone to the insights of the economic approach.

Armed with this economic-type theory, researchers in the past few decades have turned their sights on a vast storehouse of data about religion. The data come from all sources, including history and real-life stories, but most important are data from years of national and world surveys on religion. This archive of religion data has reached new heights in the twenty-first century, and it has made the testing of the economic approach possible in many areas of life.

The beliefs of religion are also part of the data. But, refreshingly, the economic approach is not in the business of contesting these. As we all know, doctrines abound when it comes to belief in the supernatural. The Immaculate Conception, the incarnation of Buddha, Muhammad's mystical Night Journey, the revelation of Torah, the afterlife, monotheism, deism, and polytheism—all of these are profound, and all of them are just fine from the economic point of view. In fact, the details of religious belief are mostly beside the point. That is because the economic approach is concerned only with the most basic human incentives—governed by costs and benefits—when it comes to how people relate to gods, to other believers, and to the world.

None of this means that anyone has to "believe" in the economics of religion. To some degree, all science is a leap of faith. Economists and sociologists believe their assumptions and have faith in the laws of statistics and markets. And economics is not without its own mysticism and mysteries. Adam Smith gave us the "invisible hand," Friedrich von Hayek offered "spontaneous order," and their esteemed peers have trafficked in economic concepts such as equilibrium, information flow, aggregates, hidden preferences, shadow prices, and even intuition. Nevertheless, a social science is different from mysticism in that it tests its theories against the real world.

In its best literary offerings, social science builds its case from fascinating case studies, puzzles, and human stories. As this book will show, the economic approach also tests its data and has stories to tell. In this process, researchers look for strong evidence. As human beings, they argue their case rhetorically as well. They enjoy winning an argument. At the same time, the goal is usually not to declare an absolute "proof" of one theory or another, for such a thing is elusive in all science. But the fact remains that some theories tend to work very well. They survive challenges and gather support. Now, in the twenty-first century, the economic approach to religion is beginning to reach that plateau. And at that plateau there is a fresh vista point, a new kind of view of religion.

To describe how we arrived at that vista, this book will follow a structure that may resemble climbing a mountain. We begin with first principles (supplies, maps, and gear) and then move to the first levels. This is where economics looks at individuals and households and how individuals think about religion. The climb eventually moves to higher levels, which would be the larger marketplace and world landscapes of religion. Here we find questions of history, modern change, the theory of secularization, and the future. Our climb up the mountain has a rest stop and canteen at the midpoint: a middle chapter to explain how the economic approach to religion got started. This is a story of people and ideas that, like the rest stop, should not be missed before we get back on the trail. At last, having reached a kind of peak, we will have time to philosophize a bit on how religion shapes economics itself and the good and bad things that religion can do.

For me to make this climb, I've relied on skilled mountain guides. The economic approach to religion has made religion a meeting ground for economists, sociologists, political scientists, and historians, who otherwise tend to hike in separate parks. In this book, a journalist will join the fray. For a quarter of a century I've chronicled the world of religion. In books I've often tied religion with something else: science, politics, law, the professions, history, and philosophy. Now it is economics. If understanding this approach was a steep climb, it was made far easier by those who responded to my interview requests and the many others whose books and articles I've drawn upon in the writing, all of whom I pay homage to in the acknowledgments and notes.

MARKETPLACE OF THE GODS

CHAPTER 1

The Economic Approach

In the aftermath of war, before the Japanese nation could rebuild itself from the ashes, its citizens began to experience a remarkable religious event. Through the late 1940s, they witnessed *kamigami no rasshu awa*, "rush hour of the gods"—a time when two thousand new religious groups sprang up, as if from nowhere.

Given the scope of World War II, the rush hour of religion in Japan hardly stopped the presses, but it has begged for an explanation. The most obvious one is political. Japan's new constitution, issued in 1946, ended state Shintoism and allowed religious freedom. Other explanations abound. The psychologist might argue that the Japanese were dealing with mental stress. The sociologist might say the rush hour was an act of collective solidarity, revealing the general laws of human society, while the anthropologist will appeal to the norms and taboos of a unique culture. Nor can we leave out the theologian. She might say that God, or spiritual forces, came down and moved the hearts of millions of Japanese. When the historian is asked, he can say only that nothing like this had happened in Japan's eventful past.

There may be a simpler and more comprehensive explanation, however, and that is offered by the economic approach to religion. At its simplest, this approach uses market models and metaphors. Accordingly, the emergence of the new political constitution in Japan was actually the end of the Shinto religion's monopoly. The religious market of Japan was deregulated. In response to the new political climate, religious entrepreneurs created 500 new groups and 1,500 others splintered off the old system, all of them offering religious goods and services.[1] This was the supply side of the rush hour, which continued well after the postwar crisis.

The rush hour had a demand side as well. Despite the postwar stress, the Japanese acted rationally by calculating the costs and benefits of joining one religion or another. The variety to choose from had grown, and their choices aimed to maximize the perceived benefits for their lives. They did not rush back to Shintoism, for example, seeking a familiar kind of psychological comfort from the past. Instead, they went religion shopping. Many chose more than one religion, creating a portfolio of investments, not quite knowing which worked best but believing that having a few was better than having just one. That, at least, is how the economic approach to life would explain the rush hour of the gods—and so many other events in religion.

FIVE MORE PUZZLES

Not long after the Puritans hit America's shores in their wooden ships, clutching their Bibles, they set up a system of laws. This included laws against working or selling on Sunday. These blue laws remained on the books of most U.S. states through the 1960s, though by the 1980s they were fast dropping out of sight. If the Puritans had looked for a good time at church on Sundays, Americans after the 1960s had a wide variety of Sabbath options. So a funny thing happened on the way to repeal of the blue laws, according to the economic view. When Americans had more choices on Sunday, what's called the "opportunity cost" of church attendance and Sabbath rest became higher. Other opportunities now competed for consumer attention: the mall, the pub, movies, or a Sunday job. In massive numbers, according to social measurements, Americans made their choice. Across the country, church attendance and contributions dropped.[2] As the economist would say, every choice means forgoing another choice. The one that costs less is typically the one that is chosen.

Travel now to Latin America in the 1970s, a time when the most exciting thing in religion was liberation theology in the Roman Catholic Church. The church had held sway on the continent for four hundred years, but now, in this decade, the bishops of each country began to show puzzling behavior. Some bishops, after years of quiescence, opposed their national dictatorships. Such dramas in Chile, El Salvador, and Brazil captured headlines. On the other hand, bishops in other countries did not lift a finger against the autocrats at a time of Latin American democratization. Why some and not others? As it turns out, the nations whose bishops opposed the dictators were the scene of the most aggressive Protestant proselytizing.[3] Latin American Catholicism had never seen such competition. And in a competitive marketplace, religions must adapt or lose customers. The only way the bishops could retain the rural and poor masses, where the Protestants made inroads, was to oppose the nation's negligent autocrats. The bishops with no grassroots competition held their peace. That, at least, is the economic approach to explaining the theological ferment of the 1970s.

As any theologian can tell us, the world beyond may be eternal, but this world is finite, and that includes the number of hours in a day. The economic view takes this problem of time allocation seriously. The 40 percent of Americans who claim they are at a house of worship each week are sorting out a budget of time and money. They travel, spend time helping, and put money in the donation box—and this is where the puzzle appears. In all voluntary organizations, 20 percent of participants give 80 percent of the funding. At first blush, it might seem obvious that the rich give more and the poor less, but this is not what the numbers suggest. Instead, those who earn less give less money but more time. Those who have less time because of higher earnings and more demands at work tend to contribute money, not time. Wealthier churches hire professional choirs to save time. Poorer churches form their own choirs to save money. Each group is giving, but in a classic trade-off of resources, each is giving what is less costly to give.[4]

Even at an Islamic bank, which claims to be a new kind of religious institution, the bank teller has to be mindful of costs. Islamic banking, which has arisen amid the modern Islamic revival, is said to be a return to the Quran's apparent ban on all interest in making loans. In this interpretation, the Quran requires a lender to share the risk with the borrower, even if the loss of money is great. The incentives are thus backward for a bank. But Islamic banks, it is said, nevertheless must give loans free and accept the losses of failed Muslim businesses. The puzzle, of course, is what incentive this bank has to give loans, and how it could possibly stay in business in the face of few profits and many losses. Under the economic microscope, the answer emerges: instead of charging interest on loans, Islamic banks charge "service fees," a substitute for interest.[5] In other words, whatever the theological packaging of human behavior, such as Islamic banking, it is a safe bet that the same human incentives are at work.

It is several hundred miles, and a great cultural leap, from an Islamic bank in Pakistan to Israel, where the economics of religion finds other universal behaviors. In the streets of Old Jerusalem or modern Tel Aviv, Israelis seem to adhere to many varieties of Judaism. Some wear a modest skullcap, others none at all. Various branches of the ultra-Orthodox differ in their hats, though a black fedora is very common. How could Jews be so different? The economic view provides an answer, and it works as well for a wide variety of sartorial differences, from the head scarves of ardent young Muslim women to the saffron robes of Hare Krishnas, a Hindu evangelistic movement. Like religion, economics also looks at the information that people signal to each other. Signals guide the marketplace. For religion, what people wear and the rules they follow signal whether they are in one group or another. Who is committed and who is not? The signal reveals who can be trusted in the murky business of life.

The new religions of Japan, blue laws, Latin American bishops, church giving, Islamic banking, and religious attire—all these are puzzles solved in new ways by the economic approach to religion. Many more puzzles await us. In many ways, the economic approach to life can seem like common sense. It is more than that, however, for it has arisen out of centuries of thinking about human behavior. Giving due respect to this fact, we should spend a bit more time looking at the whole mystique of economics. It is a world of specific jargon and models. Furthermore, the experts in the new field of the economics of religion have sketched out a certain number of basic principles that they look for.[6] Let's take a quick peek into the mind of the economist.

THE MIND OF THE ECONOMIST

Centuries ago, the Greeks began small when it came to economics. The word we use today is from their term *oikonomik*, "household management." Aristotle may have conceived of the entire community as just one big household (as did Thomas Aquinas later). But modern economics took a distinctly different direction. With the rise of classic economics in the eighteenth century, individual self-interest became a more central focus of economic theory. That spotlight on the individual made thinking about economics a lot easier, at least until it took on another layer of complexity. In the twentieth century economics tried to become a purely mathematical science, much as physics turns real objects into mathematical equations. At this mathematical juncture, economics left ordinary citizens behind. Fortunately, however, the basic concepts of economics have stayed intact and are with us today.

When people feel averse to how economists view the world, it is not only because of the abstruse mathematics. Economics has often reduced us all to the proverbial *Homo economicus*, self-interested calculating machines. In college economics courses, some professors call this Everyman by the name "Max U" (or "Maxine U"). That stands for the economic principle of maximizing utility, or simply getting the most possible benefit out of every situation in life. A later chapter will probe the history of the concept. But for now it is enough to say that it is mostly a caricature. Modern economics was founded by a moral philosopher named Adam Smith, who himself struggled with two kinds of human nature, the Max U and the moral human being. In other words, *Homo economicus* also cooperates with others for mutual benefit. As history illustrates, we are moral beings—usually as *Homo religiosus*—as well as economic animals.

A half century ago, the economic approach took on another feature that stays with us today. It is typified by an idea espoused by the University of Chicago's Milton Friedman. He called it "positive economics." Friedman argued that economics is about adopting a plausible theory and then testing it against the data. He said this at a time when most economics was prescriptive (how to shift money between rich and poor) or simply descriptive (how many cars were purchased). Instead, Friedman offered this alternative: "Economics as a positive science is a body of tentatively accepted generalizations about economic phenomena that can be used to predict the consequences of changes in circumstances." According to Friedman, the origin of a theory does not really matter. It can pop into a person's mind as an insight or be received in a dream, so to speak. "The construction of hypotheses is a creative act of inspiration, intuition, invention; its essence is the vision of something new in familiar material."[7] After that, however, the hypothesis must be relentlessly tested.

A final way to understand the economic approach is to compare it to two other human sciences: sociology and psychology. In contrast to these two, economics has typically claimed to be a more precise science, more like physics than like asking people about their feelings. This accounts for the influence of economic theory, but also its hubris, as economist Mark J. Machina readily concedes: "Many economists are of the opinion that economics has a more impressive scientific track record than [sociology and] anthropology because economists work with numerical variables such as prices, quantities, and income, rather than with qualitative variables like trust, group identification, or loyalty."[8] The same goes for psychology, which is equally difficult to quantify. But for our purposes, we will think of economics not as a supreme science, like physics, but as a middle path between two extremes.

On one extreme is psychology, which looks inside the human mind; on the other extreme is sociology, which investigates human society and culture. Each of these extremes hopes to penetrate a black box of human nature. Black boxes, of course, are those mysterious mechanisms whose inner workings are unknown, but if they can be opened, the next deepest truth can be found. In psychology, the black box is the physical brain and nervous system. Today, cognitive psychology probes how neurons and sections of the brain operate. It looks at how perception is translated into behavior. Indeed, even economists are curious: they are doing brain scans to observe which parts of the brain light up when people make consumer choices or play games of profit and loss.

On the other extreme, sociologists (and anthropologists) try to open the black box of culture. They want to find out how complex social and cultural forces impose themselves on individuals, making them act as they do. Like the number of neurons in the brain, the number of social influences in an individual's lifetime can be many indeed: nature, neighborhood, parents, family, ethnicity, religion, economic status, sex, peer groups, social networks, and on and on.

What the economic approach has tried to do is avoid black boxes altogether. The cause of human behavior may indeed ultimately lie in neurons, or it may ultimately lie in a bundle of sociocultural forces. The economist, however, has little faith that these black boxes can be opened, at least in the economist's professional lifetime.

So the economic approach tries to take a middle path: it makes a simple assumption about the behavior of each individual. The individual seeks to gain more benefits than costs and does this by a roughly rational calculation. This individual—a universal type of human being—also is presumed to know what he or she likes best and is able to compare that with other choices. This, in a nutshell, is the economic approach to *all* human behavior. It avoids having to trace billions of firing neurons by presuming the competent rationality of the person. It also avoids the miasma of culture by focusing on the individual, not on the social forces that are supposedly shaping that person's identity, hopes, and anxieties.

This avoidance of human complexity, both biological and cultural, is not for everybody, especially when economics ventures into such a complex realm as religion. Princeton University's leading sociologist of religion, Robert Wuthnow, not only doubts the rigor of the economic approach but finds it fairly dull. It "fails to illuminate about 90 percent of what I find interesting about religion," he says.[9] For others, and of course for the narrative of this book, the appeal of the economic approach is its relative simplicity.

Economics has swung to its own extremes as well, of course. After it created *Homo economicus*, it tried to reduce this human being to a mathematical entity. But fortunately for us, outside the laboratory economists don't really think people behave like mathematical formulas. Nobelist Vernon Smith, the pioneer of experimental economics, concedes the obvious among laboratory economists who turn people into mathematical robots. "They did that for modeling reasons," he says. "It can't really be that they believed this stuff."[10] As with any science, economists reach for purist models in the same way that physicists speak of frictionless surfaces—which don't exist but are helpful models in doing practical physics.

To return to religion, however, the economic approach is a way to avoid black boxes. One more black box to avoid is theology: the claim to having revealed knowledge about invisible and supernatural things. These claims will be more difficult to adjudicate than even neurons or culture. Most people take such things on faith, and that is all for the good. In the spirit of positive economics, the economics of religion simply accepts that beliefs motivate human behavior. But this behavior is always about costs and benefits. And it can be tested at three levels of our existence: the individual, the group, and the society. In the next section we will see how modern economics has done this in the purely secular sense, and then how these same models can be transferred to the world of religion.

INDIVIDUAL, HOUSEHOLD, MARKET

The economic vision builds upward from the individual to the household, the group, and the wider marketplace. Each of these human units exists in relationship to another, making life a series of exchanges: our decisions lead to our social interactions. The sociologist might speak of exchange networks as the basis for our lives, and while the economic view does not disagree, it has tended to speak of aggregates: the group is an aggregate of individual behaviors, so the safest first step is to master an understanding of individuals. The individual is the basic calculator of costs and benefits, and that is why households, groups, and larger social trends also operate on the cost-benefit principle. The individual thinks about the present and the future; therefore, so do social institutions.

At the individual level, everyone makes the same universal trade-offs, prince and pauper alike. The first universal impulse is to judge the cost and benefit of any action. This may be driven by individuals' different preferences, but the principle is the same. Everyone faces scarcity. There are limits to everything—material goods, time, knowledge, and human energy. The trade-off is about pursuit of the best possible outcome. When something costs more, individuals tend to consume less of that thing. When it costs less, they may turn to it with more frequency. The observer would not be incorrect to say that economists put a great deal of emphasis on the costs in life. The economist will admit as much, and point in particular to the foundational economic idea of opportunity costs in every life.

At one point, the Scottish historian Thomas Carlyle called economics the "dismal science," and while his remark is often misconstrued, the ordinary person may feel the same when economics is always about the cost of things. Oscar Wilde's definition of a cynic is someone who knows the cost of everything but the value of nothing. Actually, Wilde got this wrong, at least for economics. In economic thinking, the value of something can be known only in relationship to something else. After the value is judged, a person chooses one thing rather than an alternative. Every choice includes an opportunity cost—the cost of losing the next best alternative opportunity.

Far from being cynical, this emphasis on cost simply acknowledges that in the scarcity of life the value of something is judged in a context. The value of one thing is related to the value we put on another—there is no cosmic price tag floating in the ether, giving either an absolute value or an absolute price. As we will see, the economic approach to religion is also an exercise in describing something as a benefit (think optimist) or as a cost (think pessimist or realist). But the two always come together. The relatively new innovation in economics is to say that opportunities are not just material things. They are also relationships, social statuses, mental enjoyments, and beliefs. None of these opportunities—material or spiritual—is in infinite supply, in this world at least. When it comes to material scarcity, this gives us the poor of the world. But even the fabulously wealthy cannot escape deprivations of opportunity. For all, happiness and satisfaction can be elusive. Illness and death knock on every door.

In such a world, information about making the best choices can be a commodity as good as gold. The individual is a decision maker based on information. It is at this point, however, that the critics of *Homo economicus* raise the most vociferous doubts. Take the way that the psychologist and sociologist (or anthropologist) might view the economic individual. The psychologist would say that no human brain can possibly know or calculate all the information related to a choice. As a result, human beings typically make irrational decisions—driven by impulse, habit, suggestion, rules of thumb, and imitation of others. Added to that, the sociologist would say that people are shaped by their society and culture. Those public norms are imprinted on individuals, like a stamp on wax, from the moment of birth. One economist describes the contrast in particularly apt terms: "Economics is all about how people make choices. Sociology is all about why they don't have any choices to make."[11]

We will save this debate for the next chapter. But in either case, information is the key to individuals making their way in the world. The search for cognitive information, or the experience of information, is a time-consuming task for the individual. Fortunately, however, we are not alone. In many cases, we can find someone to trust, a source of reliable information. But there is also another helpmate for the individual, who is now operating at the smallest level of microeconomics. The helpmate is the bridge that can be built from the individual to the household, and then to two larger economic groups, which economists call the club and the firm.

The household is a kind of small, controlled marketplace. Within a household, people share their best information. They combine their resources—materials, preferences, talents, and time—to produce what the household itself consumes. This household production aims to maximize household satisfaction, especially in decisions involving how its members make trade-offs between time and money, quantity and quality. In this approach, the household is usually seen as having a common preference, or goal, shared by its members. But economists have also waded into more detail, theorizing how a husband and wife can "bargain" over different preferences, seeking the best possible outcomes.[12] In all, these household choices produce different results when it comes to marriage, child rearing, education, entertainment, and religion. Every household is different—but they are also all the same in trying to maximize the production and consumption of what everyone seems to want: leisure, health, status, intimacy, opportunity, hope, and emotional satisfaction.

For economic intimacy, nothing beats the household as a mediator between the individual and the market. But there is a second tier of mediators, the club and firm. Both of these are ways for participants to produce goods, share risk, and garner the best possible information. In the case of the club, the participants are volunteers who contribute so that the members can enjoy club goods. Like the household, those outside the club are excluded from its benefits. The firm is different: it produces products for general public consumption, and the more it sells, the more the firm and its employees benefit. Larger and more diverse than a household or club, the firm can gather more information, innovate more powerfully, and make collective decisions that maximize larger-scale profits. The firm does not live primarily to achieve interior happiness. It lives to expand its market share and, when possible, achieve a monopoly.

The final territory for the economic view of life is the marketplace itself. In the market, the wills of individuals are played out on the largest and most complex scales. For the entire market, price continues to be the best signal of supply and demand, a kind of information that is simple enough to allow everyone in the marketplace to think in common terms. One of the simplest laws (or beliefs) of this marketplace is that when people trade voluntarily, they all increase their wealth: they are all choosing something they value as better. The other simple law at work is that producers interact with consumers. Supply and demand strike a kind of balance. Amid this so-called equilibrium of the market, firms vie with one another, rising or falling in the process. Some firms rise to have a monopoly and, once there, must persistently struggle to ward off rivals by keeping a tight hold on the best information, innovation, and prices. There are complexities to this marketplace as well—the unintended consequences of individual behaviors. Economists call these consequences "externalities," and they can be both good and bad.

In the market, the only thing larger than the firm is government. Modern governments often step into the market when the externalities produced by one firm have a negative effect on another firm or the general public. Whatever the motive, government, representing the values and police power of a society, sets the rules for the market. The most important rules are property rights: who owns what. More than that, however, the government uses incentive, both positive and negative, to try to shape human behaviors toward particular ends. And as predictably as the sun will rise, individuals and firms in the market will try to use, evade, or manipulate these government rules and incentives to each one's greatest advantage.

ECONOMIC MODELS OF RELIGION

Top to bottom, this economic model can be translated to the world of religion, and it begins with the individual. Most individuals have been born into a world of religion, inculcated first by the family. Over time, children become freer in their responses: they can accept what is given, take on further knowledge, reject a religion, or choose another one. The choice to convert, or to commit "heresy," usually is aided by new information, a new judgment of cost and benefit, or a new production arrangement, such as a political revolution or a marriage. In rarer cases, individuals mix and match their own religious outlooks or, more profoundly, declare a new religion based on a personal revelation. That is the story of founders of new faiths, both successful and failed. As individuals, these proto-founders are the ultimate entrepreneurs in the religious marketplace.

The economic approach cannot discount that any of these individual choices are deep and real. But as a model of behavior, it insists on saying that people act in response to incentives, calculating how to maximize the outcome, either in the present or in the future. Hence, religious choice is "rational." The other important economic idea in the individual's development is the accumulation of human capital, as if money in the bank. In other words, individuals accumulate abilities, preferences, and resources they can draw upon. This capital may well include human religious capital—the knowledge of a religious tradition (personal capital) or beneficial relationships in a religion (social capital). Once this capital begins to accumulate, individuals develop a taste or habit for one religion or another, potentially maximizing their benefits.

The religious habit begins with the consumption of religion in the household, where individuals begin their lifelong journey. The household, by gathering the resources and beliefs of its members, produces beliefs and activities that include the religious life. The household, too, must calculate costs and benefits, for there is never enough time or money or energy in a day. Given these constraints, the household moves toward what it considers to be its maximum satisfaction with its religious choices and the commodities those choices produce, such as meaning, fulfillment, and an explanation of the cosmos.

As long as the benefits outweigh the costs, a household's behaviors will continue, shaping its individual members and producing more human capital (which, for better or worse, some economists call "rational addiction"). The more a habit is nursed, the easier it is to satisfy at a lower cost. Hence, most people stay with the religion of their upbringing. Most switching between traditions, in fact, is a modest leap in habits, not a radical one. By the same token, marriage in a common faith makes the best use of resources; so does sticking with one's native culture (Hindu, Christian, Muslim, or Jewish, for example). In short, human capital seems to matter in religion as much as it does in the job market or in building a bank account.

As history testifies, religion does not end with individuals or households; rather, it forms special organizations. The origin of religious groups will be a topic for later investigation, but for now it can be said that they fit our two aforementioned economic models, the club and the firm.

The religious "club," much like the household, seeks to collectively produce goods for its participants. To obtain these, members must pay a price: the price of commitment, belief, time, and money. Accordingly, the club's integrity is always threatened by free riders, who take benefits without chipping in. Strict religions solve this free rider problem by increasing the cost—ratcheting up demands on morals, dress, rituals, and free time. As we will see, the religious sect in history fits the club model. The sect survives by sending out signals—like market information—of trust and commitment. This club dynamic is pervasive in religious history. On the other hand, religions flush with free riders can certainly grow, but always under the demand for cheaper prices and under the threat of lapsing devotion and decline.

The club may evolve into a firm, which is the analogy for a sect becoming a full-fledged institutional religion. By definition, the religious firm organizes to grow and profit, using all its advantages of size, skill, information, and innovation. As firms, religions use their internal resources to produce products that win the loyalty of greater numbers of people. With a typical structure of priests (or teachers) and laity, the religious firm offers various goods and services. Some are for consumption by members and others are for sale in the marketplace. The religious firm may also produce public goods, such as charity. But as with any firm worth its salt, religious organizations must follow the laws of efficiency, productivity, and growth—in a word, profitability.

In either case, religious groups aid people in dealing with the scarcities and deprivations in life. They help people maximize satisfaction in the consumption of more basic goods: commodities called meaning, special knowledge, fellowship, and optimism about the future. As we shall see, some economists even include something they call salvation goods. By its traditions and testimonies, organized religion assures adherents that the risks of belief are worth taking; the promise of ultimate rewards is certain. In the economic view, religious groups are a venerable source of good and reliable information for making choices. The groups provide strong incentives to have faith.

As with any club or firm, a religion's internal success (efficiency, productivity, satisfaction) determines its fruits in the wider marketplace. At this macro level, religions may grow, split into rival groups, wither away, or become a monopoly. The history of religion is rich with these examples. The marketplace throws light on the rise of cults and sects, the impulse to heresy, and the fate of large denominations and state religions. In his own day, Adam Smith, the father of modern economics, began this sort of marketplace analysis, which is only now being expanded by researchers. In *The Wealth of Nations* (1776), for example, he argued that state-supported monopoly religions, with their entrenched priests and clergy, undermine religious progress. He said that more religious competition—not less—could have helped avoid the religious wars of his epoch.

This religious template of monopoly versus competition can be overlaid on every culture, often helping to explain events and outcomes among religions. In this, the United States offers a vivid, if not typical, example of a free market experience in religious history. In looking at American religion, some have called the free market (or supply-side) approach a "new paradigm."[13] But it remains to be seen what that market model can say about religions in other cultures. The debate also rages on what role the market has played in the apparent secularization of the modern world, on one hand, and in the stubborn persistence of religion everywhere, on the other.

In making its case, the economic view emphasizes the supply side of the marketplace. This is the side where new religious products are presented to consumers. While religion has often been interpreted from the demand side—namely, that people generate new psychological needs for religion—the economic approach presumes fixed desires in the individual consumer. In this view, human preferences begin not with mere tastes, as in a palate for fine food or wine, but with a fundamental appetite for health, status, leisure, well-being, and hope. Individuals search for different products to satisfy these basic wants and needs, and thus the key question becomes: What is the variety offered on the supply side of religion? Broadly speaking, therefore, swings in consumer demand do not stir change in the religious marketplace. Change is driven by new religious supplies—innovations, products, efforts, and revivals, heralded by entrepreneurs and groups of every imaginable variety.

In all these ways, the economic model translates to religion. Its ambition is to explain religion at the levels of the individual, household, group, and marketplace. The scope of interpretation can be large, but in the economic approach, the fulcrum is always the idea that the individual is economically rational. The same must be true in religion for this explanation to work. The rational religious individual, a fiercely debated idea, is worth a fuller look in the next chapter.

CHAPTER 2

Rational People and Religion

For decades, a rite of passage for many college students has been to show up at a campus psychology laboratory to participate in an experiment. In one kind of laboratory, cognitive psychologists present them with puzzles. The students try to figure out numbers, sizes of objects, and what they like most—plain or flavored yogurt, for example. In the end, the psychological experimenters report that people are not rational: they suffer from persistent mistakes in judgment. On other campuses, a different kind of researcher, the experimental economist, seems to find the opposite results. When students are subjected to competitive games for monetary rewards, they act quite rationally. They calculate how to compete or cooperate to increase the reward.

So which is the true case? Are we irrational, as the cognitive psychologist suggests? Or are we rational, as the economist declares? Economics, it turns out, has a bigger stake in this question. If people are not rational, then economic science is not doable. Religion also has a stake in the rationality debate. For centuries, religion has been dismissed as merely an irrational fantasy of human beings. Hence, for religion also, rationality is an important key to its nobility as a human choice. Without the handle of rationality, religion could not be explained any deeper than to say that it is a fog of mysteries. There is another good reason why most people want rationality to win. Despite the seeming prevalence of irrational people, how could proving that irrationality is our deepest nature possibly help the human situation? This debate, full of sound and fury, is of course prone to extremes. But it finally boils down to this: it depends on what we mean by rational.

Since ancient times, philosophers have pointed to rationality as what makes humans different from other animals. Theologians have long made the same argument. The "light of reason" was the divine gift that led humanity to know its proper destiny. This same enthusiasm for reason was adopted by the Enlightenment, which created the foundation for modern human sciences, including economics and psychology. On the eve of the twentieth century, economics had adopted its model of human rationality. For one thing, an image of the rational agent provided an anchor to understand how the actions of countless individuals made the market itself rational. More important still, this image of human action could be put into a mathematical formula.

For many, this caricature of a human agent who could be described by a mathematical formula was laughable, according to the economist Kenneth Arrow. "Hypotheses of rationality have been under attack for empirical falsity almost as long as they have been employed in economics," he says.[1] In the early twentieth century, the economist Thorstein Veblen heaped sarcasm on such an image. Forget rationality, Veblen said, for people act out of hatred and envy. They parade their "conspicuous consumption" before others, and that's what drives an economy. Figures such as Veblen and Sigmund Freud cast great doubt on human reason, preferring to suggest dark and uncontrollable impulses in human nature. Nevertheless, when modern-day psychologists turned to experimentation in quest of a scientific theory about human actions, they did not begin with Freud. They began with the classic economic concept of human behavior: the rational agent.

The two kinds of campus experiments noted above represent this scientific pursuit. If the two approaches are seen as the outer limits of a pendulum swing—swinging to the purely irrational side and then over to pure rationality—then we are clearly outside the real world. The world, and the modern answer to rationality, emerges at a middle point. We will end this chapter endorsing this middle way, but to get there, we need to explore the extremes. In this middle ground, one veteran of the debate in the twentieth century is worth introducing from the start. He is Herbert A. Simon, a pioneering cognitive psychologist and computer expert, and also a winner of the Nobel Prize in economics. His comments are a fair summary of the middle ground. "Everyone agrees that people have reasons for what they do," Simon explained in 1985. "They have motivations, and they use reason (well or badly) to respond to these motivations and reach their goals."[2]

We will look at some of Simon's work below, but for now it is helpful to summarize some of the key ideas he handed down for all future research on human rationality. Simon introduced the concept of rational choice (and the phrase) into the modern discussion. Furthermore, he said that the rationality behind this choosing is a limited rationality, which he called "bounded rationality." The human mind has limits in terms of how much information it can gather and calculate. Finally, Simon handed down a lasting and helpful distinction between objective rationality and subjective rationality.[3]

The first kind can easily be observed. In objective rationality, a person adopts a goal, makes a plan, and carries it out efficiently and consistently. For example, the entrepreneur who opens a business and turns a profit is clearly being rational; the ledger, showing earnings, proves this to be so. If he persists in this behavior, earnings are likely to grow even more. Similarly, if a theology student believes mastery of the Bible brings her closer to God, she will enter theological school. She will persist in the courses on Hebrew and Greek and earn a master of divinity degree. That degree is proof of objective rationality. This is also called utilitarian rationality. In fact, researchers are finding this kind of rational behavior in more than just human beings, for even pigeons and mice set goals and act consistently to achieve them.

However, subjective rationality is another matter, according to Simon. Depending on how a person internally perceives the world—which is hard for outsiders to grasp—that person makes rational choices. Those choices are made in an internal context that psychologists refer to as the mental frames of personal perception. The visions of wealth that dance in the entrepreneur's head, for example, or the Bible student's religious experiences make up a frame through which they perceive the world and take action. The subjective frame of mind may not exactly match reality "out there." The frame may be based on flaws in perception, such as when a man lost in the desert sees a mirage in the distance. Still, according to Simon, within that perception, the human agent calculates what to do—and that is subjective rationality.

At the turn of the twentieth century all this was up for debate, both in economic theory and in religion. It was a particular area of interest to anthropologists, as illustrated in the adventures of British anthropologist Edward Evans-Pritchard, a kind of Indiana Jones of his day. That was a time when the leading intellectuals of Europe had begun to discover and study "primitive" people in other lands. Their first, and presumably obvious, conclusion was that primitive people had an irrational mind. It was wired to be primitive. That is why, for example, such people believed in magic, which was a cognitive error: they perceived causes in the world that did not really exist. For French anthropologist Lucien Lévy-Bruhl, the primitive mind was simply faulty. It was susceptible to false reasoning. As his book *How Natives Think* (1920) explained, these kinds of minds were "pre-logical."[4]

This was the background in the 1930s when the Oxford University anthropologist Edward Evans-Pritchard rode a steamboat hundreds of miles up the Nile River to study the life of the Nuer people of Sudan. He had been studying tribes in the region since the mid-1920s, doing his first research on the Azande people. He tried to understand the logic of each tribal culture, and this invariably included its religion. Unlike the French theorists, who had emphasized collective thinking among primitive peoples, the English had a tradition of viewing the human intellect as autonomous. However, they also viewed the human mind as having evolved in stages, from primitive to modern. That mind advanced from magical thinking to religious thinking and then to scientific rationality.

For a researcher, south Sudan was an unforgiving laboratory. It has only two seasons, dry in winter and drenched with mountain rains in summer, filling the vast swamps that feed the Nile River. These two seasons shaped Nuer life. During the rains, the Nuer migrated to inland villages; in the dry season, they spread out to allow their cattle to graze on the grassy savannahs. It was in such dry seasons between 1930 and 1936 that Evans-Pritchard made landfall, pitched his tent on the shady forest edge of a savannah, and lived with the Nuer. The rains, malaria, and local wars often forced his departure, but in all, he spent a year living among the Nuer people.

The Nuer social system was a kind of "ordered anarchy," according to Evans-Pritchard. Order was found in a system of exchange and accountability that every individual was aware of and behaved according to. They thought logically about the consequences of behavior, which also had a religious dimension. As Evans-Pritchard observed, "The Nuer are of one voice in saying that sooner or later and in one way or another good will follow right conduct and ill will follow wrong conduct."[5] This way of thinking was woven into a society in which the Nuer exchanged things, albeit without specialized labor or a market economy with money. Their sense of cosmic time, moreover, seesawed according to the annual migrations. And their social system was built around a few important tribal objects: cattle, the leader's leopard skin, and a few ritual sticks and bracelets.

Despite this simplicity, Evans-Pritchard argued that thinkers such as Lévy-Bruhl were wrong when they said nonscientific minds, such as the Nuer's, were irrational. Europeans explain rain by meteorology, while African tribes believe gods or ghosts influence rainfall, he wrote in 1934 in the *Bulletin of the Faculty of Arts* at the University of Egypt, where he taught. But that "is no evidence that our brains function differently from their brains. It does not show that we 'think more logically' than savages."[6] When it came to dealing with a god, the Nuer also used logical ways of thinking. The two words they used most to speak of buying, selling, and exchanging (*kok* and *leul*) were the same words used to speak of sacrificing cattle to the supreme spirit. "Sacrifice can be regarded, as Socrates says in the *Euthyphro*, as being in a sense a 'commercial technique,' a way of doing business between gods and men," Evans-Pritchard observed. "A bargain is struck. There is an exchange."[7]

In everyday life and in religion, he found that Nuer individuals used utilitarian logic to get what they wanted and had good reasons for other behaviors. They employed objective rationality and subjective rationality. In the objective realm, their decisions functioned well enough. In the subjective realm, the Nuer lacked scientific knowledge and therefore their perception of reality was limited, but within that, their thoughts and actions were rational, according to

Evans-Pritchard. A question that was still to be solved by modern cognitive psychology was this: in what way does the human mind, not just a "primitive" mind, make regular mistakes in perception? For now, however, Evans-Pritchard concluded that the irrational savage was a creation of Europe's "armchair anthropologists." The Europeans might have had a different conclusion if they had "spent a few weeks among the people about whom they so freely wrote!"[8]

COMPUTERS, MICE, AND RATIONAL CHOICE

World War II overlapped this period of anthropology abroad. This war, and World War I, persuaded Western thinkers that even scientific knowledge does not make people behave rationally. What is rational about carnage that leaves tens of millions dead? Was Freud correct, or is human rationality still a resource to be tapped? This question prompted a new field of study, broadly called "decision theory," to develop in the 1940s.

In this pursuit of level-headed decision making, the two dominant models for rationality turned out to be economics and the new science of computer logic. The 1944 manifesto for the new movement was, logically enough, written by the pioneering computer theorist John von Neumann and an economist, Oskar Morgenstern. Titled *Theory of Games and Economic Behavior*, their highly technical book synthesized the main elements that eventually became game theory, which assumes that individuals calculate costs and benefits fairly well. During the cold war, game theory offered a helpful model to predict the behavior of the West and the Soviet Union regarding nuclear threats, since each side would logically see obvious costs and benefits to any risky military moves—and opt for doing nothing.

But for the behavior of ordinary human beings, the nature of this rationality needed to be tested in order to be understood accurately. So in 1952, the Rand Corporation held a conference in Santa Monica, California, called "The Design of Experiments in Decision Processes"—another benchmark event of this era. One of the young psychologists attending was Herbert Simon. His career would take him from mouse laboratories to observation of chess masters, work with the earliest computer software, and finally robotics. To start off, however, Simon wanted to test whether economic rationality was really at the base of how organisms worked. He reasoned that a mouse, as an organism, should operate similarly to an economic human being. The mouse had a preference (food), a means of judging options (turns in a maze), and basic budget constraints of distance, time, and hunger.

Simon proposed two major amendments to the classical economic theory of rationality, which he had been skeptical about from the beginning. In experiments, the mice proved his skepticism right. So Simon made his first amendment to economic theory by saying, as noted earlier, that rationality is bounded, or limited. Neither the mouse nor the human is a perfect computer. His second amendment struck perhaps more deeply at the heart of the classic economic view, which argued that human beings—at least in mathematical equations—will always try to maximize their benefit. According to Simon, this was highly questionable. When he let the mice run the maze, they stopped at the first choice that satisfied their "aspiration," or hunger. "Organisms adapt well enough to 'satisfice,'" Simon reported. "They do not, in general, 'optimize.'"[9]

Simon is proposing that human beings learn mainly by trial and error. They are not optimizing computers. People exhibit "approximate" rationality, which is their best possible judgment on how to achieve what they want. They often settle for good enough, not the most possible. Indeed, many people may not know what they want or what is available, and after a bit of probing they settle on something that seems satisfactory. This is a major chink in the armor of economic man, Simon explained, at least as it envisions people as all-knowing: "Neither their knowledge nor their powers of calculation allow them to achieve the high level of optimal adaptation of means to ends that is posited in economics." In his 1978 Nobel Prize lecture, he offered bounded rationality as "an alternative to classical omniscient rationality."[10]

COGNITIVE BIAS

As Simon was announcing his theory of bounded rationality, a young Israeli named Daniel Kahneman was earning his degrees in psychology and mathematics, first at Hebrew University and later at the University of California at Berkeley. He returned to Hebrew University in 1961 as a doctor of psychology and teamed up with his senior mentor, Amos Tversky, for nearly two decades of research on how human beings make decisions. This was a crucial question for the Israeli Defense Force, for which they did their early research, but also for the broader field of decision theory: how can experts help political and policy leaders make the best decisions for safety and for the public good? Kahneman, who never lost some of his idealism, notes that egotistical leaders really do not want such advice. But he continued his research just the same.

Already, Tversky had written his own book in the wake of the game theory revolution, titled *Mathematical Psychology*. One of its chapters brought to

Kahneman's attention the classic economic concept of expected utility: how an individual Everyman judges cost and benefit when the future is uncertain. This was an age-old question for merchants who shipped goods. They had to consider the risks of a storm, pirates, or shipwreck and buy insurance that was the best deal no matter what happened. Expected utility was the standard formula. In his gut, however, Kahneman believed the formula was dead wrong. It said something about how human beings calculate that seemed detached from reality.

So Kahneman and Tversky put economic utility theory to the test using students in campus laboratories. By 1979, they had published the last of a series of papers that showed that much about the economic theory of rationality was wrong—more wrong than even Simon had suggested. What Kahneman and Tversky discovered was a consistent cognitive bias in human beings: all the time, they said, people misperceive and misjudge reality. In a way, they had revived the Lévy-Bruhl idea that the human brain is miswired, prone to illogic. Kahneman and Tversky, however, put this in gentler terms. They said that the calculations of life can be so complex that the ordinary person uses various mental filters, categories, or constructs—decision rules—to simplify problems and make decisions that are often simply guesses.

With this work, the idea of frames came into common use when talking about human perception and rationality. Indeed, Kahneman and Tversky made a list of frames that tended to show up in human nature—or at least in their experiments with students, faculty, and professional groups. For example, it was found that people are most motivated by the immediate sense of gain or loss, not by some abstract calculation about the future (expected utility). Related to this, people will choose gain or loss depending on how it is described to them: most will choose the definite outcome of saving two hundred lives rather than the mere probability of saving four hundred lives. They will choose the reverse, however, if the same facts are put in a different kind of sentence.

When it comes to rationality, people don't handle numbers and statistics well, either. In one test, subjects were presented with this problem: "A bat and a ball cost $1.10 in total. The bat costs $1 more than the ball. How much does the ball cost?" The answer is 5¢. But most people answer 10¢, because their minds find it easier to split the amount into 100 and 10, and it seems about right. As Kahneman has summarized, people make decisions by intuitive rules and good guesses, not by correct arithmetic or by computer-like calculation of highest benefit. They use rules of thumb, emotions, convenience, ease of logic, and familiarity to make decisions. Plus, their memories are poor. In his Nobel lecture, Kahneman explained that deep in the brain is a rational power, but that power is often vetoed by intuition and impulse. "People are not accustomed to thinking hard, and are often content to trust a plausible judgment that quickly comes to mind," he said. The rational mind, which in Greek lore was like the chariot rider holding the reins of the three horses of passions, is not really doing that job. In Kahneman's words, the rational mind's "monitoring is normally quite lax, and allows many intuitive judgments to be expressed, including some that are erroneous."[11]

Along the way, Kahneman met a younger colleague, the economist Richard Thaler, who began to apply cognitive experiments to consumer behavior. In 1980, Thaler wrote a paper, "Toward a Positive Theory of Human Choice," that is considered the founding document of the new field of "behavioral economics," which takes into account the frames, or biases, that go along with people making choices in the marketplace. Inevitably, a cottage industry of behavioral economics books was born. It has been typified by writer Malcolm Gladwell's *Blink*, about quick intuitive judgments, and MIT psychologist Dan Ariely's *Predictably Irrational*. Both books are filled with stories of experiments, usually on college students. As Ariely explains, our choices are swayed by how we compare prices, deal with "free" offers, value objects we already own, and give up clear judgments under the pressures of reputation, social settings, and sexual arousal. "We are not noble in reason, not infinite in faculty, and rather weak in apprehension," Ariely concludes.[12]

The year he won the Nobel Prize in economics, Kahneman discussed his work and made a telling point about its goal—to help people learn to make better rational choices. "I never think of myself as having demonstrated irrationality," he recalls. "There is a definition of rationality within the context of economic theory and decision theory more broadly which is a completely unrealistic conception of a human agent. . . . We have been able to show some of the ways that people depart from this ideal of rationality. But this is not irrationality. . . . People are reasonable, they are prudent agents, it's just that the definition of rationality that is used in economic theory is, I think, a very implausible definition."[13]

MATHEMATICAL MAN

How did economics arrive at such a definition? As noted earlier, it was largely a product of an age in science when it was believed that behavior could be put into mathematical formulas. The early English utilitarian philosopher Jeremy Bentham said individuals calculated degrees of pleasure and pain and acted accordingly. In that sense, "I would not say, that even a madman does not calculate," Bentham wrote in his *Principles of Morals and Legislation* (1789).

"Passion calculates, more or less, in every man."[14] This idea of the calculating individual was increasingly turned into a machine-like operation. This is typified by the adoption of the term "margin" from the mathematical method called calculus. In everyday life, according to this new economic formulation, people make rational choices "at the margin"—the point at which an appetite is satiated and one more unit of something is no longer valuable. A cup of water illustrates the margin: the first cup of water is highly valuable to a thirsty man, but the third and fourth cups perhaps have no value at all.

This began the mathematical vision of the economically rational individual trying to achieve utility and maximization by making rational choices at the margin. The English economic reformer Philip Wicksteed called this rational self-interest a "universal and vital force," and thus this mathematical image of the economic agent entered modern textbooks, never to be turned out again. Between Bentham and Wicksteed, writes one critic, "the nineteenth-century clod, Economic Man, with his behavioral traits of insatiable greed and cold-hearted egomania was out, and a 'new' Rational Man was in."[15] It still is in, argue many modern economists, because this model of rational individuals has proven to be more successful than any other model to explain why markets themselves generally behave in rational ways, driven by human choices and by supply and demand.

Despite the findings of cognitive psychology, those who work in the fields of theoretical and experimental economics and game theory continue to argue for a reasonable fit of *Homo economicus* with how the world works. "If you are a theorist, theorists have to prove theorems," says Vernon Smith, who pioneered experimental economics in campus laboratories and won a Nobel Prize in economics the same year as Kahneman. "And you get more mileage out of very simple assumptions about human behavior. But I think it is a mistake to take that any more seriously than to say it's a model with certain assumptions and certain conclusions."[16] Just as physicists don't believe that the surface of a sheet of platinum is perfectly smooth or that the moon is a perfect sphere, economists don't really believe people are computing machines. But both physics and economics use these kinds of simplified models to explain general and complex phenomena.

If the textbook economists have created too abstract an idea of rationality, the tradition of Kahneman, Ariely, and Thaler may have gone too far in the other direction. That is the view of Vernon Smith, at least. "There is this popular interpretation that what the cognitive psychologists are showing is that we are really pretty incompetent as decision makers," Smith says. "Here's the problem. They have focused on the anomalies. Whenever they find violations, they tend to push hard on that." The world of science knows its limits as well, and one of those is that experiments are often set up to find the kinds of results that the experimenter is interested in. There's not enough time in the day, or enough money in the grants, to also conduct a series of counterexperiments to try to destroy the findings.

All in all, however, the cognitive psychologists and experimental economists are reasonable people. They want to find an essential degree of rationality in human behavior. After all, what good is irrationality? As Vernon Smith likes to say, "I think actually Danny [Kahneman] and I are closer on a lot of things than you might suppose." They are close together on other grounds as well: both operate within a historical movement that tries to understand human society by beginning with the individual as the basic unit.

Historically, this is called methodological individualism. It has a long history, perhaps best known in the English tradition of utilitarian philosophers such as Bentham and anthropologists such as Evans-Pritchard, but later elaborated by scientific philosophers such as Karl Popper and also by the so-called Austrian school of economics. For its modern rendition, we can turn to the work of the rational-choice sociologist James Coleman. Like his predecessors, he makes the case that individual rational actors aggregate into larger social groups and phenomena. As Coleman said in 1964, "I will start with an image of man as wholly free: unsocialized, entirely self-interested, not constrained by norms of a system, but only rationally calculating to further his own self interest."[17] Since Bentham's pithy assertions, there has hardly been a more succinct caricature of economic man than Coleman's—but a theoretically helpful caricature nevertheless.

In game theory, which was launched by von Neumann and Morgenstern in the 1940s, this presumption of reliable rationality is still used. According to game theory advocates, it is turning out successful explanations of human behaviors not only in markets but also in politics. Steven Brams, who has applied game theory rationality to politics and the humanities, says that the early hyperrational models, for example, have been modified to account for more complex ideas of rationality, now considering how it operates in specific environments and how it uses emotions and intuitions as tools. In experiments, people who make inferior decisions in one-shot games or tests, for example, quickly learn to make better decisions in follow-up or repeat games. Rationality improves its edge with experience. Moreover, under conditions of stress, surprise, or disorientation, people tend to become cautious and careful thinkers, not irrational. And even when they are not quite so careful, "impulsive can also be rational," Brams says.[18]

The principal idea underlying Gladwell's *Blink*, for example, has been well known in psychology for some time. People do make good snap decisions, either because the brain is hardwired to do so or because experience has trained the mind to pick up important clues fairly quickly, which leads to helpful first impressions. "We are quite capable of making those quick judgments," Brams says. "I and you and most people do it all the time. And I think that's good evidence of rationality." For thirty years in his classrooms at New York University, Brams has challenged his students to come up with evidence of human irrationality, not including mental illness. "I am still looking for good examples," he says. "I just don't think there are many." If a person sets out to commit suicide and succeeds, that's rationality in action—not irrationality. Unfortunately, the same goes for "crazy" terrorists who succeed in their horrific but rational plots.

Although the term "rational choice" was coined by Herbert Simon, a psychologist, it has been given its modern notoriety by the University of Chicago economist Gary Becker. The fact that economics has not given up on rationality was evident in 1992 when Becker was awarded the Nobel Prize in economics for extending "the domain of microeconomic analysis to a wide range of human behavior and interaction, including nonmarket behavior." At first blush, Becker's definition of rationality would seem as rigid as any in the past. "The combined assumptions of maximizing behavior, market equilibrium, and stable preferences, used relentlessly and unflinchingly, form the heart of the economic approach," Becker says.[19]

And indeed, he was unflinching in advocating this approach: "The economic approach is a comprehensive one that is applicable to all human behavior." He applied it to the human experiences of discrimination, education, marriage, crime, addiction, divorce, and fertility. Such a sweep led to charges of "economic imperialism."[20] But Becker's approach had a great influence on younger economists, and he defended it as ultimately helping the field go beyond its preoccupation with how people calculate their consumption of food, cars, clothing, and vacations. "Economists have often taken a very naive, materialistic, narrow approach to preferences and behaviors," he argues in his Nobel lecture. "We do not want to assume that everybody is a perfect calculator. There are limits to our ability to calculate. Broader preferences and bounded rationality are part of a more relevant model of rational behavior."[21] Even when these broader preferences and human limitations are taken into account, Becker has argued, the economic view of life still explains a great deal about human behavior—and probably more than psychology and sociology are able to explain.

RATIONALITY AND RELIGION

Traditionally, those who have studied the religious behaviors of human beings from a social science and psychological point of view have agreed with the ideas represented above by the French anthropologists and the cognitive psychologists.

In the first, religion is seen as a collective enthusiasm that is planted in individual minds, forcing individuals to conform rather than make rational choices. To quote the French sociologist Emile Durkheim in his influential *Elementary Forms of Religious Life* (1912), "The religious forces animating the clan become individualized by incarnating itself in individual consciousness."[22] In the second area, religion has been taken to be a cognitive bias, much as Lévy-Bruhl argued that a primitive brain was miswired. In this approach, human beings use magical thinking, which believes in causes and connections that don't really exist, just as they may decide wrongly that a bat and ball, in Kahneman's mathematical problem, should cost $1 and 10¢, respectively.

It is no wonder, then, that those interested in framing religious behavior differently—as neutral or positive—would draw upon models that acknowledge a great deal of good sense in human choices, since, in fact, most human beings have chosen religious belief and behaviors across human history. The contemporary French sociologist Raymond Boudon, though not writing on religion in particular, has argued for what he calls a cognitive approach to human rationality. He likens this broad approach to Simon's categories of subjective rationality and bounded rationality. Both of these (subjective and bounded) suggest that while in their everyday choices humans do not always master statistics and probability forecasts, they do make plausible conjectures. They have good reasons that other people also can acknowledge as good reasons. As Boudon explains it, the cognitive model is a rational-choice approach to human behavior, but broader than the economic model:

> The "cognitivist" model can be considered a general model, of which the "rational choice model" is a particular case. The "rational choice model" can be defined as the set of explanations in the form: "he did so, because he had good reasons for doing so, these reasons being of the cost-benefit comparison type." The cognitivist model generalizes the "rational choice model" by dropping the final restriction. It can be defined as the set of explanations of the form: "he did so, because he had good reasons for doing so; these reasons can be in some circumstances cost-benefit comparison type, but in other circumstances of other types."[23]

In either case, of course, the ordinary human being is not acting irrationally but with rationality. Boudon has argued that the writings of economically inclined thinkers such as Adam Smith and Alexis de Tocqueville had always recognized that people operate on both these levels, depending on the situation they are addressing. They use cost-benefit logic in some cases and plausible conjectures, theories, and rules of thumb in other cases. This can make the pure mathematical models of economics less useful, since everything is not perfectly calculated in terms of cost and benefit. But the view advocated by Boudon retains human rationality as a commonsense phenomenon shared among groups of people ("there are good reasons he will be elected") and also a rational activity in the marketplace ("I will compare prices when I buy a new car").

From this vantage, laboratory experiments may often be too artificial to judge people's real-world rationality. The experiments often involve complex problem-solving situations, Boudon argues, and they are conducted on individuals, such as students, who are usually "not trained in probability calculus."[24] The Harvard economist Richard Zeckhauser, also skeptical of the experiments, adds that the "subjects may be concerned that the experimenter is working against them," as when ordinary people deal with an auto mechanic or salesperson they do not trust, and thus the subjects employ other, defensive forms of reasoning.[25] That does not make classical economic theory any more accurate in every case, either. But the point is this: tests of cognitive bias can tend to produce their own self-fulfilling prophecies.

For example, says Boudon, a good number of the cognitive psychology studies present doctors or nurses with statistical problems related to illness, populations, and symptoms. Typically, the majority choose the wrong mathematical answers. This shows that they are not expert mathematicians. However, the fact that it is a *collective* mistake also shows that, based on particular signals, the group shared "good reasons" for its collective misjudgment. Boudon points to one study by Kahneman and Tversky that found that doctors believe depressed people are more likely to attempt suicide. In fact, the statistical analysis of raw data does not prove this to be true. Still, the connection between depression and suicide seemed logical to the doctors, based on their experience. "The belief of the physicians is not really false," Boudon says. In many cases of collective error, "beliefs could be explained as being grounded in reasons perceived by the subjects as strong, which the observer can easily understand."[26]

In the field of the economics of religion, the models of choice range across the territory opened up by Simon, Becker, and Boudon. The rational actor who holds religious beliefs and adopts religious behaviors can be doing so under the canopy of "good reasons" or that of "cost and benefit." Both kinds of rationality are trying to solve problems or seek benefits. Either of these offers enough justification to go forward with an economic approach—that is, a rational-choice approach—to religion.

Of course, many of the experts who have studied religion for a lifetime will protest against this economic imperialism, sometimes strongly and other times picking and choosing what is helpful and what is not. The British sociologist of religion James Beckford, for example, welcomes rational choice, but on a limited basis. In the helpful category, Beckford says, rational choice has helped "define religion as rational in so far as its practitioners believe that the associated benefits outweigh the associated costs."[27] But this can only go as far as objective rationality, which observes what believers do and how they do it. The economic approach is also very limited because it cannot open the black box of the mind and soul and explore why religious people experience, believe, and do what they do. To be safe, according to Beckford, rational choice is best applied to the rational action of religious groups: the groups do not have a soul, so to speak, but they rationally calculate the cost and benefit of mobilizing resources, which is much of what religion is all about. The rational mobilization of resources determines, for example, whether religions succeed or fail, grow or diminish.

Other sociologists of religion attack the rational-choice approach for the same basic reason: it cannot get inside the head of the religious believer. The rational-choice model cannot explain deep motives behind human actions, says sociologist James V. Spickard, and if religion is about anything, it's about this deep experience. "Action implies subjectivity, of which the model can give no account," Spickard writes. "A rational-choice model can duplicate the overall structure of a religious marketplace, but it cannot demonstrate that individual people think in market terms."[28]

This concern would agree with the criticism made by Princeton University sociologist Robert Wuthnow, who says that rational choice overlooks the culture that shapes individuals. A culture, or particular religious heritage, shapes the kinds of beliefs people hold and thus the kinds of things that they adjudicate rationally. Not everyone is afraid of hell, for example. "It may be rational to choose a religion that promises eternal life in heaven, for instance, if one is convinced that the alternative is to spend eternity in hell," Wuthnow says. "But the fact that many other people opt for different belief systems makes them no less rational." This can make rationality so broad that it can become meaningless or must be defined in each different cultural context—Christian or Hindu, for example. "Spirituality is sometimes the product of rational choices and sometimes the result of contingencies and influences that involve no choices at all." To wrap up this debate over the role of culture, it is worth quoting the sociologist Christopher G. Ellison, who has a warning for his friends in the rational-choice camp: "Some rational choice models of religious behavior may unduly extract individual decision making and behavior from its social and cultural context."[29]

Once again, the question arises of how much the economic approach to religion wants to open up the two black boxes mentioned in the preface. One black box is the human soul, or its psychology, and in this case religious experience. Anyone who has read William James's *Varieties of Religious Experience* (1901) can appreciate what a wonderful Pandora's box religious psychology can be: the range of human religious experience is vast, often unrepeatable, and told in the words of each person quite differently. Perhaps wisely, the economic approach has shied away from this internal realm and has instead focused on behavior.

The other black box is culture. Obviously, culture influences rational choices. A person born in West Bengal, India, or County Cork, Ireland, for example, has limited choices in religion or food. And only the rare individual in either culture makes the willful decision, against the force of cultural norms, to become a Bengali Catholic or an Irish Hindu. But as mentioned earlier, this is not the main target of the economic approach to religion. Instead, the core of the economic approach is to look at the universal nature of human rationality, applying it to religion. It has shorn away the deep psychology and the cultural complexity, for the most part. But even at this core, we can see two kinds of ways of doing things: one that is more like the economist's approach and one that is more like the sociologist's.

Fortunately, this difference can be personified, for both economists and sociologists are advocates of the rational-choice approach. We can end this chapter by looking at their slight differences, beginning with the economist Laurence R. Iannaccone, a pioneer in the economics of religion. Iannaccone proposes that people do indeed seek to maximize benefit in their choices, including religious choices. For him, this is a powerful tool in describing and explaining religious behaviors. In this model, people making choices in matters of religion are "weighing the costs and benefits of potential actions, and choosing those actions that maximize their net benefits."[30] Iannaccone acknowledges that culture shapes such judgments. Nevertheless, as an economist, he wants his model to achieve mathematical form as well. To do that, human behavior is fruitfully shoehorned into the notion of "maximization on the margin," one of those concepts in economics that continues to dominate modern-day textbooks and economics departments.

For the sociological approach to rational choice, there are no better advocates than Rodney Stark and Roger Finke, who have applied it to the religion topic for years. They like the way Simon and Boudon have fleshed out human rationality. "We prefer a formulation of the rationality axiom that softens and expands the maximization assumption," Stark and Finke write. "Human reasoning is often somewhat unsystematic and 'intuitive,' and that maximization is often only partial and somewhat half-hearted."[31]

For religion, Stark and Finke offer this kind of assumption: "Within the limits of their information and understanding, restricted by available options, guided by their preferences and tastes, humans attempt to make rational choices." That is simply the way an ordinary police detective thinks when he begins to investigate a crime: he presumes a motive and a rational plan behind the foul deeds. After that, a number of personal and cultural factors can explain details of the crime, just as growing up in Ireland or India can explain the Catholic or Hindu context of rational choices about religion. "Suppose we wish to explain why people select one church over another, or why they drop out of a religious movement following an initial period of satisfaction," Stark and Finke explain. "The rationality premise tells us to look for variations in payoffs or satisfactions, but no more than that."[32]

The debate over rationality has not produced a consensus in all the human sciences, though something like what Simon and Boudon offer has created a broad middle ground to study human beings as rational actors. There are still protests against seeing religion itself—its belief in supernatural beings and universal moral laws, for example—as anything but human irrationality in all its glory. In the economic approach to religion, all that truly matters, as illustrated by Evans-Pritchard's evidence of logical minds among the Nuer, Boudon's explanation of "plausible conjecture," and the basic human tendency to seek benefits over costs, is that people are thinking through their religious choices. The campus laboratories where cognitive psychology (Kahneman) and experimental economics (Smith) came of age are not the only test of the human capacity for rationality, with its implications for religion.

Surveys show that a large portion of the world's educated population adheres to religion as a rational and helpful pursuit. When it comes to adopting religion for rational reasons, that is, it is done by professors, college graduates, and even scientists about as much as in the general population. This may be a massive case of cognitive bias, but we may never know for sure, for the theological truths of religion can rarely be proved or disproved (as we can prove the price of a ball and bat). However, the safe bet is that these vast majorities have good reasons for religion. "We may charge these people with error, but it is difficult to accuse them of extraordinary ignorance, irrationality, or mental deficiency," write Stark and Finke. "Religious actions are embedded within their social context, yet they remain the actions of normal individuals possessed of normal tastes, normal perceptions, and a normal dose of rational self-interest."[33]

CHAPTER 3

Life in the Household

For nearly everyone, the family household is the first place where religion is experienced. The home is also the place where the earliest notion of economics—the Greek *oikonomik*—was conceived and analyzed. Whatever else religion and economics do in the wider world, they cannot escape a close encounter in the material and emotional lives of families. Economists, just like novelists and priests, have always been interested in what happens in the household, trying to unravel its mechanics and mysteries.

This is traditionally called family economics. It looks at household incomes, divisions of labor, fertility, and consumption of goods and service. It is also the model that policy forecasters use, for example, when they want to understand how government tax or welfare policies may affect health, income, marriage durability, or educational prospects. In recent decades, however, economists have refined this household analysis and some are applying it to religious consumption as well, from childhood through adulthood, into marriage, and on to the golden years and the end of life.

Public opinion polls should always be taken with a grain of salt. But when asked, just 7 percent of Americans say they were taught "nothing in particular" about religion in their upbringing.[1] In Great Britain, where there is much less religious upbringing, surveys nevertheless find that children are strongly influenced by their parents' religious beliefs and behaviors—or lack of such beliefs and behaviors.[2] In short, the household makes a difference. And the economic approach offers a way to talk about this human domain. When the new economics of the home looks at this setting, it sees production and consumption under one roof. In household economics, the parents produce, the family consumes, and, as the family grows, children also help in the production—as their consumption grows as well.

It has been said that the family is the first school. But in the economic view, it is also the first factory. The factory that produces breakfast cereal has inputs of materials, energy, and labor. Then its outputs are sold to the public. The family factory also needs inputs. The parents, and eventually the children, leave their sanctuary for the marketplace. They obtain raw materials to bring home: food, income, education, experience. Like the cereal factory, the household factory also operates under constraints. It faces limits on resources, the most basic being time and money. But then we reach the big, and obvious, difference between boxes of cereal and families. Unlike the cereal factory, the family consumes the products it produces. The family produces meals, leisure, hobbies, health, education, well-being—and consumes them all.

Of the many things that a household produces and consumes, religion can be among the most important. Arguably, human beings are more inclined to say "I am a Catholic" or "I am a Muslim" than to say "I'm an eater of food and an income earner." Religion, like ethnicity or occupation, ranks high on a person's identity scale. This suggests that the household production of religion shapes individuals and, by the same token, takes a good deal of effort to produce. As noted earlier, this effort is usually focused on a common preference that serves the entire family as a unit. However, life is never so simple—and that is why economists also look closely at how a husband and wife might "bargain" over different preferences. For policy makers, this is typically an issue of how income affects fertility and children, which are top preference issues for mothers.[3] But as we shall see, religion can also be a stronger preference in one of the spouses—and worth bargaining over.

In this household factory, the parents are the floor managers. The children eventually chip in as well. All of them bring home the inputs of religion: instruction, authority figures, rites of passage, role models, social networks, and theological ideas. These are combined with time and money and consumed, presumably because they are valued. Some economists call these consumables "salvation goods." These goods are not eaten, of course, but they are consumed nonetheless—as are leisure, education, and the emotional satisfaction of relationships. The sociologist Andrew Greeley has been more specific. He says that when it comes to religion, families consume its symbols, rituals, community experience, and heritage.[4]

At this point, the concept of household production begins to intersect with another economic interpretation of human development. Through the very experience of gathering resources, organizing them, and consuming them, people are storing up an inventory of who they are. If this were being said of a business, we would say that someone is accumulating capital. Traditionally, capital is money in the bank that can be saved to make future investments, purchases, or profits. The economists could not help themselves, and invariably the qualities that a human being stores up have also become known as capital—human capital. Adam Smith spoke of how human beings accumulate ability. But the British economist Alfred Marshall has handed down the concept a bit more specifically in his textbooks, which have shaped the modern profession. "The most valuable of all capital is that invested in human beings," Marshall wrote in his classic *Principles of Economics*.[5]

When the human capital approach emerged as a rigorous science in the 1950s, its first and best object of study was education. Storing up education, in other words, is like putting money in the bank, even though it may not seem that way for the moment. As any college student can testify, paying high tuition and spending hours in study can at times seem like a total loss of money and time. However, educational investments do pay off considerably. The experience of learning—which is a habit that leads to skills, character, and social networks—can be withdrawn from the human bank account for a lifetime. In the economic approach to religion, family production and consumption of its own religious activity stores up religious human capital that pays out over every stage of life—and, in some theological outlooks, in the afterlife as well.

Another name for human capital is habit. Psychologists and biologists have a way of explaining habit in terms of the physical body and nervous system developing routines, and this is all for the good. But in the economic view, it is also a mental process—a rational choosing of what is most beneficial and what costs less. As noted early, one famous economist has quaintly called this "rational addiction," which is a good or bad state of affairs depending on the object of consumption. We can focus on the good category: after a person invests many years in being a Hindu or Mormon, or in playing tennis or computer games, the rational choice is to continue, since time has been spent mastering this skill and the consumption continues to satisfy the person, or even increase the person's satisfaction. What concerns the economist at this point, however, is the apparent conflict between habit (capital) and tastes. We think of taste when we say, for example, that a person simply "prefers" Chinese food or Toyota cars, "prefers" being an atheist or believing in God.

ACCOUNTING FOR TASTES

Long ago, economists decided that an individual's taste, whether refined or perverse, was nobody else's business. Eventually a Latin phrase entered the economic lexicon that goes like this: *De gustibus non est disputandum*. The phrase is usually translated as "There's no accounting for taste." This seems to contradict the idea that human beings, all born and reared in households, develop what they like based on what the family household produces and consumes. Indeed, the girl born in India develops a love of curry-flavored food. When she arrives in America, now grown and working as a doctor, her preference—her taste, that is—will almost certainly continue to be for curry.

In the economic approach, however, there is an effort to look for deeper inclinations that derive from household nurture and the accumulation of human capital. As advocates of this distinction, the University of Chicago economists Gary Becker and George Stigler took on the topic of taste with, in the view of some, a resounding effect. Becker had been interested in both household production and human capital, especially in his quest to apply economic models to non-market-related behavior. To reconcile some of these concepts, he wanted to argue that human beings have enough in common that their preferences are all about the same.[6] All people want a certain set of basic goods: nutrition, security, material pleasure, status, and well-being, for example.

Human beings, in other words, are fundamentally motivated not by Toyotas or Parisian fashions but by basic needs and rational habits developed from the time of birth. Indeed, a designer dress or a British sports car may satisfy a person's desire for status, but in those cases it is status, not the dress or car, that is the basic good being consumed. Indeed, since tastes cannot be easily accounted for, economists have always preferred to focus on the more basic and simple objects at stake among consumers. As one economist explains, in "regular consumer theory, we are much more prone to classify commodities and define preferences in terms of category schemes like {'fruits,' 'vegetables,' 'grains'} compared to schemes like {'delicious foods,' 'filling foods,' 'unpleasant foods'}."[7] And so it might be with religion—people might see one religion as more delicious or filling than another, but the heart of consumer action lies at a more fundamental level. That is, each person is looking for basic religious nutrition, and its forms are typically determined by the household's experience.

That consumption is also determined by the basic constraints that exist in all human lives. Each person is born in a particular culture, for example. If you are born in the countryside of India or Japan, the available resources are typically Hinduism or Buddhism, respectively. Everyone, moreover, has constraints on time. If a family spends a good deal of time on religious activities, it has less time to seek other kinds of recreation, pursue education, or earn income.

In all these respects, the economic approach presumes that all households are similar in the natural constraints they face, time-wise and culture-wise. The same can be said about household production and accumulation of human capital. The Russian writer Leo Tolstoy famously opened his novel *Anna Karenina* with the aphorism "Happy families are all alike; every unhappy family is unhappy in its own way." From the economic point of view, the phrasing might instead say, "In their limited resources and household trade-offs, families are all alike; but every family accumulates human capital in its own way."

RELIGIOUS CAPITAL

We can all agree that the human capital of a concert violinist might look like this: She is reared in a home where music is all around. She has early lessons and practice, a trained ear, and eventually knowledge of different musicians and styles. She then qualifies for a scholarship to the Juilliard School, where there are professors and colleagues with connections. This leads to a good symphony job, a solo spot, and finally a tour and recording. This might be called human musical capital. As Becker once argued, even a lifelong connoisseur of classical music can accumulate appreciation capital and thus increase his satisfaction (that is, maximize utility) as time goes on.

But how does one accumulate human *religious* capital? First of all, it depends on how human religious capital is defined. The term, which appeared as recently as the 1970s, has bifurcated into two basic approaches. As we will see in later chapters, the definition of human capital has also been influenced by new concepts such as social capital and cultural capital. But for now, we will focus on individual accumulation of religious consumption and look at two kinds of definitions.

The economist Laurence Iannaccone, a student of Becker, has tended to continue the definition that was developed in educational and labor economics. This definition focuses on capital as skill and social connections. So in Iannaccone's view, the learning of doctrine, ritual and organizational structures, and the building of beneficial social networks all count as religious capital. An alternative definition has been offered by two sociologists of religion, Rodney Stark and Roger Finke. They put more emphasis on what is unique about religion compared to other kinds of social groups that provide skills and social connections. Stark and Finke put the case this way: "Religious capital consists of the degree of mastery of and attachment to a particular religious culture." They place a bit more emphasis on emotional attachment and are more mindful of sociology's interest in social and cultural capital, but we shall save that for later.[8]

Over the past thirty years, this concept of human religious capital has been looked at more closely, leading to these finer distinctions. But to understand its basic trajectory, we should go back again to Gary Becker, who worked in remarkable obscurity when he was first honing the concept of human capital as an empirical way to measure how education led to higher incomes. He unloosed his version of this concept in a 1962 article, "Investment in Human Capital," and later a book-length report, *Human Capital*, for the National Bureau of Economic Research. It is essentially the development of this idea in many areas of life that won him the Nobel Prize in economics. As Becker summarized in his Nobel lecture: "In human capital theory, people rationally evaluate the benefits and costs of activities, such as education, training, expenditures on health, migration, and formation of habits that radically alter the way they are."

This turning of warm-blooded and creative families into factories drew a negative reaction, at least at first. "Human capital is so uncontroversial nowadays that it may be difficult to appreciate the hostility in the 1950s and 1960s toward the approach that went with the term," Becker recalls. "The very concept of *human* capital was alleged to be demeaning because it treated people as machines. To approach schooling as an investment rather than a cultural experience was considered unfeeling and extremely narrow." After he published his model of human capital, Becker rapidly followed up with a model of how households are constrained in their use of time and income. He made this case in 1965 with the *Economic Journal* article "A Theory of the Allocation of Time."[9]

Although economics had always spoken about constraints—usually of material and money—Becker introduced the element of time as being just as important. It was a finite quantity and, in the real lives of people, it was directly exchangeable with money, as in the hackneyed phrase "Time is money." Under these constraints, and the need to allocate time, two kinds of families tended to emerge in the Beckerian formulation. One family had higher earnings per hour, so they put their time into the workplace. The other family had lower earnings per hour, so they put more time into taking care of the things they and their families needed. The first family paid for services it needed, such as child care or a gardener, while the second family took care of its own children and cut its own lawn.

The allocation of time also had an impact on the number of children in the family: having more time at home allowed families to have more children. Spending more time at work, Becker showed in social data, led to fewer children and more financial investment in each child. As social scientists have long observed, family size and allocation of time have a lot to do with religious values and behaviors as well. Families in more conservative religious traditions, such as Islam or Protestant evangelicalism, tend to have more children. They divide household labor differently, usually hinging on the woman's role as homemaker. In contrast, the urban Episcopalian family, where the wife is a lawyer and the husband a stockbroker, is likely to have fewer children and spend money, rather than time, on each child by way of day care and tutors. These two kinds of families can easily slide into stereotypes, of course. But they do suggest how time, money, and religion explain households. Each family is seeking the best benefit given the constraints on their available time and income, and this would be reflected also in the household production of religion.

The first to apply Becker's model of time and human capital to religion were the economists Ronald Ehrenberg and Corry Azzi. By the mid-1970s, a growing number of economists were applying Becker's work to such topics as health care and even suicide, evaluating how individuals assess their available costs and benefits in a single lifetime. But Ehrenberg and Azzi decided to ask a different question: what if there are multiple lifetimes, as suggested by the religious doctrine of the afterlife? So they tested the idea that if people invest for this life and the next, it should show up in their lifetime behaviors, such as church attendance and household division of labor. As Ehrenberg, now a leading labor economist, explains:

> Just as investments in education (or human capital) yield financial payoffs, we drew the analogy that investment in religious activities produced religious capital, which would yield payoffs at the end of life. The question of an afterlife is hard for a Jewish economist to conceptualize, since Judaism is a very current-oriented religion with no strong beliefs about an afterlife, but since most Christians (by far the majority religion in the U.S. at the time) did have strong beliefs about an afterlife, it seemed reasonable to assume that [an economic pattern] was out there.[10]

In their article "Household Allocation of Time and Church Attendance" in the *Journal of Political Economy* in 1975, Ehrenberg and Azzi argued that the idea of religious capital and the "salvation motive/consumption motive" made two predictions that seemed verified in social data.[11] In the first place, during high earning periods, men put in more time at work than at church. Women, who by the division of labor had more time, were more active at church. Also, in this high earning period, the household tended to increase financial donations as a substitute for time spent in attending or volunteering at church. Finally, Ehrenberg and Azzi found that as people aged, they increased their "investment" of time in religion because their peak earning years were over and the benefits of the afterlife drew closer. The findings were disputed, of course, since other models have also explained these very well-known trends in American church behavior based on household incomes, sex, and age. But an economic model for household religion had been proposed. The Ehrenberg and Azzi article is routinely credited as being the first modern extension of microeconomics to religion.

The next economist to apply Becker's model of household production to religion was Iannaccone, whose approach differed in one important respect from the assumptions of Ehrenberg and Azzi. They had taken a belief—the afterlife—as something to be invested in for final consumption. However, Iannaccone felt that the Becker model was more strictly looking at habit and the satisfaction that comes with a lifetime of accumulated habit—in this case, human religious capital. That, says Iannaccone, is the key to religious behavior, even if people do believe in immortality. "It's not about the afterlife primarily," he says. "People don't run around claiming they are thinking in terms of the afterlife."[12] Rather, they are behaving in ways that show how the accumulation of religious capital makes participation in religious activities increasingly enjoyable. This is the essence of maximization: an increase of satisfaction and a lowering of costs. Religious beliefs and knowledge of catechisms may be important in long-term satisfaction with a religion, Iannaccone says, but the habit formation is more important over a lifetime. "It's how you are raised in the environment that you are in." His 1990 article "Religious Practice: A Human Capital Approach" became the second benchmark in applying an economic approach to religion.

Ehrenberg and Iannaccone had opened up a new door on household religion. As seen in their two different approaches, the household is a dynamic system of trade-offs, producing and consuming, judging cost and benefit, living for the present and planning for the future. Each household may be located in a different culture, which defines resources and constraints. But after that, the household process functions the same way for everyone.

In regard to the production of religion, we can explore all the possibilities by following the point of view at each age: we begin at childhood, then meet these individuals again as young adults, a time when they make choices about marriage and their own children. With a modicum of humility, the economic approach to religion makes predictions about what will happen at these different ages. It claims to explain, for example, the ages of religious commitment, conversion, and the various degrees of participation in religion. It also claims to explain ratios of attendance to financial contributions, rates of switching among religious traditions, trends in marriage choices—and also, finally, what happens when people get old.

HOUSEHOLDS MAKING TRADE-OFFS

Who can say what an infant, a few weeks or few months old, may experience during an initiation rite in a religious tradition? It may be the cold dab of water or holy oil in a baptism or christening, the smell of incense in a Catholic or Hindu setting, or the warm rumble of assembled voices singing hymns. Whatever the experience, it starts the process of accumulating human religious capital. Psychologists have studied this sturdy world of infant perception, which by its biological nature is inclined to view the world in a religious way. The growing child has a sense of reality having been created and designed. The child also sees objects, such as animals or trees, as persons animated in a similar way to the human beings who first define the child's existence.

Depending on the tradition, children will be exposed to religious services, often in groups with other children, and will begin a process of learning the tradition, whether it is in a Sunday school or a Muslim madrassa. In the Christian traditions where baptism comes only after the age of consent, teens will make their profession of faith in a public display of white robes and splashing water. These are the rites of passage that every culture provides for its youth, and according to the best interpretations of human development, they leave a strong mark in memory and self-conception. As it will turn out, the religious upbringing of the child will become one of the great threads of continuity with the parents.

In comparison, few children today follow the same profession as their parents. Take two examples from Great Britain. One study of modern Anglican bishops, for instance, found that just 6 percent of their children also went into ministry. Most of the clerics' kids became businesspeople, managers, and schoolteachers, but also police officers, artists, lawyers, journalists, and social workers. Still, the carryover of religious affiliation remained strong.[13] The same thing happens when parents are not involved in religion, according to a massive survey of British households. If parents did not consume religion, the children ended up just as unaffiliated. Parents going to church and believing did not by any means guarantee the same in their children, but in ordinary households, the parents' religion, as human religious capital, did mostly rub off on the offspring.

One way to think of the household factory is to consider an elaborate Thanksgiving meal. Money is spent, physical resources are brought into the home, the chef applies time and skill, and the family consumes not only the food but also the good feelings of the event. There may have been other things to do, such as sleep or go to a restaurant. But the available time was dedicated to producing a superb holiday. Religion can be seen the same way. For the American experience, one of the most universal indicators of this investment is household use of the Bible, the basic text for Christianity. Although knowledge of the Bible (Bible literacy) is fairly anemic in the United States, Bible sales and ownership point to how American households produce and consume religion. More than 90 percent of Americans own a Bible, and the average home claims three. In turn, some estimates put Bible sales at nearly a billion dollars a year.

This does not prove that a home is a Bible knowledge factory, of course. But it suggests how religion can be an investment of time and money—an investment in religious capital in the home. According to surveys, Americans of high school age most often cite their church as the source of their Bible knowledge (72 percent), but the home comes in second (40 percent).[14] In combination with the church, the household is making cost-benefit choices about producing religion for family consumption. If the Bible is learned and its precepts practiced in a home, then the parents and children must have a degree of skill in producing and consuming that experience. They must also spend time. The average automobile trip to church these days is equal to one commute to work, according to the U.S. Department of Transportation.[15] In a commuter age, when people live farther and farther from their churches and synagogues, spending the time to travel is a significant investment in household religion.

The home investment can also be illustrated in cultures where religion is more of a household event than something done at church or synagogue, typical in the United States. At the foot of the Himalayas, West Bengal is the most densely populated state in India. It is also a religious marketplace centered on the home. The predominance of bhakti Hinduism, which is more popular and devotional than other forms of Hinduism, is one reason that the number of festivals and temples in West Bengal continues to increase. Trips to a local temple or guru take time—and usually involve leaving a few coins behind.

Despite the great number of temples and festivals, Hinduism in West Bengal is mostly a household event. A survey of its households found that 89 percent of respondents spent money for "performing religious rite at home," which might include household shrines, foods, flowers, incense, gifts, and other accoutrements. Religious expenditure in the average West Bengal household was 2.6 percent of all household expenditure, which otherwise largely went to food, energy, education, medical care, and housing. Again, if a West Bengali spends one or two hours a week, or several rupees a month, on household devotions, that time and money are taken away from other activity (recall, this is the proverbial opportunity cost). The investment is worth the cost, apparently: West Bengal households report several benefits from household religion, including "mental peace," "improve[d] state of health," "financial affluence," and the perpetuation of "family tradition."[16]

The story is not too different in modern Tokyo. On the whole, Japanese do not join religious organizations. If they practice religion, they draw selectively on elements of Buddhism, Shintoism, Taoism, Confucianism, and on occasion even Christianity. They visit shrines on holidays, in times of distress, or to ask for good fortune. Marriages draw on Shinto and Christian tradition, while funerals draw on Buddhist services. However, the primary activity is in the home, where families maintain a small Buddhist shrine, the butsudan. Surveys of Tokyo-area homes show that nearly all extended family groups (90 percent) maintain a butsudan in one member's home. More than half of all nuclear family households also have a shrine.[17]

From the viewpoint of household production, then, religion is mixed with material concerns. Three of these are disposable income, fertility (the number of children), and even the weather. All of these can be related to religion in terms of allocation of time and resources.

In the 1990s, one of the leading team studies of how Americans give money to their churches was faced with a mystery. As with most nonprofits, in churches 20 percent of the people give 80 percent of the donations. This is the "80–20 mystery." As the sociologist Dean Hoge said, "This phenomenon begs for theoretical explanation, especially since it occurs in widely varying situations, from large impersonal parishes of 4000 members down to rural churches of 50." This is the classic "skewed character" of contribution, Hoge added, and it "alerts us that givers are very different from each other."[18] In the household production model, the difference is in how different families trade off time and money. Religious participants who earn more at work will spend less time volunteering at church but will make up for that by higher contributions. Why this pattern comes out 80–20 may be a mystery of statistics. But in the economic view, it hinges on how different families allocate their resources.

Meanwhile, the way that households combine religion and financial resources also throws light on fertility rates—how many children a family has. In this view, household production of religion seems to tell us something about fertility in the strongly Catholic countries of southern Europe, among ultra-Orthodox Jews in Israel, and among Mormons in the United States. After the 1960s, the number of children in Catholic families in Italy, Spain, and Portugal dropped dramatically—and it was not because more women went into the workforce. Rather, the dramatic changes of the Second Vatican Council of 1962–65 led to a decline in the number of nuns and priests, and hence a drop in church-related services available to families: schools, day care, and the rest. With less of this available, Catholic mothers not only stopped going to church as much but also stopped having as many children. Unfortunately for the church as well, "the reduction in Church-supplied services led also to lower levels of religious involvement among Catholic laity," according to this study.[19]

The opposite happened in Israel, where the growing political clout of ultra-Orthodox Jews prompted the government to give their families more subsidies. As a result, the fathers spent more time in religious study and the mothers had more children. In this case of household production of religion, monetary services provided by government, not the religious group itself, allowed Jewish families to focus more time on religion, which included the value of having children. Similarly, the Mormon Church endorses large, loving families as a religious virtue. But when financial support drops away, even Mormons have smaller families. On average, they have larger families than non-Mormons, but the rise and fall in number of children follows the same economic trends that dictate all American fertility rates. Only extra church rewards will motivate having more children, as is often seen among Mormon leaders or wealthy Mormons.[20] In summary, the religious values of a family are bound up in household production, which must consider the balancing of time and money.

Even the weather is something that households factor into religious production. Depending on the weather, churches draw greater or lesser attendance; this is something that leaders of religious congregations have long observed— and fretted over. The economic approach offers a peek at what may be happening. Religious attendance is seasonal, as everybody knows. Most people go to church at Christmas and Easter. They flock to synagogue during the High Holy Days. At other times of year, attendance differs. In one study in sunny California, church attendance drops most during spring and early summer.[21] The good weather, in other words, raises the opportunity costs of going to church. Greater value is placed on outdoor activities, recreation, or spring cleaning. West Cost clergy know the pattern. That is why one pastor said they "pray for rain." In rainy England, the pattern seems opposite: the clergy pray for a break in the rain so people will come out of their homes. In either case, the weather is a material factor in religious behaviors.

"SWITCHING" AND CONVERTING

Each family's household production of religion can have different intensities. The truly devout, presumably, go to church rain or shine. The intensity of religion, moreover, can be seen in how the family uses time and money. It could spend more time at church, or pay for private religious schools and religious summer camps. Either way, the economic approach predicts that the more human religious capital an individual has, the less likely he or she is to switch to a different religion. This, in fact, is what tends to happen. It has prompted church historians to speak of religious affiliation in the Untied States, for example, as "glacial"—it does not move much. "The majority of church members never change denominations," says Kirk Hadaway, who spent a career measuring affiliations. "Further, when Americans do switch, they often remain within the same broad denominational family."[22]

This glacial effect is predicted by the human capital approach. Economists also have another explanation for such stability in consumer choices: in rational economic choices, people often stick with the status quo, what they are used to.[23] Or as Samuel Johnson once said, "To do nothing is within the power of all men." That may be true, but the human capital approach offers insight on why people mostly stay with the religion they were born into: they do so because it becomes more satisfying with time. Familiarity breeds not just comfort but also mastery. When people switch churches, moreover, they tend to join ones with a similar worship style. Those divisions over liturgical similarity typically show up in a person's enduring preference for a "low-church," informal style of religion or a "high-church" style with lots of ritual.[24]

To make a sharp departure from a religion, in turn, is to lose a longtime investment. As Greeley argues, in a church upbringing, a person learns how to participate and "consume" such things as symbols, rituals, community, and heritage. "In the case of each of these benefits there will be considerable cost in giving up their utility," he says. Changing has costs: "It is difficult to learn the rituals, protocols, and doctrines of one religion; why bother learning another when the extra benefit does not seem all that great?"[25]

And yet the typical headline in research on religion is how much people switch—how much they change affiliations and beliefs. Does this destroy the human capital argument? It depends on how we approach the numbers. For example, the 2008 headline on a Pew Forum on Religion and Public Life survey of 35,000 adult Americans was this: "Change." It declared that nearly half (44 percent) "have either switched religious affiliation, moved from being unaffiliated with any religion to being affiliated with a particular faith, or dropped any connection to a specific religious tradition altogether."[26] If one looks at the data differently, however, what stands out is really a lack of change. Most people stick with their tradition.

In traditions that invest more intensely in human religious capital the retention rate is highest. For example, Hindu, Catholic, and Jewish groups lose the least number of adherents over their lifetimes. In America today, 90 percent of Hindus were reared in that tradition, and the same goes for 89 percent of today's Catholics and 85 percent of today's Jews. When Protestants switch, furthermore, they typically move to similar kinds of Protestantism. For example, 84 percent of Protestants surveyed in 2008 said that they were reared as Protestants. They may have changed from Presbyterian to Methodist, or evangelical to Pentecostal. But the Protestant similarity—the human religious capital—seems to dictate a continuity.[27]

For all the main U.S. religious groups, the primary attrition has been into growing alternatives in American religious experience: nonbelief, Buddhism, innovative sects, or so-called New Age spirituality. Switching is an important phenomenon, and it goes hand in hand with the ability of people to apply their critical and free judgments and to make rational decisions about costs and benefits. But the phenomenon of human capital (or habit or inertia) means that the vast majority of people do not change their religion.

Clearly, as a drama, the human capital approach is fairly dull. It does not predict radical upheavals in religion. In modern times, upheaval is what we might expect. That is what happened with the Walceks of Placentia, California, a Catholic family with nine children. They appeared on the cover of *Time* magazine in 1993.[28] From a human capital point of view, all nine, having gone to church and parochial schools, were good candidates to stay Catholic. Yet most of them did not. Emil and Edward "dropped out of church, and stayed out." Mary created her own unstructured worship of "God's creation," and Rosie "drifted into the Hindu-influenced Self-Realization Fellowship." Chris chose Unitarianism, while Theresa sought a Higher Power in a twelve-step program. Ann was about to marry a non-observant Jew but called it off when he turned to observant Orthodoxy. As *Time* reported, these "spiritual journeys" typified the nation's baby boomers.

Through the lens of the Walcek family, human religious capital did not amount to much. But their story illustrates one other insight in the economic approach to religion: if a person is going to convert to a new tradition, it will typically happen in early adulthood. The analogy is with career choices. When they are younger, men and women change careers more often, looking for the one that suits them best. In youth, less capital has been stored up and so less capital is lost with a change. Studies of conversion or apostasy—the conscious choice to accept or reject a particular faith—show that it takes place far more often at a young age. As the economist Iannaccone explains:

> Religious switching, like job changes, will tend to occur early in the life-cycle as people search for the best match between their skills and the context in which they produce religious commodities. Over time the gains from further switching diminish as the potential improvement in matches diminishes and the remaining years in which to capitalize on that improvement decrease, whereas the costs of switching increase, as one accumulates more capital specific to a particular context. Conversions among older people should be very rare.[29]

The stories of change are always interesting. But most of the studies talk about glaciers. Trends in religious affiliation over the past quarter century show "high rates of religious loyalty," says one study, which also confirmed that when "individuals switch religious affiliations, they are much more likely to choose one similar to their original faith."[30] In other words, people tend to select a next affiliation that conserves or maximizes their religious capital.

MARRIAGE AND INTERMARRIAGE

So far we've looked at individuals as children in families or as young adults, but the next test of the economic approach is whether it can explain religion and marriage.

For decades in Canada, the government statistics office had done what the United States has rarely done: it asked Canadians who acquire a marriage licenses their denominational affiliation. In the United States, with its belief in separation of church and state, the census has asked Americans about their religious background only a very few times in the nation's entire history. So Canada is unique in having large amounts of data on this topic, and these show a strong pattern: people tend to marry within their denomination. Lutherans marry Lutherans, and Anglicans, Catholics, Baptists, and Jews tend to do likewise in overwhelming majorities. The one bit of U.S. data that seems to show the same trend was an unpublished census survey in 1957 that included questions about marriage and denomination. While the American scholar who unearthed the 1957 data emphasized that "interreligious mating is much greater than is generally acknowledged," the pattern was still about 80 percent marriage among people of the same religious denominations—about the same as the Canadian statistics and the Pew survey mentioned above.[31]

That 2008 study of 35,000 Americans shows that intermarriage by religion has increased, although not among traditions where religious capital is emphasized or is fairly distinct in a person's upbringing. For example, 81 percent of all married Protestants are married to other Protestants, 78 percent of married Catholics married someone of the same affiliation, and the same goes for 69 percent of Jews. The highest rate of same-faith marriage is among Hindus (90 percent) and Mormons (83 percent), where the household focus on religious capital is presumably higher than in most other faiths.

Among Protestants, black and evangelical Protestants are far more likely to marry in the same faith. This again may be due to a more intense accumulation of religious capital. Just 12 percent of black Protestants marry non-Protestants, for example. The same goes for just 15 percent of evangelicals, who participate in a more intense and orthodox version of Protestantism. The greatest rates of intermarriage are among the growing number of "unaffiliated" Americans.[32] According to the human capital viewpoint, this is what we would expect: if one or both spouses have lower amounts of religious capital, they are more likely to intermarry.

One of the most celebrated marriages in British history was that between Charles Darwin and Emma Wedgwood, given so much attention because of Darwin's revolutionary work on the theory of evolution. The young Darwin had studied theology and intended to become a country parson, but he gave it up. His family and in-laws were hardly that religious, either—Anglican, Unitarian, and agnostic, for the most part. Emma, however, was quite religious. While Charles did not convert to her faith, in his writings on evolution he desperately tried to avoid offending her religious sensibilities. Darwin and his wife married in the Anglican tradition. By this time, Darwin had already completed his seafaring adventures in the Galapagos Islands but was not too long out of his theological studies. Although in time he became a committed agnostic, his marriage to the devout Emma illustrates that they had some common Anglican religious capital going at the time—as the economic approach predicts.

Both Charles and Emma were independently wealthy, so it would be hard to argue that their joint Anglicanism made their household production more efficient. In general, however, a marriage between rival traditions incurs a cost, in the economic view. Secular studies of divorce, for example, show that divorce is more likely between spouses who have different religious backgrounds. On the other hand, belonging to the same religion has practical benefits. When the time comes to have children, for example, the "economy of scale" kicks in for the same-faith couple. It is easier to attend the same church or synagogue, donate to the same cause, and rear children in a single tradition parents agree upon.

Religious intermarriage can indeed be a smashing success. But in the human capital view, it requires a sober look at benefits and costs. One celebrated marriage of our time is that between the celebrity journalists Cokie Roberts (Catholic) and Steven Roberts (Jewish), who told their story in an engaging book, *From This Day Forward*. They testify to the challenges of bridging Catholic and Jewish families, participating in two kinds of religious observances, and rearing children in both religions. The challenge began on the wedding day, as they recount: "Could we really be both, Catholic and Jewish? Could our relations with our parents, and each other, survive the stress? The whole process, painful as it was at times, taught us a great deal about solving problems, showing patience, focusing on what was truly important."[33]

From a strictly economic point of view, marriages that take such a double focus introduce new stresses and inefficiencies. That is why in the economic approach to religion, the prediction is that one spouse will convert to the religion of the other spouse, usually following the spouse who has the strongest commitments and attachments and thus the greatest amount of religious capital. This is a kind of spousal "bargain" over religious preferences, where the stronger preference is followed, perhaps with something else agreed to in return. For all practical purposes, in the Darwin household Charles circumspectly followed Emma—it made for efficient householding. He did not force her to become an agnostic like himself, nor did he emphasize his agnosticism to the point of introducing antagonism into a marriage that, by all accounts, was harmonious. Nor did she insist that he be pious. As a solution, Charles simply remained reticent.

Lesser-known families also follow household efficiencies, argues the economist Iannaccone. "As long as it is costly for different household members to worship in different contexts there will be an advantage to marrying 'within one's faith,'" he says.[34] To evoke Tolstoy again, every family is different in its household chemistry, and this must be especially so in two-faith households. But it is evident that the prevailing trend is to rear children in a single tradition. In contrast, Cokie and Steve Roberts took up a noble challenge. They received letters of praise, they report, but also letters of doubt, such as this: "But if the children are baptized Catholic, then they are not Jewish. Likewise, if they are not baptized, then they are not Catholic."[35]

THE END OF LIFE

When the economic models of Gary Becker were first applied to religion by Ehrenberg (1975) and then Iannaccone (1984), each highlighted a different aspect. Ehrenberg argued that belief in the afterlife was part of the religious capital that people wanted to withdraw from the bank, so to speak, as they aged and came closer to facing death. Iannaccone doubted whether such a belief really matters in storing up human capital. Instead, he argued that religious activity increases in old age because of habit formation—the increased enjoyment of consuming a religion known for a lifetime.

In the years since, both approaches have been used to study how individuals change their religious behavior between youth and old age. What is clear is this: religious activity does increase with age. At the same time, however, it is generally not old people who are having dramatic conversions, either between faiths or from disbelief to belief. True, Cardinal Henry Newman, Malcolm Muggeridge, Tony Blair, and Newt Gingrich all converted to Catholicism late in life, and with a great deal of publicity. But these are the exceptions. According to the human capital approach and the available data, most such dramatic changes occur in the younger years. Meanwhile, higher church attendance by older people is well documented around the world. Taking just one example, the *Field Guide to U.S. Congregations*, an exhaustive survey, found that the average age of worshipers is fifty and the single largest age group in the pews every week (36 percent) is forty-five to sixty-four. One in four worshipers is retired, nearly twice the U.S. national average.[36]

From a purely human capital approach, as seen in Iannaccone, these old-timers are enjoying the fruits of the religious knowledge, skill, and attachments they accrued over a lifetime. They are at the end of the lifelong economic curve of earnings and investments. When rearing children, the couple put a great deal of time into earning money, building the household, and establishing social networks. They had little time for other "leisure" activities, such as church or synagogue. When children leave the nest and couples are in their peak earning years with more free time, an increased investment in religious capital is likely. However, at a certain point saturation is reached and other cost-benefit factors emerge. In old age, earning power goes flat. Declining health can also curtail investment in religious activity.

In other words, this is the pattern that all the social data show in people around the world who have families, earnings, and a religious affiliation—and who are getting older. If Iannaccone puts a focus on consumption satisfaction, the Ehrenberg approach has looked at how people have invested in their religion for a lifetime in expectation of being rewarded in the afterlife. Indeed, Ehrenberg and Azzi suggested that religious investment increased in old age as the time of reckoning approached. This idea strikes most people as plausible, including Iannaccone (though not in his consumption and habit formation model). Facing death is a universal human experience, and every religion has offered what some call an eschatological answer: what happens in the end?

In the United States, mostly among Christians and to a lesser extent among Jews, the afterlife is a chief consideration in religious belief. Interest in the afterlife, according to studies around the world, increases with age. One survey of Catholics and Protestants in the San Francisco Bay area tested the common assumption that approaching death brings anxiety, and anxiety leads people to seek more answers in religion. However, aging people don't necessarily look for doctrinal answers, according to the survey results. They don't become more orthodox, in other words. But they do immerse their minds in preparation for what may come next. They do plan for the next life, but with a caveat, the study said: "The widespread notion that men become increasingly pious as a means of overcoming the ravages of time is true only if piety is carefully defined as private devotionalism and belief in an immortal soul."[37]

This also seems to hold true in West Bengal and Japan, where the aging population has also been studied. In West Bengal, the average expenditure for all types of religious activities increases with age, especially after forty. Religious behaviors of men and women notably shift. Women begin to focus more religious activity at home, since most temples are very crowded or inconvenient to visit. For older men, "the maximum religious expenditure was observed at the place of Guru," or the ashram, according to this study. Men moving toward retirement, in other words, seek the fellowship of male peers in a religious context. Around Tokyo, aging is the strongest determinant of whether a Japanese individual believes in kami (Shinto gods), angel-like buddhas (bodhisattvas), ancestral spirits, the afterlife, or reincarnation. Since Japanese religion is not organizational, people do not rely on it for social support. Near the end of life, however, they draw upon religion's solutions. As one study says, older Japanese "become progressively more religious." Another study sums it up precisely: "Eschatological beliefs increase with age."[38]

According to the human capital approach, however, most human beings are not going to change religions late in life or have deathbed conversions. Habits are already strong. A lifetime of investment has been made. In the case of Charles Darwin, a group of Christian propagandists tried to evoke a quite different picture. For decades, a famous pamphlet circulated in the West telling of Darwin's last-minute conversion to evangelical Christian belief. Historians tracked down the source of the story and showed that the tale, dramatic as it was, could not have been true. From a human capital viewpoint, this makes sense: Darwin would not be likely to make any such dramatic shifts in belief so late in life. His investment in doubt and disbelief had been a great investment indeed.

In this review of the household, the individual and family have been the crux of the matter. The emphasis, however, has been on production and consumption, habit formation, marriages that seek a good amount of efficiency, and lifetime investments that are called in as the sun sets. Intentionally, this approach has not probed into what we will call "bargaining with the gods"— the more detailed cost-and-benefit analysis that is unique to religion. This continues to be a story of upbringing and habit formation. But now that story will look more closely at the ways people hold intellectual beliefs and the ways religious organization teach these ideas. We are not yet at the largest scale, that of the marketplace of religions, but a step before that: the point at which human beings judge the risks of life, their ability to trust others, and the validity of the consumer products called religious belief.

CHAPTER 4

The Gods of Risk

When the Metropolitan Life Insurance Company erected the tallest building in the world in 1909, it had no religious purpose in mind; the Manhattan tower simply testified to Met Life's commitment to staying in business. Even that motive, however, is not too different from what motivated the builders of Salisbury Cathedral. Built in the thirteenth century, Salisbury still boasts the tallest spire in England. For centuries, this massive house of worship has told consumers that Christianity was in business. In fact, the Gothic grandeur of Salisbury inspired the building of another skyscraper in Manhattan, occupied by another major firm, New York Life, which calls it the "cathedral of life insurance."

In more ways than just tall buildings, religion and insurance have a good deal in common. They have a strong parallel in how they speak to the desire for risk aversion in human nature. They also offer guarantees about the future. Cathedrals and skyscrapers house businesses and are vehicles of great art and architecture. But they are also a form of advertising and reputation building. In short, these great buildings instill consumer confidence, which is what consumers need in a world of risk. Every individual faces uncertainties in everyday choices, especially in long-term investments. Religion is no different.

This comparison of the secular insurance industry with the spirituality of religion can be a jarring one. Fortunately, we have an outstanding religious personality to help us make this transition. In seventeenth-century France, Blaise Pascal offered a religious calculation of risk and insurance. While sacred scriptures from the Bible to the Quran have texts about investments and risk, costs and payoffs, Pascal brought it to mathematical perfection.

At age eighteen, Pascal invented a calculating machine for his father, a tax collector. As a young man, he traveled with his worldly friends to the gambling salons of bourgeois France, where he helped them calculate the probabilities of dice rolls. In the end, and in consultation with Pierre de Fermat, Pascal invented probability tables. In dice, for example, one could take the probabilities of rolls with one die, add that to the probabilities of the other die, and calculate possible outcomes when rolling both. Toward the end of his short life, Pascal devoted all his thought to religion. But he left behind the basic method for judging risk used by modern insurance adjustors. They look, for instance, at the number of fires in a decade, deaths per unit of population, and car accidents among teenagers. Then they calculate the probability—that is, the risk—before writing policies on fire, life, and auto insurance.

In his last year, when he was ill, Pascal jotted down the ultimate insurance calculation for religion, now called "Pascal's wager." Pascal was able to offer a precise calculation on the risk of religion because he presumed exact numbers, much as can be done with a 6 on a die or the thirty-eight numbers on a roulette wheel. In religion, Pascal argued, there were only two numbers: either God exists or God does not exist. If God exists, there are only two possible outcomes, heaven or hell.

Faced with these odds, the most rational gamble is belief, Pascal argued. It is not rational, he wrote, to "hoard your life rather than risk it for infinite gain." If God does not exist, the person who wagers on belief merely suffers a small loss of earthly enjoyment, albeit for no reason. But if God does exist, then wagering on disbelief is the worst bet of all, as the choice of disbelief trades a short period of enjoyment in life for eternal punishment in hell. Wagering on God is the better bet: "If you gain, you gain all; if you lose, you lose nothing," Pascal said. "Wager then, without hesitation."

What Pascal did not address, however, was a future of many possible choices. This is the future of uncertainty, which, by definition, offers no numbers that can be calculated. In religious terms, for example, uncertainty would mean that the future is controlled by an unknown number of gods. Life may offer many possible roads to salvation. What is more, there could be many different types of heavens and hells that people will find as their final destinations. Pascal's simple picture is enticing and profound. But in religion, as in much else, life is a combination of numerical risk *and* non-numerical uncertainty. Some things can be calculated. Other things, it seems, must be left to chance or to fate.

To cope with both of these existential concerns, we all look for tools to engage in risk management. Here again, the parallels between economic life and religious life can be striking. In particular, the economic approach to religion can throw light on this similarity in three areas. First is the concept of risk and insurance. Then we turn to how consumers and suppliers try to verify the reliability of goods. Finally, in both economics and religion, human beings are searching for knowledge that allows them to best handle risk, costs, and benefits; when it comes to religion, this is knowledge about the gods, the after-life, and even hell.

RISK AND INSURANCE

Since its founding, the insurance industry has been in search of a particular kind of person: a customer who is risk averse. This is the individual who will pay a premium now to avoid a potential greater loss in the future. All human beings show a significant degree of caution, but risk aversion varies. As police, parents, and psychologists know, young people, age eighteen to twenty-five, make up the age group most prone to risky behavior in regard to drugs, driving, sex, and crime. However, this proneness to risk taking may continue in life. The Wall Street broker working on commission goes out on risky limbs. In contrast, the schoolteacher responsible for a group of children avoids risk at all costs.

The attempt to reduce risk to mathematical formulas, and hence to put it under human control, has been perennial. In the late eighteenth century, the mathematician Daniel Bernoulli tried to offer one formula for how all rational people will make the calculation of risk. While his concept of expected utility is still a textbook example for economics, it is clear that people judge risk in more ways than any single formula can account for. Since the 1970s, an entire industry devoted to risk analysis has arisen. Like Pascal at the gambling table, it has adopted the mathematical approach to calculating probabilities in different scenarios. In these cases, the goal is to lose the least amount of lives or money in a loss situation.

It has become clear, however, that everyone judges risk a little differently. Today, the experts speak of subjective risk, based on how people perceive things. This differs from the objective risk that risk experts calculate in the spirit of Pascal's probability tables. But human perception of risk is not entirely arbitrary. As noted, teenagers take more risks. There is a difference between the sexes also. Women are more averse to risk than men. This could be an outcome of social roles or biology. But whatever the case, for our purposes it is significant that women are more likely to participate in religion as well. Does that mean that religion speaks to risk aversion? Is religion an escape from risk?

There are plenty of examples to the contrary, of course. Martyrs have been torn up by lions, burned alive, and exposed to mobs who are antagonistic to their beliefs. This is definitely risky behavior. Missionaries go to risky locations to spread the good news. In less dramatic terms, religious believers may risk stigma and discrimination to adhere to exotic or minority religions. Even adopting a religious belief system is risky—it may turn out to be wrong after a lifetime of investment. To believe in any religion is to risk disappointment. "Promised rewards may never materialize, the beliefs may prove false, the sacrifices may be for naught," the economist Laurence Iannaccone says.[1] In the economic approach, then, we should look for ways that religious believers try to gain consumer "assurance" of the quality and benefits of a religion, and also consumer "insurance" to take away the risks of future dangers.

For the modern world, the debate on risk took a new turn in 1964. In that year Australia became the first nation to require that cars be fitted with seat belts. Europe soon followed, and in the United States, it was New York State that imposed the first mandatory seat belt laws in the mid-1980s. In the surrounding debate, manufacturers complained of extra cost, libertarians resented government intrusions, and risk experts cited a new calculation problem: how do people behave when they are "insured" by a seat belt?

The overall practical benefit of seat belts has been accepted: they obviously decrease deaths. But who can say how human incentives and risk are working? It has been argued, for example, that when people snap on the belt, they drive more recklessly, since they feel "insured" against risk. Indeed, there is strong statistical evidence that when people drive cars with antilock brakes, airbags, and seat belts they have more accidents but fewer deaths. (This introduces the topic of moral hazard, to which we will turn in a moment.) But the predominant logic used by insurance experts is that people who refuse to use seat belts or who smoke cigarettes are, by nature, risk takers.

In understanding religion and risk, seat belts and smoking have become handy indicators. People who make risky choices when they drive or light up also show a behavioral pattern in regard to religion: they are less involved. These kinds of risk takers attend church less, according to the findings of one study. In this economic calculation, risk takers do not attend church because they put "more value on current earthly activities and [have] less concern with potential future consequences."[2] In this study, certain kinds of people are said to be strongly motivated by momentary satisfactions in life, such as smoking a cigarette or not buckling up. They have, it seems, no interest in the long-term outlook of religion. Economists call this choice of the present over the future "time discounting." In one sense, time discounting means that the consumer simply wants immediate gratification. But in another sense, it means that the consumer is valuing a thing—such as having a dollar—less and less the farther in the future that it can be obtained. By contrast, others prefer delayed gratification. They save for a rainy day.

At least traditionally, religion falls on the side of investing for the future. It counsels restraint in day-to-day gratification. In this sense, of course, religion and economics could not be more different, since the latter generally encourages optimal consumption—you can have it now. But in looking to future rewards, religion sets up a situation of uncertainty. As the study relating church attendance and seat belt use (and smoking) suggests, people treat religion "like other goods that exhibit uncertainty and that provide for a delayed expected future payoff." Some people feel that getting something now is a better bet than an uncertain promise of getting something in the future. This might be an apt description of a teenager. On the other hand, another type of person likes to plan for the future. For example, surveys find that people who go to church tend to be more educated than the general population. When it comes to a time preference, these individuals may be showing a basic liking for investment in the future: putting their time into education *and* into religious participation.

The sociologist Andrew Greeley, who likes the analogy between religion and insurance, makes the case that religion can provide both goods to be consumed in the present and goods that are saved up for the future. In both cases, the opening assumption is an economic one: there is a cost to being a religious person. In that religious choice, an individual faces a great deal of uncertainty, going on faith, as it were, that the religious product is good and reliable. For example, Greeley says, "information regarding the existence of God or the afterlife is notoriously imperfect and does not appreciably improve with time."[4] Still, most people choose a religious explanation of life. They choose it either to insure against an ultimate loss or to lessen damages along the way. Think of taking out fire insurance that will entirely replace a destroyed home. But also think about the insurance investment of installing a sprinkler system, which may help avert greater damage should a fire break out.

For Greeley, belief in God and the afterlife is like fire insurance. But faith also provides an immediate payback, he says, because in the here and now it gives people a sense of meaning and purpose. In economic parlance, faith "raises utility independent of whether the afterlife exists." This practical earthly reward is something that Pascal, for example, left out of his wager, perhaps because his temperament made him see religion as a denial of worldly enjoyment.

Greeley includes earthly satisfaction in the package. He also argues that the insurance analogy can be extended to explain why different people have different levels of religious commitment. With insurance, the more expensive the policy, the greater the coverage. "Faith is costly to maintain," Greeley explains, and some people will be willing to pay more than others. Those who pay more are the highly committed religious people. They will pay the highest price to guarantee eternal salvation. Fortunately, according to human religious capital, that price becomes less of a burden over time. A large amount of religious capital, Greeley says, "lowers the cost of maintaining a given level of faith."[5] Hence, the believer can move up to higher levels of satisfying faith, the cost being less. In many religions, devotees speak of the "joy" of paying the price—perhaps because it becomes easier with practice.

As illustrated in the seat belt problem, insurance can influence human behavior in good and bad ways. That is why the insurance industry has identified the problem of moral hazard. If insurance is handled badly, people may lose their moral compass. They may find it easier, and to their advantage, to behave badly. In all insurance, people move their risk to a third party. In car insurance, it is moved to the underwriter. In religion, the third party is typically God. But once someone feels covered—by the underwriter or by God—what guarantees her good behavior? This is the moral hazard problem. And the high-stakes nature of moral hazard became dramatically apparent to the American public on Monday, March 17, 2008.

That morning, the eminent bank JPMorgan Chase & Co. was used by the U.S. government to bail out Bear Stearns, a New York investment firm that had behaved very badly. To avoid the appearance of a government bailout, JPMorgan agreed to borrow U.S. funds and buy all of Bear Stearns's stock. Essentially, that Monday morning marked the beginning of a panic that sparked the great 2008 stock market crash. It also marked a global debate on moral hazard: should companies such as Bear Stearns be "rewarded" for their incompetence and greed? In the next case, the U.S. government decided that moral hazard was a problem, so it refused to bail out Lehman Brothers, which immediately crashed into bankruptcy on September 10. In the next few days, the global financial situation went into meltdown, so concerns about moral hazard were again put aside. Governments poured billions of dollars into banks that had taken irresponsible risks—perhaps like teenagers.

As this intense period illustrates, judgments of moral hazard can be complex. The same applies to the economics of religion. In one kind of religious system, a lifelong investment in the insurance of the afterlife can certainly motivate moral behavior—and less risky behavior. At first glance, moral hazard would not be a problem. Why is that? Unlike Met Life or New York Life, the underwriter in religion is the supreme being, who can see our behaviors and, it is said, read human hearts. In this view, people insured by God (by way of their faith) would not risk bad behavior. But again, the incentives of insurance are never so easily understood.

In religion, unlike much else in life, there is a doctrine that God offers the world grace, that no matter how badly people behave, they can be forgiven. Some clever car insurance companies advertise that they offer accident forgiveness—say, for a first accident or a minor scrape. But there is nothing like divine forgiveness. So why behave well if all is forgiven? This is the question that one economic interpretation posed to Christian history. In the Middle Ages, for example, the institution of regular confession had become a central practice of Catholicism. With each confession, individuals felt their sin was erased. With this assurance, arguably, they more easily went back to cheating in business and philandering in marriage. In the debate over how Catholic culture shaped early European economics, it has been argued that thanks to confession, it was easy to opt for enjoyments and appetites—gluttony, promiscuity, sloth, and so on—because all could be forgiven.[6]

The point in this economic interpretation is that the Protestants rejected confession and had a different idea of forgiveness. In the classic thesis of the Protestant ethic, this version of Christianity says you are uncertain about ultimate forgiveness, so you behave well daily. Hence, Protestants, especially Calvinists, became superb capitalists and people of business. For Protestants, the only insurance against the future was faith, not works (such as going to confession). But we should also recall that even Protestants varied on these incentives. Martin Luther, for example, told his followers that it was their faith, not their behavior, that endeared them to God. To make his point, he urged them to "sin boldly," because in contrast to lowly sinners, God's ability to clean them up for heaven only amplifies the glory of the Creator.

On the whole, however, religions have offered precepts that included a kind of insurance. As the Bible succinctly puts it, people reap what they sow. That is why in addition to insurance, religions provide moral guidelines, much as New York State imposed seat belt laws. In religion, the guidelines range from the Ten Commandments and the Sermon on the Mount to the Quran, the Buddhist sutras, and the Confucian Analects. Each offers ways to avoid risk. These moral maxims suggest that right behavior produces good rewards. As a backup, moreover, many religions also provide an ultimate insurance, especially those that offer a supreme being or the belief in an afterlife. Across the ages, religious teachers have warned against individuals "losing their souls" by making the wrong choices. They have also suggested that, in the end, the universe will judge, or forgive, all the mistakes made during risky behavior.

From the human point of view, then, religion is a form of risk management. In the study of human culture, anthropologists have made the case that entire societies develop rituals and traditions to reduce a feeling of risk. In the 1948 classic *Magic, Science and Religion*, anthropologist Bronislaw Malinowski argues that tribal cultures use ritual to guard against the loss of identity and order. In the same spirit, Mary Douglas's *Risk and Culture* claims that each culture has its own "worry budget." Each uses religious rules, such as when the ancient Hebrews had food prohibitions, to avert the risk of "pollution" by outsiders. "Each form of social life has its own typical risk portfolio," Douglas says.[7] Organized religion—a collective production of belief and ritual—is one way to identify those risks and to avoid them as a group.

In the next chapter, we will look at how religious groups can protect collective goods from loss, but for now, it is worth considering how individual consumers find ways to deal with the risks of religious choices. One particular way, proven across history, is to own a "diversified stock portfolio," to use an apt economic analogy. As economist Iannaccone explains, religious risk can be spread across many investments. "Rational religious investors have reasons to avoid specializing in a single religion or class of religious acts, preferring instead to diversify their investments over a number of them," he says.[8] It's the mantra of all investment advisors: diversify. Some stocks will fail, others will succeed—and the portfolio as a whole can be expected to increase in overall value.

In ancient Greece and Rome, it was normal to call upon several deities to insure against losses in life, or to request blessing and good fortune. Later Roman emperors had many household gods, and it was Augustine, among other church fathers, who questioned whether diversified portfolios offered as good an assurance of salvation as putting all one's stock in the biggest going concern, the "one true God." The history of polytheism is a story of portfolio diversification. This was true in the Greco-Roman world and is the case with most Eastern religions. The idea of yoga, for example, springs from Hinduism. Then it developed as a form of meditation in Buddhism. This practice lent itself to individual use, or consumption, and soon yoga, meditation, and other practices were being joined to devotion to one god or another in the pantheon of Hinduism, or the multiple bodhisattvas, angel-like beings, in Buddhism. The diversified Christian portfolio today might contain yoga or meditation. For some Buddhists, Jesus is a bodhisattva.

In the 1970s, the so-called New Age burst on the American scene, bringing a revival of alternative American spiritualities, interest in new Eastern imports, and literary forums such as the *Whole Earth Catalogue*.[9] The next decade saw Shirley MacLaine's spiritual autobiography *Out on a Limb*, the "cosmic convergence" event in 1987, and the growth of roving marketplaces—the Whole Earth Expo, Whole Life Expo, and now New Life Expo—that offered an array of beliefs for anyone building a spiritual portfolio: meditation, herbs, yoga, crystals, séances, angelology, astrology, Tarot, and all the rest. Lest this "expo" marketplace be tagged only to alternative beliefs, mega-expos by the National Religious Broadcasters or Christian Booksellers Association prove that evangelicals have a portfolio marketplace as well. In any case, the New Age is actually the old age. It is really only the most recent burst of human interest in using as many "spiritual technologies" as possible to reduce the risks in life. There is no requirement to join a group. Brand loyalty is typically weak. Portfolio religion is like shopping at many boutiques, meeting many providers, covering several spiritual bases in life.

As is well known, even people who belong to established religious traditions—Catholic, Protestant, Jew, Hindu, Muslim, and Buddhist—hold beliefs not sanctioned by their traditions. Christians may believe in UFOs and Muslims in astrology. For orthodox gatekeepers, such mixing of beliefs and practices is a cheap cafeteria religion or a messy smorgasbord of faith. But in the economic analogy, it is one sensible way to cover as many risks as possible. One compelling case of a diversified portfolio in history is the "rush hour of the gods" that occurred in Japan after World War II. As we've seen, new religions proliferated, multiplying the different ways that Japanese consumers could select what they liked from Shinto, Buddhist, Confucian, and Taoist goods and services. For most Japanese who engage in religion even today, this choosing of bits and pieces is common. But it can be just as common in the West.

PROOF OF QUALITY

In East or West, the religious consumer faces the same problem: how to verify the quality of a religious good. One way, as we've seen, is to sample many in hopes that some of them are genuinely effective. But as with picking a brain surgeon, we'd like to pick a religion that is safe and effective from the start. So let's return to the skyscrapers and cathedrals. In the world of supply and demand, consumers want a good product and sellers want to win consumer confidence. This goes for all goods in the marketplace, but especially for something that economists call "credence goods."[10]

Credence goods are items whose quality cannot be judged before or after purchase. We buy them because we trust the credibility of the supplier. Examples of credence goods abound. Consumers must trust a medical diagnosis, for instance. They must accept the word of a mechanic who says the transmission needs repair. The same goes for the services provided by counselors and therapists. In many such cases, we turn to a third party to gain proof of reliability. Doctors, mechanics, and therapists all need a license. Producers offer warranties and money-back guarantees to reassure consumers. And they advertise, which, as we will see, can be a signal of reliability.

Religion is the credence good par excellence. It is taken on a great deal of trust, and that is why history is littered with efforts by religions to win public confidence. Buying a used car or taking on a large mortgage is an experience of doubt and angst, but it is probably nothing like choosing a religion. Once again, Augustine comes to mind. His *Confessions* are about the struggle of making the choice. In contrast, there is no such great literature on the human anguish involved in choosing cars, refrigerators, or insurance (although the stories of choices on medical treatments can approach such drama). If Augustine's *Confessions* probe religious doubt, most of his other writings try to prove the validity of the Roman Catholic faith. He wants to build consumer confidence. He points to the proof of prophecies, the rise of Roman civilization, the success of saints, and the grandeur of the Roman Church compared to the absurd and whimsical pagans.

Augustine's arguments persist, but every religion must continue to make its case as reliable and valid. Religion can't offer a warranty, so it must use every other means. "No church offers a money-back guarantee to a soul that is dissatisfied with his or her afterlife experience," writes the economist Robert Ekelund.[11] In religion, therefore, the demand for credibility, honesty, fairness, and sincerity in religious institutions and leaders goes far beyond what is expected of business firms. By worldly experience, everyone knows he or she can be hoodwinked, especially when it comes to credence goods. "Unfortunately, sellers of credence goods have incentives to cheat consumers by overstating the product's merits (and so raise its price)," writes economist Brooks B. Hull. "Buyers and honest sellers of credence goods gain if honest sellers can somehow assure their honesty." So, for example, a church cannot prove eternal life. But "it can assure consumers that priests *sincerely believe* in life after death and believe that certain steps must be taken to achieve it."[12]

Many other features of religion try to signal this honesty, or at least the absence of gross self-interest. Clergy and priests usually make sacrifices above what lay members do. Celibacy is the classic example. When adopted in the early Middle Ages, it was said to model the celibate Christ. But it was also a clear way to tell the masses that children of priests were not inheriting church wealth. Another sign of disinterest was the lionizing of martyrs, displayed in statues, great narratives, paintings, and saint's days. This held true for Catholics in particular, but no less for Anglicans, Quakers, and Christians in general. Martyrs could be trusted—they walked the walk, not just talked the talk. Religions have also typically provided the service of pointing out heresy. By unmasking impostors, a religion can bolster its claim to be a better product.

Taken in this way, organized religion is a veritable cascade of credibility-proving behaviors. For the tens of thousands of religions that attempted to start up in human history, we can assume that very few passed this credibility test. Those that have survived most successfully are the great world faiths. Still, no religion, large or small, is immune to losing its credibility. It can be attacked by the village atheist or sabotage its own credibility by scandals of sex, power, and money, which in recent years have been the bane of some evangelists and Catholic priests. Nevertheless, clergy are still ranked high as trusted figures.

Religion persists in validating its credence goods. It licenses its clergy and gurus. Within Christianity, the age-old debate over "credentialed" spiritual leaders continues. In some contexts, clergy must undergo psychological evaluations and criminal background checks. They must earn degrees in theology, pastoral work, and ethics.

The building of Salisbury Cathedral was also a way that a religious tradition verified its bona fides. This is akin to one effect of advertising. Consumers want to decrease their cost of searching for information about satisfying products, so advertising appeals to them. Advertising also shows that a company has nothing to hide.[13] In addition to these signals, long-term investments, such as skyscrapers and cathedrals, signal that money is being sunk, or even lost, to send out free information about the firm's reliability and longevity. Even religions, like business corporations, want repeat customers long down the road. Firms spend great amounts of money on impressive headquarters buildings, logo images, and advertising.[14] In 2009, the tallest building in America, which is Chicago's Sears Tower, came under new ownership and changed its name. Now owned by the Willis Group, the Willis Tower, the tallest in North America, signals a business commitment to its worldwide market of customers.

The same pattern may be applied to the rich architecture of every religion. Often we know other religions best by their temples, not their theologies. In the old days, building a cathedral signaled "that the church has made a substantial long-term commitment to maintaining customers' satisfaction," according to economist Hull.[15] "Should it fail to serve members, the church forfeits the investment in the cathedral." The main body of Salisbury Cathedral, completed in 1258, took a mere thirty-eight years to erect, which explains its consistent architectural style. But its expansive grounds and towering spire were added gradually over several more generations. In Cologne, Germany, the cathedral begun in 1248 was not completed until the nineteenth century. In naming it a World Heritage Site, the United Nations described it as "a powerful testimony to the strength and persistence of Christian belief in medieval and modern Europe." Such examples range from St. Peter's Basilica in Rome to Notre Dame Cathedral in Paris, a site that draws tourists nearly on par with the Eiffel Tower.

The religions of Asia have also used architecture to broadcast the reliability of credence goods. Cambodia's ornate and ancient Angkor Wat temple, built over a generation to honor the Hindu god Vishnu, later became an enduring symbol of Buddhism's presence in the region. Such projects continue. In New Delhi, India, the world's largest Hindu temple complex opened in 2005. The Akshardham complex is the city's primary tourist attraction. It is a project to give credence to Hinduism. The mainstream missionary group behind it has also erected classic Hindu edifices around the world. The Islamic complex in Mecca, goal of the annual hajj for the faithful, is a long-term investment that signals the relevance of the faith. Fortunately for Islam, Saudi Arabia's oil industry has made it far easier to invest in the upkeep of Mecca, a dramatic advertisement for the perpetuation of Islam.

This proof of commitment is applied at the level of congregations as well. The Willow Creek Community Church, a megachurch near Chicago, took this to heart when it was trying to draw "seekers"—who shunned church—to its worship services. A visitor's first impression was to be one of Willow Creek's permanence, quality, and "Main Street" ambiance. The church, which increased its draw to 15,000 on weekends, looks like a well-groomed, bustling community college by a shimmering lake. "First impressions are lasting impressions," says building manager Larry Dahlenburg. "We don't even like using any 'out of order' signs anywhere in the building because we see that as sending a message that 'it has been broken for some time.'"[16]

Credence goods are also verified by the fact that growing numbers of people flock to them: can everybody be wrong? People flock to celebrities, and similarly, economic consumer theory speaks of the "superstar effect." Specifically, this is about the market mechanics whereby only a few stars, rather than a goodly number, make extraordinary amounts of money.[17] In the case of religion, the main point is the public attention given to a celebrity or a product. When an aged pope, old-fashioned and proud of it, gathers a million teenagers, as did Pope John Paul II, a kind of superstar effect is taking place.

But actually, the superstar effect is fairly limited in religion. It might apply to the pope, the Dalai Lama, Billy Graham, a televangelist, a quasi-religious self-help guru such as Oprah Winfrey, or a best-selling religious author. The more common concern is a good showing in local religious activities, the grassroots of any religion. Anyone who visits an empty church on Sunday senses its relative powerlessness. The more people flock to it, the more its beliefs are verified. At megachurches, this is called the vortex effect—greater attendance generates more attendance. This idea is widespread in such phrases as the "best-seller effect" and "the rich get richer."

A final form of credence is the very coherence and rationality of a religious system. If a religion and its teachers want people to have confidence in a onestock portfolio, that stock must include a fairly powerful explanation of how life and the universe works. In this view, religion is a rational pursuit that fights the chaos in life and tries to bring coherence. In other words, religion is perhaps more an explanation than an amorphous experience. A religious system "is first of all a cognitive system," argues the cultural anthropologist Melford

Spiro. In religion's attempt to push back chaos, it presents propositions. These can be both pleasant and unpleasant, but as a result, human beings have statements of clear benefits and costs. People tend to believe in the whole package, Spiro says: "The pleasant and the unpleasant beliefs alike continue to be held because, in the absence of other explanations, they serve to explain, i.e., to account for, give meaning to, and structure, otherwise inexplicable, meaningless, and unstructured phenomena."[18]

Not that the gods of human history have never been chaotic and irrational. In some cases, they have been more fickle than soap opera characters. The Greek and Roman gods often were victims of mortal passions and moods, hardly a boon for the humans below. Some Jewish, Christian, and Islamic views of God also concede that he may indeed be arbitrary, hiding his agenda, confusing mortal humans with a bombardment of contradictory words and deeds. In game theory, in fact, it has been argued that in a competitive game with humanity, God gets what he wants most with human beings by keeping them in fear and suspense. He gains the upper hand by his "arbitrariness," his being ambiguous and covert about his real intentions.[19]

Nevertheless, religious systems have tended to offer a rational ordering of life. By virtue of this, the most comprehensive systems draw large followings. As the sociologists Rodney Stark and Roger Finke have stated simply: "An individual's confidence in religious explanations is strengthened to the extent that others express their confidence in them."[20] It is all part of avoiding risk and building trust in a credence good such as religion.

GOD AND THE AFTERLIFE

Two of the most common beliefs deemed rational, assessed as helpful in avoiding risk, and backed by centuries of testimony and adherence are these: the existence of a high god and the reality of an afterlife. As Pascal knew well when he proposed his wager, people respond to incentives—and both heaven and hell have been strong ones when it comes to the afterlife. For economic thinking, these incentives make sense. But there is also a puzzle: from an incentives point of view, why did the belief in a single God who dispenses heaven or hell come into such dominance in history? Particularly, why hell? What benefit could there be in developing such a negative product for religious consumption? Who would buy it? For incentives, however, the concept of a good, wise, and all-powerful God is easier to understood, so we will begin with this topic.

The origin of monotheism, or belief in a single or highest God, is an event lost in history. But what seems clear is this: as history moved forward, more and more people adopted monotheism rather than polytheism. In the economic view, there is a logic to this process—a process related to credence goods. There is a reason humanity began to find that high gods were more reliable than small local ones.

In *A Theory of Religion*, the sociologists Rodney Stark and William Sims Bainbridge present a sweeping, incentive-driven theory on why high gods became prominent in human belief. Stark and Bainbridge build their case on principles of market exchange. They also draw upon the insights of Malinowski, the anthropologist who studied religion. Malinowski argued that when rational human beings find practical ways to solve problems in the world, they no longer rely on gods to micromanage those concerns. In other words, they give up magic. When agricultural skill increases, the spirit or ghost in the plant is no longer evoked. As medicine solves problems of health, the attempt to control spirits in arms, backs, and headaches disappears.

Finally, the historical human experience has led the world to believe in one, or a few, gods "of greater scope," high gods that solve more general types of human problems. "Gods are of greater scope when they perform a wider range of activities, offer a greater variety of rewards, impose a greater variety of costs, and when the sphere of their influence is more universal and less local," Stark and Bainbridge write. "Thus a god of weather is of greater scope than a god of wind, or a god of rain."[21]

Such higher beings also offer larger-scale explanations about existence itself—the meaning of life, suffering, hope, death, and the afterlife. If the deity becomes too general, however, supplying no specific exchanges or rewards in daily life, it can easily become so vague that it is irrelevant to human concerns. Typical cases of overgenerality in the highest deity are the impersonal Taoist "force" of the universe, or the Deistic clockmaker God of the Enlightenment. In *Star Wars*, the "force" was with them, and although it lacked any personality, it at least provided a very practical benefit: with it, you can win sword fights with villains.

Between the extreme of impersonal forces and on-the-spot magic, humanity has tended to choose a personal God, or gods, of great power. Magic is too easily disproved. The impersonal force becomes faceless. A high but personal God is the best combination. This all-providing deity cannot be proved or disproved the way magic can be disproved. So if God is accepted, as Pascal recommends, humans can engage in personal exchanges for the highest rewards imaginable. The modern belief in a supreme being is not universal, but it is pervasive. Belief in a traditional God is extremely high in the United States,

Ireland, Poland, Spain, Italy, and the countries of Latin America and Africa. If the idea of a "universal spirit" is added, even citizens in the more secular countries of Europe show that a majority believe in some kind of supreme being or benign cosmic force.

Compared to a benign Creator or universal spirit, the belief in the afterlife or in its worst outcome—Pascal's hell—is less amenable to human belief. There is a strong correlation between monotheism and these two beliefs, of course, but it is more complicated than that. Around the world, belief in the afterlife is a bit less prominent than belief in God. Most Jews, for example, don't adhere to the notion of an afterlife even if they think God exists. By the same token, many people who believe in a universal spirit (not a traditional God) also give credence to immortality. Finally comes hell—an idea that, if we adopt Pascal's harsh image, has declined as a modern belief. Even in the United States, fewer than half of believers assent to a hell. To illustrate the preference, more people believe in angels than believe in the devil, the CEO of hell.

As the world increasingly adhered to a belief in a single God, it also invariably developed the image of God as judge as well. He is the supreme adjudicator of justice, reward, and punishment. This is the story of the biblical religions of Judaism, Christianity, and Islam. From an economic view, these three are, in their traditional forms, typically known as the "high-risk religions." Each offers a potential major threat at the end of existence, and believers are in the market for ways to reduce that risk. To highlight this quality of so-called Western monotheism, it has been contrasted with the lack of eternal risk in Asian religions.[22] In the Eastern worldview, there is no powerful deity looking at the scale, checking off a list in the Book of Life. Furthermore, Asian religions are not exclusive, but are happily syncretistic.

From another point of view, however, this may be giving monotheism too much uniqueness in offering ultimate judgment. All religions that speak about the unknown future, especially after death, are dealing in risky outcomes and risk avoidance. It is well known that historic Buddhism and Hinduism, and their popular and supernatural versions today, speak of supernatural consequences. Asian religions include their own forms of risk. According to a major survey of beliefs in modern Taiwan, a Chinese society with a vibrant popular Buddhism, Taoism, and Confucianism, "a low-risk religion should not be misrepresented as a non-risk religion." As with monotheism, "there is always a certain amount of uncertainty and risk inherent in Eastern religions."[23]

Take Buddhism. It has a strong doctrine of karma and rebirth. Most Asian traditions have strong sanctions against wrong thinking, lack of devotion, or an evil heart. In Asian literature, indeed, there are images of hell that would make

Dante's *Inferno* look like a country club. Therefore, in Taiwan at least, the people who participate most in its indigenous faiths are in fact avoiding risk, according to this survey of Taiwanese religious belief, the largest such survey ever done. Even in Asian cultures, it concludes, "being irreligious constitutes a form of risk-taking behavior," and the gods, or the forces of nature, will notice the deviance and extract a cost.

The Taiwan study suggests that across all world cultures irreligious thinking and behaviors are considered to be risk taking, either for the eternal consequences or for the social deviance that might follow. A high God, in other words, is not always necessary to produce incentives in human beings to avoid risk. Nevertheless, monotheism still provides us with the superlative doctrine of what avoiding risk is all about—the doctrine of eternal hell. We can look at its development in Christianity in particular to see the role that such beliefs can play as incentives, a matter of judging costs and benefits. There is clearly no benefit from going to hell, but it may engender other positive rewards. The two examples we will look at are the incentives that surrounded the rise of the doctrine of purgatory, a temporary safe house from hell, and also the ability of hell to produce better behavior on earth. In particular, hell seems to have been an early and long-term guarantor of property rights, a central topic in economic behavior.

The ancient world in which the Catholic Church developed its doctrines of the afterlife had many alternative views to offer. These included reincarnation, eternal sleep, annihilation, progressive growth, and universal salvation. All these influenced Christian thinking, but in the long run the orthodox doctrine of heaven and hell emerged. As the great Catholic theologian Anselm of Canterbury expounded, anything less does not reflect God's justice and power: "There is eternal happiness, and eternal unhappiness."[24] In the thirteenth century, however, an innovation was added: the doctrine of purgatory. Christians had always prayed for the dead, suggesting their belief that ultimate fates could still be altered. But now it was official—people bound for hell stopped instead at purgatory to be purged of their sins and, one hoped, to become candidates for heaven. The doctrine was declared officially in 1445 at the Council of Florence, but as evidenced by the important role of purgatory in the Italian poet Dante Alighieri's widely read *Divine Comedy* (c. 1320), this midway realm of the afterlife was popularly taught long before.

In the economic view, purgatory has an obvious benefit. For individuals on earth, there is hope that their loved ones can still arrive in heaven. The living also have this benefit when they die. The church had incentives as well. It could use the doctrine of purgatory to motivate public behaviors. For example, to help a soul move from purgatory to heaven, people on earth not only had to pray but also had to do good works and make amends for the sins of the departed. One of those sins was unpaid debts: believers were thus motivated to pay the debts of their dead loved ones. From a property rights point of view, purgatory was far better than a costly debt collector.

The Church also taught that believers could help loved ones progress through purgatory by making donations. At the same time that this doctrine arose, so did the first popular religious orders—the Franciscans and Dominicans. As mobile agents, they played an important role in collecting the penances and donations related to loved ones in purgatory. This amounted to a vast financial collection system related to a credence good, which was trusted because the friars—who lived by vows of simplicity and poverty—were trusted in their teachings about penance, heaven, hell, and purgatory. Of course, this eventually went overboard. The Dominican friar Johann Tetzel became known in sixteenth-century Germany for his catchy advertising copy, such as "Won't you part with even a farthing [for] an immortal soul, whole and secure in the Kingdom of Heaven."[25] The idea of paying money to avoid cosmic risk struck individuals such as the Augustinian monk Martin Luther as a bit corrupt. And so it was that the Protestant Reformation was a revolt against the widespread practice of indulgences—paying money to get, among other things, relatives out of purgatory and into heaven.

But even Luther believed in hell, and a fiery one indeed. In Pascal's wager, the "infinite gain" of heaven is arguably the positive benefit that a person can focus on. But in the economic way of thinking, the prospect of hell still seems so negative that we wonder why it developed at all. The doctrines of heaven and purgatory offer obvious benefits to consumers who seek to "optimize their utility," as the economic textbooks say. But what benefit does hell offer? One answer has been risk-avoidance behavior, since believing in hell provides an uncertainty that people want to avoid by being good. As we've seen so far, the motivations of risk avoidance are complex, as illustrated in the moral hazard problem. Presumably, the doctrine of hell solves that problem: God is the all-seeing judge. He knows who wore a seat belt or made risky investments and who did not, and will issue punishments accordingly.

Arguably, then, a belief in God as judge, or in hell as a consequence, can motivate moral behavior in individuals. In later chapters we will see evidence of this in people's work ethic and economic productivity. For now, we can look at how the doctrine of hell can influence societies at large. This idea has been called the "supernatural punishment hypothesis." This says that cultures with a sense of ultimate consequence (such as hell) tend to behave better, both in finding rules of cooperation and in protecting property rights. In economic terms, such societies produce public goods that benefit everyone. Religions have always taught this kind of behavior as a duty. We have the Ten Commandments, the New Testament, and the Quran, all of which can also be read as property rights manuals. But when people fail to do their duty, other incentives must be brought in to encourage social order. One of these has been the cost incentive suggested by the doctrine of hell, the nub of the supernatural punishment hypothesis.

To test this hypothesis, one study looked at measures of cooperation in 186 societies and compared that to whether each society historically had high gods, supreme beings able to distribute rewards and punishments. The study admits that finding this kind of connection is as much art as science. Nevertheless, in nearly all cases, a modern society has a higher measure of cooperation—and public goods—if it has a long tradition of a higher god who oversaw justice in this world and the next. Furthermore, "high gods are significantly associated with societies that are large, more norm compliant in some tests (but not others), loan and use abstract money, are centrally sanctioned, policed, and pay taxes." This provides at least some support for the economic idea of religious incentives and disincentives at work, since "supernatural punishment may be associated with cooperation among societies."[26]

Another way to look at hell is in its role in supporting the social contract, one piece of which is a person's right to own property without threat of loss. Today, every modern society has a vast system of laws, contracts, courts, and police to enforce this common assumption in society. But this was not always so—and those were times when belief in God and hell played an important role in protecting property. This begins to explain a pattern of belief in history, argues Hull, the economist. "Religious enforcement will be more important in situations where temporal enforcement is relatively inefficient."[27] The religious doctrine of hell, in other words, will tend to emerge at a transition point in a civilization, a period when that society moves from the simplest property arrangement to a vastly more complex one, as seen in the modern world.

In early human societies, property exchanges took place face-to-face in small groups. If a tribe wanted another tribe's property, it simply took it and killed the enemy. However, society expanded to include many tribes, and for this they needed rules to govern property. This would be a society of moderate complexity, still lacking full bureaucratic systems of law, courts, contracts, and police. In the economic view, this would be a time for religion—with its divine court—to emerge with strength. At moderate complexity, a divine judge is helpful in enforcing social order. However, in massively complex technological societies—such as our modern world—religions no longer can speak to the enormous complexity of contract management, although religious ethics certainly can play an important role. In the modern world, legal bureaucracies step in.

This history of property rights might explain why doctrines of hell have fluctuated in intensity. The image of hell in early Christianity, for example, seems to have been milder or less emphasized. Eventually, the church found that such a mild hell did not sufficiently motivate individuals to invest in eternal rewards by curtailing immediate earthly benefits, many of which involved property-related sins. In turn, the doctrine of heaven may not have been motivating the best behavior, either. As a result, the theologians increased the harshness of the hell doctrine, emphasizing the "fear of the Lord." This theory also presumes a consumer curve: that people will not stay at extremes for too long, but will adjust to an equilibrium, a moderate balance of costs and benefits. Too much heaven can undermine consumer confidence, but too much hell can also do the same.

The stronger use of hell seems to be most helpful at times when societies do not have an effective and just system of law enforcement. Thus, Hull argues, the strong doctrine of hell may be "more important in cultures of intermediate complexity."[28] The most terrifying doctrine of hell—we can think of Dante's *Inferno*—may play this role at a particular time, but it cannot last. The public, as consumers of religion, will always be calculating how to take advantage of both heaven and hell, comparing the costs and benefits in relationship to other earthly goals and opportunities. Perhaps the most obvious such pattern is that as a society modernizes, offering more assurance of property rights, there is less need to preach doctrines of hell to curb cheating.

This has been the story of Europe, writ large, and of Puritan New England on a smaller scale. In early Puritan days, when the wilderness ruled, the images of hell offered by Jonathan Edwards's sermon "Sinners in the Hands of an Angry God" and by America's first best-selling book, *The Day of Doom*, were helpful enforcers of social order. "Not surprisingly, Puritan hell doctrine became more severe in times when the family, community, and government were relatively weak," Hull explains.[29] That strictness faded, however, as society became more ordered and complex. The threat of hell was replaced by the threat of lawyers, police, and courts. In time, new incentives drove other kinds of theological innovations. In American Protestantism, the terrifying and judgmental God of the Old Testament was soon replaced by the loving cosmic presence of Jesus.[30]

In his short life, Blaise Pascal was a virtuoso in the mathematical sciences, helped shape French literature, and gave us a classic religious enthusiast, though often an abrasive one. Pascal's wager still is with us as a sterling piece of economic and religious logic. In the nineteenth century, another great religious philosopher, the Danish writer Søren Kierkegaard, castigated Pascal for reducing religious faith to such cold calculation and pursuit of personal gain. True religion, Kierkegaard argued, is a "leap of faith," not a calculation. As we have seen, faith is a perennial kind of human response to risk. Still, the credence good called religion needs constant verification, for it is always being challenged by competing products, such as laws or earthly tools that can substitute for the work of the gods, even though finally only the gods can supervise the ultimate costs and benefits.

Kierkegaard not only emphasized the almost irrational leap of faith but also was an absolute loner. He wasn't interested in organized religion. In his cultural context that meant the Lutheran Church in Scandinavia. Kierkegaard was not a joiner, to risk an understatement. But as the next chapter shows, organized religion has been absolutely essential to supporting belief—as a credence good—in the human marketplace. This is why, in fact, religions have formed. They have built cathedrals and temples to announce, as have the modern insurance companies, that they are open for serious business in the world.

CHAPTER 5

Why Religions Form

By all accounts, the founder of Buddhism, the Indian prince Siddartha Gautama, did not plan to start a religion. From the day of his first sermon, given to five disciples in a deer park in northern India, his message stayed the same: "Work out your own salvation with diligence." He taught this while wandering for forty-five years. At first, his most ardent students imitated the wandering. Then they began to organize, especially for shelter in the long rainy season. They set up the first monastery and prescribed rules for behavior.

On his deathbed, the Buddha would not have called this a new religion. But the seeds were clearly there, providing clues for an economic approach to asking why religions organize in the first place. Today, Buddhism is the fourth largest of the world faiths. From its scant beginnings, its success would rival any multinational corporation's. Its antiquity, complexity, and diversity—ranging from atheism to supernatural beliefs—have prompted some to say that Buddhism really doesn't fit the definition of an organized religion. All the same, its historical story, as the economic approach might tell it, has features that are similar to all faiths that move from a founding moment to being a major institution in the human marketplace.

By one estimate, history may have produced some 100,000 different religions, the vast majority short-lived and obscure. Textbooks today speak of seven world faiths, and yet who could have picked them as winners in their earliest days? For most Western readers, the accounts of the founding of Judaism and Christianity are most familiar. But even their survival and growth boggle the mind if one considers what it was like to be an adherent at the very beginning. The Jews were a small and harassed tribe surrounded by rival tribes and overpowering nations with many gods. Jesus was a young man from Nazareth who wandered the countryside. "Can anything good come out of Nazareth?" people said. Jesus offended the establishment by saying he had fulfilled prophecy. He also preached enigmatic things about God, love, and the end of the world.

The extremely poor odds that Buddhism, Judaism, or Christianity might, in their own day, become great world movements has many economic analogies.

To make this comparison, however, we will have to leap from the sacred to the profane—from the God seekers of old to the food seekers at McDonald's today. In 1937, nobody had heard of Dick and Mac McDonald, two brothers who ran a hot dog stand at a small airport in Monrovia, California. They moved east of Los Angeles, over the mountains, to start a new restaurant along Route 66, catching travelers with a regular drive-in with carhops. Hamburgers sold best. So by 1948 they converted to a hamburgers-only drive-through with a "Speedee Service" system. For the first sixteen years, the brothers ran a solo operation. Then in 1953 the first franchise opened in Phoenix. Today, of course, we speak of the McDonaldization of the world.

The venture of the McDonald brothers might have remained a single operation, one of the millions of kiosks that set up and then close down in the world marketplace. Even today, most new businesses fail. Similarly, the Buddha's sermon might not have outlasted his lifetime. The same goes for the three-year ministry of Jesus. This comparison opens the way for some economic thinking about the origins of religion. Economists have asked, for example, why firms come into existence. Why isn't the human marketplace simply producers and buyers making exchanges? As the Nobel Prize–winning economist Ronald Coase once asked, why firms? "Production could be carried on without any organization," he argued.[1]

In the same year that the McDonald brothers opened their hot dog stand, Coase published his article "A Theory of the Firm" to explain why firms come into existence. He concluded that firms are not simply a clump of workers and supervisors, as may have been seen in Egypt during the building of the pyramids. Modern firms help a producer reduce costs and increase benefits. To do this, firms organize and tend to grow to a certain size. That size balances the efficiency of having inside employees making outside contracts, all with the goal of producing and selling more—to make a profit. The same might be said of religion. The firm is a kind of ecological organization. So is a religion, which balances internal resources with outside market forces.

Economists also sought a theory for smaller groups that formed around production and consumption goals. Thirty years after Coase's work, the future Nobel Prize–winning economist James Buchanan described the formation of "co-operative membership" groups that he called "clubs." In his 1965 article "An Economic Theory of Clubs," he similarly used the principles of cost and benefit to explain why people form voluntary and dedicated groups.[2]

In forming a club, the chief question is the "size of the most desirable cost and consumption arrangement," Buchanan said. That arrangement hinges on the number of other people with whom each member must share the benefits. In the best club arrangement, all club members invest themselves. As a result, together they produce the optimal amount of club goods for the membership to share. The other key to this arrangement, moreover, is the ability of the club to exclude free riders, people who take benefits but do not contribute. When a club demands commitments of time, money, or loyalty, for example, free riders quickly look for the exit. In short, the most desirable club, says Buchanan, is one of high dedication, exclusivity, and shared consumption. If it were otherwise—and free riders took over—there would be no club at all.

With these two models—the club and the firm—the economic approach offers a way to answer the question of why religions appear in history, and what the process is by which that takes place. This leap from the profane to the sacred—the use of economic models for religion—can raise immediate protests. In religion, it has been said, we don't ask people to pay costs but only to give out of generosity and caring. Religion is not about efficiency, survival, and profit, but about sacrifice and love—even martyrdom.

The story of Francis of Assisi, for example, might defy the club or firm models. Francis gave away everything, as did his small roving band of followers. They took no benefits and, presumably, let free riders join—or did they? In fact, joiners of the Francis of Assisi club faced very high entry costs: poverty, exposure to the elements, social stigma, and exclusive commitment. Those who stuck with Francis received an exclusive benefit, or club good, which was the religious experience of "living like Christ" and a small social network, or safety net, as it were. At the start, the Franciscans survived on the club model. In time, they evolved into a firm. The Franciscans became one of the most powerful and property-rich forces in medieval Europe. The Franciscan question of poverty finally became so explosive in the fourteenth century that Rome and the order, like two competing firms, engaged in a deadly battle over market share that included excommunications, exiles, vast transfers of property, and executions.

But we now return to Buddhism. Obviously, the teaching of the Buddha did not remain as a kiosk in northern India. The first monastic group he organized was called a sangha, which, as we will see, follows a club model. The sangha evolved into a kind of firm and franchise across history. Indeed, the sangha has lasted for two and a half millennia—a record that a firm such as McDonald's is very unlikely to match.

BUDDHISM: FROM CLUB TO FIRM

The factual story of Buddha is so ancient that it is lost in the mists of history.[3] However, the traditional account of his life is well known. From a worldly point of view, Siddartha was a fortunate young man. He was the son of a noble and therefore probably in the second-ranking caste of Hindu society, which was surpassed only by the hereditary Brahmins, a class that produced Hindu priests who conducted the chief religious rituals in society. The Brahmins, moreover, were considered to be highest on the earthly ladder of reincarnation, soon to reach heaven after their current lifetime. All the other ranks of society, from nobility to soldiers to servants, were destined to return to the world in a higher stage if they produced good karma—that is, good behavior—in the current lifetime.

When the young Gautama secretly wandered out from the palace grounds, he was shocked to find on the streets of India aging, illness, and death. He also saw for the first time the wandering ascetics who were trying to escape, in a single lifetime, the sad and perpetual cycle of rebirth in the suffering world. At age twenty-nine, Gautama decided to leave behind his palace, wife, and infant. He wandered the forests with a shaved head and bowl. He tried yoga and asceticism for six years. But after meditation under a fig tree, he was "awakened" to true reality: there was a Middle Way between indulgence and asceticism that could lead to enlightenment in a single lifetime. It was not an easy way, however. The story is told that the evil one taunted Buddha, saying there were probably no other humans who could follow his severe path. Buddha replied, "There will be some who will understand." So he traveled to the Sarnath deer park near the sacred city of Banaras. There he found five old friends from his yoga and asceticism days. He preached to them his essential teaching: the Fourfold Truth and the Eightfold Path.

That first group, which formed the sangha, imitated Buddha in his wandering and teaching, though they had to meet occasionally to support each other and, practically, to find refuge from the three-month rainy season of northern India. In the first year, in fact, a friendly Hindu ruler in one of the two kingdoms where Buddha did his teaching provided him with a monastery, as did a wealthy banker in another location. The locations were isolated wooded areas. The monks provided labor to restore and maintain the buildings. For sure, this arrangement gave the monks food, shelter, and a livelihood. But their more noble goal was nirvana, the extinguishing of the cycle of rebirth. To achieve this, they had to follow a path of right thought and behavior. This became formalized in a set of strict monastic rules, called the Vinaya, which became the heart of any Buddhist "club."

The first puzzle is why, amid so many wandering monks and so many Hindu festivals, rituals, and personnel in India, the small Buddhist group managed to survive. As the historian of religion Houston Smith observes, "Unlike Hinduism, which emerged by slow, largely imperceptible spiritual accretion, the religion of the Buddha appeared overnight, fully formed."[4] According to tradition, a hundred years after Buddha's death, there were still only several hundred monks considered worthy enough—that is, they had achieved enlightenment—to attend a reported council. For over a century, from an economic club point of view, the Buddhist assembly had stayed strict enough to retain its efficiency and endure.

Clearly, the cost of membership remained high in the early sangha, while the benefits produced by the monastic community certainly must have proved significant. Not only did membership in the club require a full-time commitment, but the monastic rules were designed to separate members from the surrounding environment, even as monks wandered and increasingly took on social roles as trusted third parties, matchmakers, teachers, and physicians. The first glimpse of a full-scale religion came when the Buddhist sangha allowed lay membership. Eventually, one branch of monks was also allowed to marry and have children. At the start, however, Buddha demanded a full commitment to the path of enlightenment, so the early club was one of celibate and elite practice. As most religions that have survived know well, it is the adult converts who keep the zeal, not the children of converts. A completely celibate order, therefore, can help avoid a second- and third-generation dilution of the original club commitment.

The history of religion is rich with illustrations of how barriers were kept high at the club level by codes of diet, dress, and behaviors. Some of these required obvious sacrifices and the taking on of "stigmas" that helped draw lines between club members and the outside world, and which helped encourage more internal participation. From the celibacy of a priesthood to the earlocks of ultra-Orthodox Jews, the vegetarian diets of Jehovah's Witnesses, and the ritual garments and two-year missionary requirements (in white shirts with ties and name badges) for Mormons, such high levels of commitment are signals of trustworthiness within the club, if often taken as useless religious oddities by the outside world. For the first Buddhist monks, these signals were the Vinaya they followed, plus a shaved head, begging bowl, and robe.

The nature of the club signals was a major debate in early Christianity. After Jesus' death, some argued that followers of "the way" had to be circumcised and follow strict dietary rules, as inherited from traditional Judaism. These were both the costs and the signals necessary to follow Jesus, according to the so-called Judaizers. For the Hellenizers, there were other spiritual signals that would suffice. The apostle Paul, in hopes of reaching the Gentiles, argued for liberty in regard to eating and declared that believers could be "spiritually" circumcised. After Paul won the debate, membership continued to have its costs. Now, however, it was the cost of facing synagogue police and Roman officials who, as a matter of patriotism, required Christians to worship Rome's many gods. A few early Christians set a very high price for membership in the club, which was death in the Roman Colosseum.

In understanding why a religion survives in its earliest stage, the sacrifices and stigmas, according to this application of the club model, pay off in the long run. There are no free riders. Nascent religions pass the early Spartan test of efficiency and a future in the marketplace. As Ernest Hemingway would say of prose, these club religions were "all blood and muscle." The other key economic point is that this club behavior is rational. Club members weigh costs and benefits. They feel they are coming out with a satisfying profit. Otherwise, they would not continue.

This pursuit of apparent hardship might seem starkly contrary to most consumer behavior, where earthly creature comfort is the typical payoff. But that is where the club of religion is different. "Efficient religions with perfectly rational members may benefit from stigma, self-sacrifice, and bizarre behavioral restrictions," economist Iannaccone explains. "These costs screen out people whose participation would otherwise be low, while at the same time increasing participation among those who do join."[5] In the case of early Buddhism, the monks who took on those bizarre commitments were rationally calculating the benefits, and for certain monks, some of those benefits were social and material, not just spiritual.

In the club model, social welfare is also a club good that the members generate together. The early Buddhists had their monasteries in the woods. Their begging became more organized, and both savings and regular patronage from the public must have developed. In modern times, the club model has been studied in a variety of religious settings around the world, especially in ultra-Orthodox Judaism and in madrassa-based Islam. In these cases, higher religious commitment coincides with greater assurance of social welfare. In modern Indonesia, for example, the rate of men and women joining Islamic study groups increased during an economic crisis. Those who put more effort into study and religious activity gained access to club goods, which included financial resources in emergencies, something the secular society could not offer. "The role of religion as a provider of insurance is broadly consistent with club goods theory," economist Daniel L. Chen says of the Indonesian case.[6]

Once Buddhism had stabilized as a club, it could develop a public clientele without creating a problem of free riders. The Buddhist sangha began providing goods and services for consumers. At this point, it was on its way to becoming a firm. Where the monks had settled, they built ties with the population, and indeed, lay Buddhists began to pursue their own forms of enlightenment. The laity also funded the monks. In turn, the monks provided spiritual services, much the way the Hindu Brahmins had traditionally done in Indian society. The Buddhist monasteries were separate from the world, but they nevertheless became a key feature of secular life. Historians suggest that merchants and traders were the characteristic patrons of the monasteries, which often stood along trade routes such as the legendary Silk Road.

After Buddha's death, the gradual transition of Buddhism from a club to a firm, or even a franchise, was evident in the earliest internal debates, which concerned the leadership succession and a clear statement of the Buddha's teachings. Most at issue, however, was the Vinaya—the strict rules for membership. Tradition says that the first council to meet after Buddha's death focused on this concern, and by the second and third councils, coming a century and more later, schisms had developed over membership requirements. As is common, the debate was between the orthodox and the lax. The first wanted high costs for the benefits, the second lower costs. Buddhism began to splinter, each branch offering a different set of incentives. This first branching of Buddhism produced eighteen sects, only one of which ultimately survived (today called Theravada Buddhism).

The dynamic of strict and lax trends in an early religion is well known and shows how club development is a dynamic affair. According to studies, the conversion and defection rates in small religious groups that try to keep high standards and avoid free riders are far greater than in large and low-cost organizational memberships. For example, it was easy to join Hinduism and hard to leave, because it was so open and woven into Indian society. To join early Buddhism, however, required a severe break. We can presume that people quitting, or being ejected from, the strict sangha was as frequent as people trying to join. This, at least, is the pattern of modern-day sects and religious cults. By keeping its standards, Buddhism retained its identity through the rough spots of the founding centuries. In time, the tradition was solid enough to enter the religious marketplace. Now it faced the test of survival as a firm.

To become an important religious firm, Buddhism needed a significant foothold in the market by which its goods and services could reach a public of consumers. This step was achieved by political good fortune, not necessarily by outselling the diverse system of Hinduism and the entrenched Brahmin class that was in control. One can also think of when the Roman emperor Constantine made Christianity, still a struggling network of clubs, the official religion of the Roman Empire in 325 C.E. Six centuries earlier, this had happened for Buddhism in India.

In the middle of the third century B.C.E., a local warrior-king named Ashoka Maurya conquered neighboring kingdoms and expanded India's territory to an extent that would be exceeded only by the British Raj (1858–1947), or rule, millennia later. Feeling guilty about the carnage of conquest, it is told, Ashoka embraced Buddhism. He tolerated all religions, according to ancient inscriptions, but seemed to establish Buddhism as the favored one. He built temples and stupas and sent Buddhist emissaries to the west and east, probably rooting Buddhism in the soil of Southeast Asia, where it has prospered. But even with Ashoka in the picture, the rise of Buddhism as a full-fledged organized religion can be evaluated on purely economic models.

As a humane dictator, Ashoka used Buddhism to establish what economics calls a "natural monopoly," which seeks efficiency of services rather than opportunistic profit. This is typified by the public utility—a railroad, mail service, telephone system, or electricity grid—which in many countries is a quasi-governmental monopoly. The irony of Ashoka's actions is not lost on historians. At first Buddhism was anti-establishment. It offered an iconoclastic path that challenged Hinduism's authority, ritual, speculation, tradition, easy salvation, and sacred mysteries. In casting these aside, the Buddha urged only private mastery over body and mind. Eventually, Buddhism itself became a tradition. "The religion that began as a revolt against rites, speculation, grace, and the supernatural, ends with all of them back in full force and its founder (who was an atheist as far as a personal God was concerned) transformed into such a God himself," says Houston Smith. "After his death all the accoutrements that the Buddha labored to protect his religion from came tumbling into it."[7]

When the Buddhist religion is seen as a firm, all these accoutrements, in fact, become necessary and welcome developments. Long before Coase offered his theory of the firm in 1937, the philosopher Adam Smith looked at the churches in Scotland and elsewhere and concluded that they had organized for efficient business. "The clergy of every established church constitute a great incorporation," Smith said in *The Wealth of Nations* (1776).[8] In particular, Smith was concerned about the monopoly nature of corporations, as typified by mercantile policies and state churches. The modern theory of the firm, however, is just as interested in how firms can operate efficiently, and how they organize themselves for a single purpose: to increase resources and revenues.

Economics also has a long tradition of looking at the production of "public goods," which typically are produced by governments and can be consumed by everybody. The usual examples are public highways and national defense, paid for by taxes. Everyone may pay different taxes, or none, but everyone gets equal access to highways and protection from outside invaders. Without doubt, religions also produce public goods. They teach people to behave well toward others, contributing to moral education, literacy, and the golden rule. They also operate vast charitable projects that take care of the needy. However, these good works have a limit if a religion is to survive. Ultimately, even a religion must behave as a firm. It must produce goods and services, sell these to consumers, generate revenues, and do all this efficiently by techniques such as the division of labor, pricing, specialization, and product diversification.

LABOR, PRODUCTS, AND SPECIALIZATION

The division of labor and specialization could be seen fairly early in both Buddhism and Christianity. Famously, the apostles of Jesus divided up between those who made money waiting on tables and those who traveled to seek converts. In Buddhism, the core experts were the *arhat*, or enlightened few who achieved what Buddha had achieved. In the twentieth century, the German scholar Max Weber called these types of individuals, in every faith tradition, the religious virtuosi. Even from a practical point of view, there is no shame in a religion having such specialists, Houston Smith reminds us. "Religion is no less complicated than government or medicine," he says. "It stands to reason, therefore, that talent and sustained attention will lift some people above the average in matters of spirit; their advice will be sought and their counsels generally followed. In addition, religion's institutional, organized side calls for administrative bodies and individuals who occupy positions of authority, whose decisions carry weight."[9]

This division of labor, and the specialization of religious leader, required a new structure. An early insight into this fact was offered by the French thinker Emile Durkheim. For an actual religion to function, he said, it needed a group experience, symbols, and keepers of those symbols, the priesthood. Across history, individual teachers—a shaman, a healer, or a wandering monk—might offer a particular service. But this is the proverbial one-time exchange between a client and customer: a spell, prayer, ritual, palm reading, or astrological chart. Durkheim called these services "magic," not religion. Magic does not need a social structure, but religion does. "In history we do not find religion without Church," he said. These organized religious bodies can span a tribe, cover a nation, or reach across populations, organizing themselves on one theological system or another. But in contrast, Durkheim said, *"there is no Church of magic."*[10]

Even in the concept of the firm, there are management and employees, all of whom work together for the firm's existence—and to produce goods for public consumption. By the same token, the leadership of a religion produces spiritual goods that are consumed by the members, much as any firm produces a product that goes to market. Second, the religious product must compete successfully with alternative products or else the organization will no longer be able to survive. The firm, in other words, must take consumers into account and innovate products accordingly. For every religious club that wants to become a religious firm, this question of product is crucial.

While it may be said that most religions provide a similar product—an explanation about life and its supernatural forces—concrete doctrines, practices, traditions, and cost-benefit formulas vary widely. Religions can provide a place to gather, a social identity, a place to rear children, and a network of friends and associates. But, of course, other things do this as well—guilds, neighborhoods, armies, and social classes. As noted in chapter 3, religion is the ultimate credence good, for it asks followers to take risks and carry costs in hopes of expected future returns. No doubt many a Buddhist initiate struggled on the path to enlightenment, asking whether the Vinaya was worth the prospect, perhaps elusive, of nirvana in this lifetime. In this sense, the religious firm is essential to guaranteeing that its products are the real thing. Stated simply, "religious institutions exist to reduce (or at least appear to reduce) the risk of fraud and misinformation," says economist Iannaccone.[11]

THE MEDIEVAL CATHOLIC FIRM

Firms do more than this, of course. The classic definition of a business is that it seeks "rents," an arcane phrase that originated in early nineteenth-century English economics. Seeking rents is simply seeking to make a profit, with the profit strategy determined by alternative choices consumers have in the market (such as renting land cheaper nearby, as the old English case study explained). In short, the firm exists to make profits. At this point, the cynic about religion can say, "I told you so," but this may also be taken as simply a benign and necessary fact of life. Any institution needs to pay its way. It needs to cover depreciation, waste, and loss, invest in growth and the future. Perhaps the Achilles' heel of religion—in terms of cynicism—is that it uses beliefs, not just earthly goods, to earn money. So the cynic can indeed have his moment, but now we move on to the more interesting facts of life.

To study a religious firm, nothing serves better than the Roman Catholic Church in the medieval epoch, and fortunately, a team of economists led by Robert B. Ekelund has been doing this for twenty years. In 1981, they began to study "public choice"—that is, rent seeking and profit making by firms or governments—in early Europe. And there was no firm as successful as the Church itself.

From the eleventh century onward, the papacy, led by the "lawyer popes," created one of the most efficient centralized systems in the world. Management flowed from the papacy and the Curia, wherever it happened to be (sometimes the papal throne moved about, other times it remained in Rome, and for one long stint it was in Avignon, France), down to the bishops, who had to come to the pope to acquire the accoutrements of their authority. Church law became the common law of Europe.

Monasticism was an early product of feudal Europe, with monastery estates being stand-alone affairs in a fiefdom or part of a network, which began under the Benedictine Rule. Monastery systems, too, came under the authority of the papacy. New kinds of monasteries arose as well, typified by the Cistercians. Their goal was to return to a more strenuous monasticism. When they moved to the open frontiers, the Cistercians developed a caste system of labor, land management, commodities, and capital. They emerged as the first multinational corporations. It was not a stretch, therefore, when Ekelund and his colleagues titled their book *Sacred Trust: The Medieval Church as an Economic Firm*.

To analyze the medieval Church as a firm, they recognized that public goods were part of its product line, for indeed the Church enforced laws, solemnized marriage, administered the courts, and enforced some property rights. Nevertheless, the Church was also in the business of selling salvation goods in a wide variety of forms, delivered by different providers and offered at different costs. "Suppliers of religion, whether ancient or modern, encounter the same basic problem as a business," Ekelund writes. "They must decide on the nature and quantity of services to produce and the price to charge. As with businesses, the solution to these problems depends in part on the type of market structure within which a firm operates."[12] Very large churches do face a free rider problem, but at these larger scales, free riders can become a benefit: a growing base of customers to buy the goods and services.

To serve this large consumer population, the medieval Catholic Church became a vertically integrated industry, able to dominate the marketplace and develop new products to adapt to a changing environment. It was the harbinger of what today is called the multidimensional firm: a head office, divisions, and agents in the field, all following a chain of command with accountability moving upstream to the head office, where cash accumulates and then is strategically invested again for the most profitable yields in various divisions.

Such a firm has challenges, of course. One is to keep its agents in the furthest reaches in concord with the interests of the head office. The same challenge faces religions, according to economist Ekelund. "The typical pattern of supply within religious institutions involves the use of intermediaries, or agents," he says. "The role of these agents has evolved over long periods of time and across various cultures. The shaman of early societies eventually gave way to the priests of later civilizations."[13] In addition to ensuring that agents have incentives to generate profits up the chain, the head office must also find ways to be sensitive to local changes in markets, where surprise events can change consumer behavior, or where consumers themselves can be confronted with alternative choices.

Fortunately for the Roman Church in the Middle Ages, it had a veritable monopoly. But as in any market, monopoly is always open to challenge, especially in local settings. One of the great competitive challenges was the heretics, who in one colorful episode moved across southern France. The Church took measures to compete with them on their own product terms by backing the grassroots friars, such as the Dominicans. But the Church also employed violence. It was not the first time, but the use of violence against heretics became more evident than ever in the thirteenth century. It was used in tandem with the Crusades in Spain and then in the Holy Land. Of course, when it is available, violence is a very effective way to stanch competition.

Nevertheless, for many centuries the Church did not have any serious competition. In this somewhat stable circumstance, a firm still tries to increase revenues. As history records, the Church found many ways to do this. In many areas, it could simply tax the public and charge tolls for use of its many resources. The Church also regulated career advancement in the priesthood, monasteries, and religious orders; the rites of baptism, forgiveness, and burial; and ultimately the power of excommunication. As Ekelund and his colleagues documented in some detail, Church regulation in all these areas shifted and adjusted to generate the greatest amount of revenue. Three examples are illustrative: penance handbooks, the development of the doctrine of purgatory, and finally the doctrine of usury, or charging of interest.

In a competitive market, according to economic theory, innovation and lower prices are a firm's key strategy to increase profits. A monopoly situation, however, offers different dynamics. One typical dynamic is price discrimination, which is the practice of a firm adjusting its prices to produce the best possible outcomes with different consumers. In one study of Starbucks, it was noted how at different stores and at different hours coffee prices changed to make the most of people who would pay more or less, given their needs for coffee—especially during the morning rush hour.[14] Similarly, the medieval Catholic Church charged what the market could bear. "Price discrimination allows a seller producing religious outputs at the same cost to successfully sell the same item, or virtually the same item, at different prices to different customers," Ekelund explains.[15] The evidence is the Roman Catholic penance handbook, which lists different payments for people of different wealth. The poor could fast, pray, or join the Crusades as soldiers. But the rich were encouraged to give money instead.

As noted, monopoly is never absolute. The Church still had to make the most of a diverse consumer environment. We saw in chapter 3 how the doctrine of purgatory may have motivated people to pay their debts, both secular and to the Church, but it was also an innovative theological good that some people, worried about hell, would pay for on earth. Purgatory was a third way between heaven and hell, and for the right offering, access to it would be granted by a priest, friar, bishop, or decree of Rome. This again is the story of indulgences, a practice that was a primary grievance behind the revolt called the Protestant Reformation.

Profit maximizing in the Church perhaps was most evident in its banking and collections practices. For theological reasons, it upheld a ban on usury, or loaning money for profit. The medieval records show, however, that the normal economic incentive of profit drove Church practice. It could be said that the ban on usury was a way to make sure that public wealth was not siphoned off to lenders but instead was available for paying tithes. What the record shows more concretely, however, is that the Roman Curia, or head office, loaned money to its own divisions in the field—bishops, monasteries, or religious orders—at high interest rates. This allowed Rome to collect rents downstream, a very normal profit-making practice of the multidimensional firm.

The Catholic Church long benefited from its monopoly on religious products and services. But invariably, all monopolies are forced to adjust, since the public invariably loses interest in some products, competitors try to come up with alternatives, and either the firm itself becomes unwieldy or its consumer public becomes too large to be served in a local and sensitive manner. For Roman Catholicism, the end of that monopoly came with the sixteenth-century Protestant Reformation. Suddenly, vast numbers of Catholics, including many of its priests and political patrons, were offered a variety of alternative ways to obtain the precious product of salvation. This story of competition is a larger pattern saved for a later chapter.

THE BUDDHIST ENTERPRISE

The evolution of Buddhism from club to firm took a far different trajectory than did the centralized Roman Catholic Church, but the principles were similar. As best as historians can tell, after Emperor Ashoka endorsed Buddhism, he also presided over a great council that aimed to "purify" it of heretics, that is, competitors. Despite such efforts, after Ashoka's death, Buddhism entered its great sectarian period, a time of historical splits in its own ranks and a revived challenge of competition from Hinduism, which was also going through a revival. In the centuries on either side of Ashoka, Buddhism was still a rather elite and Spartan tradition. The people supported the monks, and the monks, characteristic of the Theravada tradition, provided the rituals and metaphysics to bless the kings.

Inevitably, however, the masses had to gain access to Buddhist products and services as well. There were also eager suppliers of a more popular version. This dynamic produced the greatest split of all in historic Buddhism. What arose was a popular Buddhism for everybody. It was easier to adopt and offered a wide array of supernatural helpers for everyday life. The leaders of this popular Buddhism called it Mahayana, or the "big raft," denigrating their elite rivals as offering only a "small raft" (that is, Hinayana, taken to be a derogatory alternative name for Theravada). Mahayana broke the Theravada monopoly, with its more elite, strict path, and did this by offering the help of deities called bodhisattvas. They were individuals who, having achieved enlightenment, returned to earth to help others assuage suffering and gain grace, or salvation. Naturally, Buddha himself was the chief bodhisattva, a kind of Christ figure who would come again. But meanwhile, popular and devotional Buddhism grew, filled with deities, rites and chants, and wondrous metaphysical speculations.

With its populist appeal, Mahayana challenged not only Buddhist elites but also the Hindu system of Brahmanism. In the strict caste system of India, Brahmins continued to ally with governments in their role of providing rituals for the public. But now the Hindus had to meet the Mahayana Buddhist market challenge. To do this, Hinduism underwent its own radical innovation between 100 B.C.E. and 100 C.E. This period saw the rise of devotional Hinduism, captured in the great religious stories of the Bhagavad Gita. The stories offered not only new national myths but the promise of salvation by way of daily devotion and practices. Indeed, this revival is the root of modern evangelistic Hinduism, from the bhakti movements to the Hare Krishnas. Now Hinduism had a product to compete with the bodhisattvas. Indeed, over centuries of competition, the deities all began to mix in a plethora of supernatural helpers.

Mahayana Buddhism continued to spread, and one of its greatest success stories is the rise of Tibetan Buddhism, which developed unique approaches to the Mahayana rites and metaphysical systems. Islamic invaders from the north finally expelled Buddhism from India, but its masters landed on their feet all across Asia, especially in Tibet. By the twelfth century, Tibet flourished as a new hub, and marketplace, of Buddhism. At the time, Mongols ruled Tibet through a secular system of wealthy clans. Four main Buddhist sects flourished, divided across thirteen regions and several clan patrons. One region dominated, and that was crucial to Mongol rule.

This changed with the rise of the Ming dynasty, which, based in Beijing, conquered Tibet and took a hands-off policy. When the four Buddhist sects of the early Mongol era dominated, what economists call monopolistic competition existed. But under the Ming, the market was opened up. Former top monasteries lost power. The patron system was in disarray. New sects arose. One of them was the Geluk sect, which in a few more centuries would dominate all of Tibet. Today's Dalai Lama, for instance, is the leader of Geluk Buddhism. The international politics in Tibet, just as they are today, were always crucial to which Buddhist sect gained prominence, usually with the help of armies. However, the economic story is one of product innovation and powerful marketing techniques.

In Tibet, the final competition to be the top Buddhist group had come down to the Geluk sect versus the powerful Karmapa sect. The key to gaining ground was acquiring the wealthiest patrons. For this, the sects had to offer enticing products. The Karmapa had a leg up with its doctrine of the reincarnated lama, a spiritual figure said to be a Buddha returned. The Geluk sect, founded by the charismatic Buddhist teacher Tsongkapa (1357–1419), needed to innovate to win similar patronage. Luckily, after Tsongkapa died, his successor declared that the Gelukpa, too, had an incarnated Buddha—the Dalai Lama. "The introduction of the incarnate Dalai Lama represented a technological improvement," says political economist Rachel McCleary. "The Gelukpa could now directly compete for wealthy patrons."[16]

Avoiding secular politics in the beginning, the Gelukpa focused on religious products. While mass monasticism was common in Tibet, the Gelukpa excelled in recruitment, in building monasteries in the emerging power center of central Tibet, and in mobilizing scripture production and "printing" methods to swamp the market with its orthodox teachings. On the club model, the Gelukpa retained a strict core and heightened specialization. They ordained abbots, required celibacy, pursued mastery of complex scholastics, and enforced orthodoxy. The Gelukpa soon gained a monopoly in central Tibet. With fixed costs at home, it could expand its market share—with literature, for example—at little extra expense. Other Buddhist sects could no longer compete, for their start-up costs were prohibitive. The final coup de grâce, however, was military might, not Gelukpa marketing.

Fortunately for the Geluk sect, they had sided with the Mongol warlord who defeated his rival, a warlord with whom the Karmapa had allied. Thousands of monks were killed in sieges, and monasteries were burned to the ground. Military victory, of course, is only tangentially related to pure economics (a civil war, for example, is called a "negative externality"). Nevertheless, the Gelukpa ascended on economic mechanisms, from club discipline and product innovation to mass marketing. "The Geluk school was one of the last religious groups to form in Tibet, yet it rose to become the state religion around the middle of the 17th century," says McCleary. "Having won, the Geluk sect continued to be an exclusive club, and, rather than showing religious tolerance, concentrated its resources in its institutions."[17] It took over the market. Geluk Buddhism is one of the few religious monopolies in history to endure until the present (only to be today in deadly competition with the military might of Communist China).

RELIGIOUS CLUBS AND FIRMS TODAY

History is rich with examples of religious clubs and firms, but we also have cases today. During the 1970s, for example, Western societies saw the rise of a few hundred "cults" and "new religions," many of which operated on club models. In this view, rational people joined these groups because the benefits—the club goods—were worth the costs of club membership. By keeping the costs high, so-called cults did not allow free riders. As in all clubs, they created various kinds of costs as barriers to exclude people who were not willing to pay the price.

One such barrier can be geography. If a religious commune sets up in Manhattan or downtown San Francisco, for example, its proximity to city streets guarantees it will be flooded by free riders. The commune becomes a soup kitchen. In contrast, in 1981 one of the Eastern sects, the followers of Indian professor-turned-guru Bhagwan Rajneesh, opened a commune at Big Muddy Ranch in the boondocks outside Antelope, Oregon, population 130. Only highly committed people would pull up stakes and go to a place that lacked suburban amenities. Many strict religions continue on the club model, requiring what economist Iannaccone calls "sacrifice and stigma"—dress codes, moral codes, eating codes, marriage codes—to keep the membership focused on the internal work of producing club goods.[18]

The club model in religion can also have an impact on worldly activity such as business and trade. Today, a visitor to Manhattan's legendary diamond district will still see a carryover from days of old: ultra-Orthodox Jewish men in black coats and hats ambling between the trading floor and some 2,600 diamond businesses crammed into a single block of West 47th Street (at Fifth Avenue). For some, it is like a Jewish shtetl, or village, in the heart of Manhattan, but that ambiance is fast changing under the weight of new technologies, such as sales on the Internet. Still, the diamond district is the hub of a $15 billion business, and the ultra-Orthodox are at its center due to club economics.

As the economist Barak D. Richman argues, "Jewish predominance in the diamond industry is explained by the community's ability to enforce contracts that few others can."[19]

That enforcement derives from the way ultra-Orthodox diamond dealers and cutters, motivated by the club goods of their religious community, decide that honesty is the best policy (and dishonesty the worst). In a club, people can be excluded from benefits, which can happen with expulsion from the Orthodox faith. Trust is a key part of membership, and trading diamonds is an especially dramatic test of this value. Diamonds are tiny, easy to steal, and worth millions. Since the diamond trade began centuries ago in Holland, Orthodox Jews have handled the product with the least amount of loss. Even today, the Jewish diamond cutter is called a "diamond-studded pauper." He will not steal diamonds because he would either have to flee or be denied the community goods of his religion, which may also resort to excommunicating him. Visiting the diamond district, Richman asked one cutter, "Why don't you just take them?" The man, smiling, replied, "Where would I go?"

It is more than coincidence, according to the club principle, that the other group famous for its honesty in handling diamonds is a Jain sect in India, the Palanpuri. The Jains, even before Gautama, staged a protest against the Brahmin monopoly and have lasted until today. The Palanpuri also are bound by strict honor codes and the risk of being excluded from club goods, namely, their inclusion in a closed religious community. The Palanpuri were known not only for cutting diamonds but also for carrying millions of dollars' worth of the gems safely between Indian villages and cities. Indeed, they have made India a new rival to Antwerp and Manhattan for the international diamond business. The Palanpuri also work in New York's diamond district. The ultra-Orthodox see them as commercial rivals, of course, just as the Internet is a new rival. But they also are partners at times, and the two perceive their common legacy. Both groups are equipped to make sure the honorable diamond trade is not ruined by an excess of free riders.

Like clubs, the world of larger and more open religious organizations faces the same issue of reaching optimal efficiency. While the club controls its internal affairs quite well, the religious firm must deal with the fact that it offers public goods, attracts free riders, and is always challenged to keep up its market share of consumers. The religious firm needs enough consumers to survive and grow. Economists have also wondered about the optimal size of a firm for it to succeed. This has been such a difficult thing to measure that the Nobel Prize–winning economist George Stigler reverted to what he called the "survivor technique."[20] In his study of the steel, auto, and oil industries, Stigler found that firms of many sizes succeeded in gaining the best market share. In other words, those that survived by having an adequate market share had found the right size.

Studies of American churches in the marketplace have arrived at the same conclusion. Churches come in many sizes, each with a particular kind of market share and each with strengths and weakness. One set of studies of Lutheran churches in the United States, for example, found that size and level of contributions are determined by competition, free riders, and cost-effectiveness.[21] In Birmingham, Alabama, the Christ Lutheran congregation draws about twice as much weekly attendance and revenue as Christ Lutheran in Pittsburgh, even though both congregations have the same number of members on their rolls, about 650 people. Both are in industrial cities. But the two churches have different experiences. In Birmingham, Alabama, there are few other Lutheran congregations. Therefore, a dedicated following shows up in Birmingham. Free riders see no benefits in joining a minority group, such as the Alabama Lutherans, with their limited resources and lack of social connections.

It's different in Pittsburgh, where there are many Lutheran churches. Most of the Lutherans go to a few large and popular congregations. With high attendance, these churches raise high revenues, but the per-person giving is actually lower than at the small churches. In other words, the big, popular congregations have a considerable bevy of free riders, those who go for the social connections and the many programs that a larger church can provide. At the smaller Christ Church in Pittsburgh, the congregants who attend services are a dedicated holdout. At some point, the large Lutheran churches can no longer siphon off small-church members: these small congregations offer an intimate experience that is not possible at a larger church. At the small churches, members get all the attention they need. They stay and donate generously to keep it that way. Just as Stigler found different sizes in the steel, auto, and oil industry, churches also find a cost-effective balance and then tend to stay at that point. Each needs enough market share to survive, but growth is always a precarious challenge.

The big exceptions to the growth challenge, of course, are the modern-day megachurches, which seem to grow like giant mushrooms after a rain. Large churches are not new in American history. But the abrupt rise of them since the 1990s has thrown light on the topic of the most effective size for a church. Maybe big *is* better. One team of economists first thought of the phenomenon this way: small churches were like mom-and-pop retail businesses, while megachurches were like big-box retailers (think Wal-Mart, Costco, etc.).[22] But that model did not work because one other economic principle seemed to dominate in megachurches: the principle of entrepreneurship.

Megachurches are not cookie-cutter imitations set up here and there, but original enterprises built by entrepreneurial personalities, who usually don't meld easily with head offices and bureaucracies. As the Austrian economic historian Joseph A. Schumpeter provocatively argued, entrepreneurs are a creative response to stagnation. Their "creative destruction" of old ways opens the door for progress.[23] Entrepreneurs shake up the normal course of business. They also draw criticism, and there has been much heaped on rapacious megachurches for altering the religious landscape and, it is argued, stealing members from smaller, struggling churches.

Besides being the product of entrepreneurs, megachurches have also prospered, according to economists, because they employ an economy of scope. Traditionally, a firm makes a profit by the economy of scale: a larger scale of production cuts costs, allows the firm to reduce prices, and hence increases sales and profits. However, every church provides public goods that earn no profit. Anyone can walk in a church door and consume what they like. Accordingly, large churches draw free riders, who contribute nothing or the minimum. Nevertheless, even with free riders, a megachurch can generate revenue and participation by the economics of scope. It can offer a wide variety of products and services. In this sense, the megachurch is like the mall, not the big-box store. Not for nothing did the *New York Times* call the megachurch a "minicity." Not only does each megachurch have its own distinct personality, it also has a remarkable variety of things to attract interest.

The megachurch has a mission as well, and this is what the management guru Peter Drucker, writing in the *Harvard Business Review*, said that firms can learn from megachurches. Churches organize to get things done, grow, and reach out.[24] Naturally, such a successful megachurch as Willow Creek Community Church, located outside Chicago, eventually became a topic of study at the Harvard Business School. Despite the impression of some of Harvard's young go-getters, who felt that religion is a matter of spontaneity and free handouts, Willow Creek founder Bill Hybels argued that even Jesus was an efficient manager. When it comes to saving souls, Hybels said, reaching market goals, and not being simply laissez-faire, is important. "It matters that we align our staffs and leverage our resources," he said. "Jesus was not the least laissez-faire about building the kingdom." The task of a church leader is to build "prevailing" churches.[25]

The latest object of fascination is the phenomenal Lakewood Church of Houston, where pastor Joel Osteen turned his father's congregation into a throng of 25,000. They purchased the former Houston Rockets stadium to serve larger audiences. In 2007, members put $43 million in the offering plate. Broadcasts of worship events drew $30 million. Osteen's best-selling books add still more. Osteen presents a religious product that combines both an evangelical faith and a "positive thinking" gospel, both very much in demand in the American marketplace of religion.

As a religious firm, Lakewood illustrates how, despite the way free riders may harm clubs, they turn out to be a market resource for well-adapted firms. Operating on weekends much like a large sports event or concert, the megachurch lowers every possible barrier to people attending. As Osteen explains, "I wanted to reach the mainstream. I mean we've reached the church audience."[26] In its entrepreneurial pastor, the church has a strong brand name. Osteen is the "smiling pastor." When it comes to an economy of scope, Lakewood has twenty distinct ministries, many at the campus but others that have been parlayed into national speaking events, books, and other products.

In a religious firm such as Lakewood, economists have pointed to the management structure and the way megachurches make free riders a key component of their growth strategy. For a start, the core staff of a typical megachurch uses the efficiency of a division of labor but also generates the benefits of a club. A typical core staff is a chief spiritual officer (pastor), chief executive officer (administrator), and chief financial officer (accountant). Their staff further divides up specific duties. Moreover, the staff is highly dedicated: to be a part of it, as in a club, they must invest time and donations in the church. According to one study, a large megachurch needs at least 15 percent of its membership to have club-like dedication, with at least 5 percent highly dedicated.[27]

With that core, the megachurch can generate guaranteed manpower and income. With this, it can deal with its fixed costs, which are the building and the product, such as the Sunday service and educational and social service activities. In regard to the core product—the religious message—it doesn't cost any more to give it to one more person, and hence the economy of scale kicks in in a remarkable way. Megachurches can invite massive numbers of free riders at no extra overhead cost. They can do this by satellite broadcasts as well as by having thousands of seats in the sanctuary. By increasing the free rider audience, the megachurch has a larger market for participation and revenue. Every megachurch seeks to bring casual visitors to a higher commitment—to brand loyalty.

This is always a challenge, since free riders, as economists know, like their situation. According to a Harvard Business School study of Willow Creek, its first big challenge was to "convert" the 10,000 participants it brought each week. "How could Willow Creek assimilate the growing number of unconnected visitors when it promised them anonymity in its services?" the study asked.[28] New data on megachurches show that this conversion process consumes a great deal of megachurch activity; large numbers of visitors still come and go. As the sociologist Scott Thumma says, based on 2008 surveys, "It takes a lot of effort to get people inculcated to the life of the church."[29] Many people are very new. In the Thumma study, six in ten megachurch members had attended five years or less. Seven in ten had attended another church, and only 4 percent had been in a megachurch "all my life." In other words, says Thumma, "there's a lot of circulation of folks."

But that, combined with the core, is the optimizing model of the megachurch. There are low entry barriers. The church provides lots of public goods to free riders in hopes of creating brand loyalty—higher commitment and higher donations. However this turns out, there is much else working for this market approach: the superstar effect, the buzz of what's happening, and the vortex effect of big, anonymous, and entertaining events. "Individual choice is the key," Thumma says. "The motto is, 'Preach the ideal, accept the minimum.'"[30]

We began this chapter by asking why religions form into groups, growing more and more. Why not thousands of individual gurus, or millions of tiny religious kiosks? As in all economic approaches, religions form to allow individuals to create the most effective means to ensure that the benefits are greater than the costs. They seek individual goods, but also goods that can be produced only by joining a group. Furthermore, people rely on each other to define how satisfying these goods should be. As the sociologist Darren Sherkat summarizes, "Religious goods are not simply 'experience' goods which must be consumed in order to be evaluated; rather, these goods must be experienced in communities which direct us on how to evaluate them."[31] In religion, the club and the firm have turned out to be the most effective ways of generating these group benefits and acceptable costs. Hence, people join religious groups with eminently rational motives. That rationality holds whether they enter a strict club with high demands or a wide-open popular religion with few entry costs. The religious club and firm are rational as well, as if creatures in their own right. They use cost and benefit to generate resources, survive, and grow.

Up to this point, we've traced the economic approach to religion through the ranks of the individual, household, club, and firm. Now we can pause before moving on to the great marketplace of the world, and ask: where did this idea of the economic approach to religion come from, anyway?

CHAPTER 6

History of an Idea

The founding of the economic approach to religion has typically been traced to Adam Smith, the eighteenth-century moral philosopher. He analyzed religion in terms of competition and monopoly, looked at the incentives of individuals, and discussed the importance of church-run schools in accumulating skills, which we now call human capital. He also said that the clerical leadership ranks are like a great "incorporation," and he noted how sects, like strict clubs, can be energetic and highly productive.[1]

Smith was part of the Enlightenment. So he also drew a lot of his ideas from the Greco-Roman classics. Socrates, indeed, spoke of religion as bargaining with the gods. The ancients spoke of incentives, private property, and economic cost and benefit. In the fourth century c.e., the Roman statesman Themistius pleaded for tolerance of religious pluralism before a long succession of powerful emperors, most of them Christians, either Catholic or Arian. Themistius argued the merits of religious choice and competition, since all human nature had piety but individuals sought their own ways of worship. "A complete absence of competition fills us with lethargy and boredom," he declared to Emperor Jovian. But by allowing the coexistence of pagan and Christian sects, there is a "beneficial contention from pious observance." And this leads to a helpful "zeal in religious affairs: mutual competition and rivalry."[2]

The modern reinvention of the economic approach to religion has its own distinct origins, however. The question of who invented the modern version is akin to the question of who invented the Internet. Its origins began broadly in modern mathematical ideas, which came to fruition during World War II as computer logic. Information theory followed, as did the development of information "packets" and "switches" in the 1960s, leading finally in 1990 to the first proposal for what became the World Wide Web. Early on, theologians and science fiction writers also contributed the web idea. The Catholic visionary Pierre Teilhard de Chardin, for example, spoke of an information "noosphere," making him a favorite among early Internet entrepreneurs, who today envision a vast computing "cloud" around the planet.

In a similar way, the economics of religion has many predecessors but, arguably, a small contemporary group that catalyzed its current popularity. The
critical elements began to fall into place after World War II. The key intersec-
tion, as this story will suggest, is a combination of new theories about human
behavior with new data about religion. All this, beginning in the 1970s, was
shepherded forward by new institutions and new personalities. For economics
to address religion, religion itself has to be able to be studied scientifically. For
religion to be studied scientifically, it has to be measured, and that means
obtaining data on how people act and what they believe. The easiest way to find out,
of course, is to ask them—to conduct a survey.

DATA AND THEORY MEET

Public surveys date from the nineteenth century in Europe. As the art of public
polling came of age in the 1940s in the United States, however, it also fell under
acute suspicion after it predicted Harry Truman's defeat in the 1948 presidential election. There was a good deal of social science wrist slapping and a con-
gressional investigation. To avoid future mishaps, a new technique of statistical
sampling was adopted as the standard. It surveyed a random sample of citizens
and generalized to the entire population. For social research, this required
massive data collection centers, which first arose at academic centers such as
Columbia University, the University of Michigan, the University of Chicago,
and the University of Washington, Seattle.

Half a century before, the U.S. census had stopped asking citizens question
about their religious affiliations. Small religious groups had protested, with political success, against such census head counts, believing they could lead
to discrimination. In 1924, a group of social scientists from New York City traveled
to Muncie, Indiana, to begin a massive survey of rural Protestants, a project that
turned out to be a full study of an average American town—called Middletown in
one of the most famous case studies in American sociology. In the 1940s, some
opinion polling or census surveys gathered information on religious affiliation,
but by comparison to other social topics, religion lagged behind. In contrast,
groups such as veterans, voters, unions, adolescents, and the mentally ill were all
being understood on a national scale by the new survey-and-analysis approach.

The religion vacuum began to be filled after the 1950s, when "a series of major
surveys described every aspect of the religious beliefs and practices of Americans
in such detail that little remained to be discovered," recalls one researcher.[3] One
of those watersheds came in 1958. At the University of Michigan, the sociology

unit had been doing an annual Detroit Area Survey since 1951. When sociology professor Gerhard Lenski was put in charge of the 1958 round, he added questions about religion. The result was the first random sampling survey of U.S. Catholics, Jews, white Protestants, and black Protestants, comparing details on religion with income, class, age, marriage, family size, work satisfaction, and so on. The survey team also interviewed clergy. When published, Lenski's *The Religious Factor* did not report any bombshells. Religion predicted attitudes as much as class did, for example, except in voting. Each group existed in a "socio-religious subcommunity" that was less tolerant of outsiders than, for example, the public-minded churches they attended. Perhaps most surprising, religion was not just for the dispossessed: the educated and well-off also showed high participation.[4]

For those interested in the scientific study of religion, Lenski's opportunity was the envy of the hour. Their day would come, however. At the University of California, Berkeley, the sociologist Charles Y. Glock arrived to set up Berkeley's Survey Research Center around 1960. As a professor at Columbia University in New York, he had done some survey work for the Episcopal Church. So at Berkeley he set up a subset of the Survey Research Center, the Research Program in Religion and Society. About the time of his arrival, Glock wrote that no study of religion in America, past or current, "meets even the minimum standards of scientific inquiry."[5] He tried to change that, and the opportunity came when a large Jewish organization, the Anti-Defamation League, was willing to put a large sum of money behind a survey of American religious beliefs, especially regarding anti-Semitism. Hence, in 1963 Glock's program produced the next big survey of American religion. But before we look at these collections of data, it is important to see what was happening in the same period with theories about human behavior—which include behaviors in religion.

At Harvard University in the 1960s, there was a great rumbling over how to study human behavior. For a generation, the classic sociological ideas of Harvard's Talcott Parsons had set the agenda. In the tradition of the French thinker Emile Durkheim, Parsons taught that all individual behavior is a by-product of group behavior, which imprints norms on individuals. It was a typical sociological view: making group forces the most powerful influences. In this view, all the sectors of a society, including religion, functioned to glue the society together and create individuals who followed its norms. This is the functionalist view of religion, and it came to dominate American academia, thanks to Parsons. But it was soon to be reversed. The first step was the influence of the organism-focused behaviorism of B. F. Skinner, but the final break came with the work of sociologist George Homans. As Parsons's Department of Social Relations at Harvard crumbled amid academic disagreements, a formal Department of Sociology emerged in 1970, with Homans as its chairman.

In the previous two decades, Homans had advanced a view of the human being that he (and others) called methodological individualism. As in economics, from which he mined many of his concepts, Homans said the proper object of social study was the individual making exchanges with other individuals. This was the "contrast between the social contract theory and the social mold theory," Homans said in his 1950 book *The Human Group*.[6] In other words, did humans make rational exchanges with each other, judging costs and benefits, or were people molded and shaped by larger social forces, like hot metal poured into a cultural cast? Homans argued for the exchanges.

Homans began at Harvard studying English poetry and aiming to be a newspaper reporter, but when that job was scuttled by the Depression, he stayed on to study social science. After serving at sea in World War II, he returned to academia and applied his gift as a wordsmith to arguing for exchange theory. In this, Homans acknowledged his debt to "elementary economics," which, when added to social psychology, could provide a few simple axioms for all human behavior.[7] These were, in short, that humans sought rewards and avoided losses. People made these judgments in terms of past experiences, repeat exchanges, opportunities, satiation, and future hopes.

In 1964, Homans was president of the American Sociological Association, and at its annual meeting held in Montreal he gave a talk that he would count among his signature manifestos. Titled "Bringing Men Back In," Homans argued for a return to the study of individual agents, not social systems that reputedly shaped all human actions. With mock apologies, he denounced the dominance of the functionalist school. The problem was that functionalism could not explain why people behaved the way they did. For instance, when sociologists try to explain the rise of the British textile industry, it is obfuscating to speak of "systems of action," but helpful to say: "Men are more likely to perform an activity, the more valuable they perceive the reward of that activity to be." Those rewards need not be material, said Homans, arguing that social science must return to individual actions: "Let us get men back in, and let us put some blood in them."[8]

During his presidential address, two other elements presaged the emergence of the economic approach to religion. For one thing, Homans cited the University of Chicago sociologist James Coleman, who was using the economic principles of rational choice in the study of social phenomena. By then, rational choice was emerging as a central feature of the Department of Economics at Chicago, as we will see later. On the second front, a graduate student who was working with Glock at Berkeley's Research Program in Religion and Society was in the Montreal audience. His name was Rodney Stark, a tall North Dakotan, former college fullback, and army veteran with a growing interest in the scientific study of religion. For Stark, Homans's speech was a turning point.

Before becoming Glock's student and completing a doctorate in sociology, Stark spent a year as a newspaper reporter for the *Oakland Tribune*. He had earned a college degree in journalism in Denver in 1959. A *Tribune* editor once sent him to cover a UFO conference, the Oakland Space Craft Club, and as Stark later recalled, his feature article on the fringe group was "well received," so he got more such assignments. As he became interested in alternative groups, he realized just how many dotted the U.S. landscape. In another news assignment, Stark went to interview the pastor of an Italian Catholic parish. This was on the eve of the Second Vatican Council. The pastor took Stark to the front steps of the church and pointed across the street to a white frame church with a huge vertical neon sign on the bell tower: "Jesus Saves, Italian Pentecostal Church." Gesturing at the neon sign, the pastor explained to Stark, "Everyone over there came from over here. Every time you are tempted to cut corners, remember that."[9] What Stark remembered, to great effect in his future work, is that religion lives or dies in a competitive marketplace.

Between 1963 and 1968, Glock and Stark launched a project to expand beyond Lenski's work. A random sample of 3,000 churchgoers in four northern California counties was treated to nearly 500 interview questions, many on religion. The project also recruited Chicago's National Opinion Research Center to ask many of the same questions of a national random sample of nearly 2,000 people. In all, the 1963 study was an early layer of bedrock, for eventually many more strata were laid down by other surveys, both in the United States and abroad. Glock and Stark mined their survey for all they could get. They announced a three-book study, the first appearing in 1968 as *American Piety: The Nature of Religious Commitment*. Stark was turning out to be not only a gifted writer but a fast one, using the journalistic knack of cutting through much chaff to find a kernel of wheat. The two final books of their three-part series were mostly written. At that point, however, Glock and Stark disagreed over the goal of the project, dooming it to incompletion. In the spirit of Homans, Stark wanted to put theory into the books, presumably exchange theory. As a veteran of social science, Glock felt that their mission was to collect data, not theorize.

CHURCHES, SECTS, AND CULTS

The 1963 surveys, and a few others at Berkeley, provided Stark with a gold mine for his first journal articles. He wrote on everything from beliefs in the afterlife to the connection between religion and mental health, anti-Semitism among

Christians, and the beliefs of graduate students, professors, and professional theologians. This was the 1960s, however, and as one of Stark's colleagues, John Lofland, recalls, the counterculture, the antiwar movement, and the new religious "cults" had, all at once, exploded on the sociological scene. Even in the fifties, Lofland said, his work at the University of Wisconsin on religious behavior was belittled as not "relevant." But that changed overnight when exotic religions became part of the 1960s upheaval. "Suddenly, 'trivial' and 'obscure' questions such as conversion, missionizing, and faith-maintenance and many other questions became 'hot' and timely topics," Lofland recalls.[10]

The hottest topic was cults. Lofland and Stark managed to track down one of the first Unification Church missionaries to America, a Korean former professor named Young Oon Kim, and Lofland, like an anthropologist with an island tribe, studied her first small American following. He called it, with an excellent sense for book sales, a "doomsday cult." If not for the outburst of new religions in Japan in the 1950s, and a similar American event in the 1960s and 1970s, sociologists of religion might never have returned to the topic of how religions form, or their dynamics as cults, sects, and churches. But now cult formation—and the origin of mainstream religions—became the hottest of topics for research, doctoral dissertations, and academic careers. It was a topic that Stark, among others, would take up with relish and fair-mindedness. Indeed, at a time when many social scientists said religion was a product of mental illness, Stark found in his surveys that religious people were the most mentally well adjusted of the population sample.

The only jobs open, however, were in the training of criminologists, and so Stark took his first professorship at the University of Washington in Seattle to do just that. Although the religion topic was on a back burner, Stark continued to experiment with his theory of religion. He followed the example of Homans, who set down a few formal propositions about human behavior. Stark did likewise, but he was in pursuit of a much greater elaboration and thus many more axioms than Homans would concede. (In the final statement of his *Theory of Religion*, published in 1987, Stark presented seven axioms, 104 definitions of concepts, and 344 contingent propositions.) But it all came in Homansian baby steps. In the mid-1970s the project moved forward thanks to a new stimulus. A recent graduate of Harvard, William Sims Bainbridge, arrived in Seattle as a new sociology professor, and he and Stark hit it off. Bainbridge had famous Baptist missionary leaders in his ancestry, and though he is a "lifelong atheist," he was taken by how early Christian missionaries spoke of pitched market competition between religions around the world.

As per the era, Bainbridge also specialized in the exotic. At Harvard he did his doctoral work on space flight enthusiasts, who eventually formed a kind of futuristic cult. He also wrote on Shaker communes, utopian groups, psychiatric cults, Scientology, the occult, and the rise and decline of Transcendental Meditation. Meanwhile, Bainbridge was influenced by Homans's exchange theory and the new work, typified by the up-and-coming sociologist Mark Granovetter, on networks, or how through exchanges individuals developed strong and weak ties that had a lot to do with success in life and the flow of information among people—a topic that might sound very economic. Either way, when Bainbridge and Stark met, they had both been cultivated by the new ideas of the era: exchange, exotic religious groups, and networks. They also wanted to add the complex mind—the cognitive ability of belief—to the simpler exchange behaviorism of Homans. In any case, they said RIP to functionalism.

To bury the old approach, they honed an ambitious new sociological model that they built upon learning theory, economics, and exchange theory. When it was done, their collaborative book, *A Theory of Religion* (1987), was a "full-length deductive theory of religion."[11] It began with a theory, in other words, and then tested it against data. This was the idea being espoused by Milton Friedman in economics and the philosopher Karl Popper in science. But before jumping in with both feet, Stark and Bainbridge sent up a few trial balloons. In 1979 they published the article "Of Churches, Sects, and Cults: Preliminary Concepts for a Theory of Religious Movements," followed the next year by a wider proposal: "Towards a Theory of Religion." The latter article, in addressing the nature of religious commitment in the individual, presented seven axioms that remained central to their future work. For our purposes, two important ones were these:[12]

(Axiom 2) *Humans seek what they perceive to be rewards and avoid what they perceive to be costs.*

(Axiom 5) *Some desired rewards are limited in supply, including some that simply do not exist [in the physical world].*

In these two alone, an economic approach to religion was fast emerging. As Stark and Bainbridge viewed the world, individuals organized themselves according to exchanges, thus accounting for groups and power structures. People faced scarcity of resources. Every choice for one thing was a denial of another thing. People also tried to solve problems in how they lived their lives and understood reality. In the latter case, religion offered explanations, and the exchange of belief systems was an important human reward. Individuals made religious commitments and joined groups—cults, sects, and churches—on the basis of judging the costs and benefits of the explanations. Founders of religions, priesthoods, and organized religion all supplied these explanations. And, as history testified, consumers were eager to have them, whatever the cost.

In his long career as a sociologist and writer of major college sociology text-books, Stark evolved to a narrower definition of religion. With Glock in 1965, he stated that human belief systems were "over-arching and sacred systems of symbols, beliefs, values, and practices concerning ultimate meaning which men shape to interpret their world." However, one branch of the systems was humanistic and the other religious. All religions affirm "the existence of a supernatural being, world, or force, and predicate their ultimate solutions on this assumption." Nearly four decades later, the Stark model was pithier still: "Religion is concerned with the supernatural; everything else is secondary." As in all else, "in pursuit of rewards, humans will seek to exchange with a god or gods." Religion sets "the terms of exchange."[13]

After their joint publication of *A Theory of Religion* (1987), Stark and Bain-bridge parted ways. In the experience, they learned how to build a juggernaut of ideas. For example, everything in *A Theory of Religion* was essentially present in nineteen journal articles they had worked on, compiled in an anthology (*The Future of Religion*, 1984), and then summarized in a final tome. That accom-plishment was met with both admiration and skepticism in professional circles. But what most irked sociologists of religion was the way that Stark had opened the door to a potentially pernicious invader: economists.

ECONOMIC RUMBLINGS IN CHICAGO

At the University of Chicago, economics was making a name for itself in this period. The school was stacking up more Nobel Prizes in economics than any other academic institution. Despite its diverse faculty, its most prominent members were champions of the neoclassical, free market, laissez-faire—and rational-choice—revolution that took on Keynesian "big government" eco-nomics. And they seemed to have won the battle, both politically and cultur-ally, with the election of free market advocate Ronald Reagan in 1980. Well before that, however, the "Chicago School" had a name for other reasons.

The school's founder, the midwesterner Frank Knight, wrote on markets and risk and was a fierce believer in the democratic free market's ability to curb corruptions of power. Wright was only the first generation. Soon to follow was a second generation, best known for its free market thinkers who grabbed newspaper headlines, the Austrian Friedrich von Hayek and of course Milton

Friedman. Both opposed central planning and favored deregulation. Among professional economists, however, Friedman was best known for his 1953 essay "The Methodology of Positive Economics."[14] Here, he proposed a deductive method much like Homans's in sociology: start with a theory, then go test it against the data, whether in case studies, historical records, or statistics. As noted earlier, this overlaps the method used in Stark's *Theory of Religion*: start with a vision of how the world works, then test it relentlessly. Mere data— prices, products, and statistics—could not explain how people behaved or how they likely would behave the next time.

At Chicago, the third generation began to emerge in the 1960s, and none was more prominent than Friedman student Gary Becker. Positive economics stirred Becker's imagination. With it, he conceived of economics expanding its explanatory power to the entire human experience. Like Friedman (who had trained in physics and mathematics), Becker was a mathematical whiz. Reared in Pennsylvania, he headed for Princeton to do math and economics but, find- ing them "sterile," turned to sociology—with no better luck. "I found Talcott Parsons, who was then Mr. American Sociologist, impossible to read," Becker recalls. "I tried and I said, 'I just can't make it as a sociologist. I can't under- stand this stuff.'" So he went back to economics—and on to Chicago, where the ideas of Friedman and others reignited his intellect. Now, he felt, "econom- ics could deal with the problems I was interested in," which turned out to be economic approaches to racial discrimination, educational inequality, and more.[15]

Becker encapsulates his economic approach to human behavior in an anec- dote of his own experience as a professor at Columbia University. He was late for an appointment with a graduate student and could not find parking. He parked illegally, made the appointment, and did not get a ticket. Afterward, he tried to put his on-the-spot existential experience in economic terms: how high a fine was he willing to risk to get the time he needed, and how much value did the police put on enforcing the parking law? This scenario, he concluded, was how people calculate life every day. As he later said, "the economic approach is a comprehensive one that is applicable to all human behavior."[16] For his part, he would apply this economic model—complete with mathematical equations and reams of hard social data—to discrimination, education, crime, addiction, divorce, marriage, and fertility. The term "rational choice" had been around since the 1950s, but Becker, more than anyone, put it on the map of modern economics.

Historically, Becker reached back to philosophers such as Adam Smith and Jeremy Bentham. Smith had touched on the topic of what is now called human capital, or the accumulation of habits and skills. Bentham argued that human beings had a scale for calculating pain and pleasure, making choices accordingly. Along with University of Chicago colleague George Stigler, Becker presented a more refined economic model of these age-old ideas: "All human behavior can be viewed as involving participants who maximize their utility [rewards] from a stable set of preferences and accumulate an optimal amount of information and other inputs in a variety of markets." [17] He applied this to studies of the family and the household, where the constraints on optimal inputs were time, resources, size of family, and other factors. In short, he created a new household economics.

Well before Becker was awarded the 1992 Nobel Prize in economics for this kind of work, the complaint against his "economic imperialism" was heard, and it sounded much like what sociologists of religion had said about Stark's theory—both were reductionists who insulted human mystery and spontaneity. In no way, however, were Becker and Stark in the same professional orbits. Stark was a man of the western states, a bit countercultural himself, and never part of the Ivy League circuit. Becker was of the eastern Establishment, a hard-nosed economist who moved easily between Princeton, Columbia, and Chicago. But for putting down the first floorboard of an economic approach to religion, both Becker and Stark were crucial. Each also had a student who incarnated their ideas. For Becker it was Laurence Iannaccone, and for Stark it was Roger Finke—both of whom completed doctoral work in the mid-1980s. With proper credentials, they began hacking through the jungle of economics and sociology in search of a new species, which they called the economics of religion.

STUDENTS OF THE REVOLUTION

A midwesterner, Finke studied social work for his first degree at Concordia College, a Lutheran Church–Missouri Synod school in Nebraska. Interested in social work, crime, and delinquency, Finke headed for the University of Washington in 1976, mainly to study social statistics with its leading expert. There, at the Seattle campus, he met Stark, who was training criminologists as well, and they discovered their common interest in theories of religion. Hence, in 1984, Finke emerged with a doctoral dissertation not in criminology but on the demographic growth of church attendance over a few hundred years of American history.

The topic of criminology had taken them into interesting territory. They looked at crime and religion in the Roaring Twenties, cults in the Jazz Age, and the role of chain gangs. During one of his many ponderous searches in early twentieth-century American census statistics, Finke finally discovered an anomaly that would change his career. Since its founding as a science, sociology had argued that urbanization undermined religion: city folks got secular while country folks kept their superstitions. To the contrary, however, Finke found dusty census figures showing that religious participation increased as people moved to the cities. "So at the very time when the population was getting more educated, more urban, more industrialized, you saw an increase in the overall level of [religious] involvement," Finke recalls. "Exactly the opposite of all the things I had been taught."[18] Stark was intrigued also, so they began digging.

The first quarry was Finke's findings about the late nineteenth century. Then they looked at U.S. cities in 1906. Next, they reached back to the American colonies in 1776. They were applying theory—about exchanges, free markets, and competition—to data, musty as they were. By unearthing the old church information, Stark recalls, Finke began a small revolution. His was "the first major effort to test the deduction that pluralism invigorates religious 'firms' and thus results in higher overall levels of religious participation."[19] By 1983, Stark had already begun to write articles using the novel term "religious economies." In 1986, he and Finke published on the census data. Finally in 1989 they offered a sweeping summary (that was also the topic of Finke's doctoral thesis): "How the Upstart Sects Won America, 1776–1850."

In cheering on the "upstarts," Stark and Finke soon became known as the sociologists who challenged the venerable old school of church historians. The old view, typified by Sydney Ahlstrom of Yale, is that the well-groomed Puritans moderated themselves, became the upper class in America, and then expanded out to create America's Protestant establishment, a middle class in which all sects, outliers, and underlings aspired to have membership. A contrary view, however, was already evident in the work of historian Sidney E. Mead, who argued that American religion moved "from coercion to persuasion." This story was not of merger into a cumulative mainstream but, as government backed off, of sects competing in the open landscape. Earlier in the century, Yale's H. Richard Niebuhr had also (like Ahlstrom and others) lamented that Christian groups were so fractious, that is, denominational. In other words, Niebuhr saw the sectarian competition clearly but pined for amicable unity.

In contrast, Stark and Finke celebrated the jostling marketplace. Tearing a page from Adam Smith, they noted how the big, lazy churches were outsmarted by the clever, active, and entrepreneurial little guys. The title of their 1992 book captured this spirit: *The Churching of America, 1776–1900: Winners and Losers in Our Religious Economy.* "The economists were very favorable to the book," Finke recalls. The social historians were also pleased—but most of the church historians were not. "They viewed it as social scientists coming in and saying, 'We know it all.'" As Stark recalls, they were in fact saying something like that:

they had used data and theory to "challenge many chapters in the standard narrative of American religious history."[20]

The dean of church historians at the time, Martin Marty, fired the main salvo. "The authors enjoy using a kind of 'in your face' approach to 'religious economies,'" Marty wrote in a book review. "Most students of American religion use some economic insights and market metaphors, but Finke and Stark reduce everything to the language of 'regulation,' 'cost and benefit,' 'maximizing,' 'collective production,' 'good bargains,' 'opportunity costs,' 'consuming' and so on."[21] Soon enough, references to a "supply-side" religion would also creep into the debate. This added some political electricity, since "supply-side economics" was the rallying cry of the Reaganauts who had ruled politics through the 1980s. For those offended by the intrusion of economics on religion, perhaps the worst was still to come. After all, Becker was keen on spreading his economic gospel to all human behavior. And now Iannaccone, his student, began taking economic equations right into the sanctuary.

About the time that Stark and Bainbridge were putting the final touches on *A Theory of Religion* and Finke left Seattle for his first teaching job near Chicago, Laurence Iannaccone was finishing up his doctoral dissertation under Becker. He had applied Becker's models of human capital and household consumption to explaining religious participation. By now, Iannaccone was teaching at Santa Clara University. On his own time, he worked on writing his first journal article. He knew Stark's work, for in fact his dissertation used the 1963 San Francisco Bay area religion survey to test his economic model. At the end of 1985 Iannaccone sent a draft of his article to several sociologists of religion. Stark was the only one to respond. The economics of religion was about to take another important turn.

Iannaccone was born in Buffalo into a family of Italian immigrants. Earlier in the century, the family had broken from Catholicism to join a dissenting branch of the Jehovah's Witnesses, which itself had splintered off from the early Adventists. It was rich American church history, and young Iannaccone had a front-row seat on the sectarian religious experience for eighteen years of his life. Still, his father had a Columbia University Ph.D. in education. He was a "wandering academic" who went to jail as a conscientious objector, set up summer church camps, and taught at several universities. The family ended up at the University of California, Santa Barbara, and Laurence went off to Stanford to study mathematics. Then in 1977 he headed for Chicago, considering pure mathematics but not exactly enthused. Looking for alternatives, he had an interview with James Coleman, the noted sociologist. Coleman said that sociology was in utter disarray. "You should think in terms of economics," he advised. "Rational-choice economics."[22]

Eventually, as a student of Becker, Iannaccone mastered his household economic models. But, given his own background in strict Protestantism and his wife's Mormon background (she was earning a Ph.D. in social psychology), Iannaccone was interested in the sociology of religious groups as well. "Around the dining room table, I was trying to see how the society and the church are pulling people in different directions, drawing little budget constraints and so on," he said of his early musings. Finally, he presented an ambitious thesis idea to Becker: to apply human-capital and rational-choice models to household religion *and* sect formation. Becker knew his student was biting off too much. He urged a narrow focus, as seen in the resulting 1984 dissertation: "Consumption Capital and Habit Formation with an Application to Religious Participation." "Becker was enthusiastic," Iannaccone recalls. "He probably saw it as one more brick in the edifice of rational choice."

Iannaccone was breaking new ground, but he was not the only one. The acknowledged start of applying Beckerian principles to religion came with Corry Azzi and Ronald Ehrenberg's 1975 study, "Household Allocation of Time and Church Attendance," which stirred rebuttals and discussion for another couple of years. The article had coined the terms "religious capital" and "salvation motive." "At the time, most people not connected to the Chicago school were not very interested in our work, just as they did not take Gary Becker very seriously," recalls Ehrenberg, now a Cornell University professor who specializes in the economics of labor and higher education. "The National Science Foundation turned down a research proposal that I had submitted to do new work in the mid-1970s and I moved on to do other things. I was happy to see in more recent years a resurgence in interest in the topic."[23]

In the early 1980s, the University of Southern California economist Timur Kuran, trained at Princeton and Stanford, launched his work on the interaction of economics and religion, much as Adam Smith might have—but without much peer enthusiasm. His first-of-its-kind journal article in 1982, which explained and critiqued the rise of "Islamic economics," suddenly made him the world expert on the topic, at least to journalists and conference organizers, he recalls. Most fellow economists grimaced. "You are losing your marbles," they said. "If you are going to do this kind of work, move to a theology department. It has nothing to do with economics."[24] About this same time, the economists Brooks Hull and Frederick Bold were crafting a working paper, "Would You Buy a Used Car from This Priest?" that applied the law of asymmetrical information to religion, as a Nobel economist had done to used cars. The Israeli economist Shoshana Neuman used Becker's human capital model on the religious lives of Israeli workingmen. And in 1987 the economist Robert Ekelund and his colleagues began their fifteen years of writing on the medieval church from the point of view of public choice, or the church as a complex profit-making firm. Later still, the Harvard-trained economist Eli Berman began applying club models to sectarian groups, including the new breed of religious terrorists, Hamas, Hezbollah, and the Taliban.

Before this ferment had begun, Iannaccone, who landed a teaching job in 1982, completed his dissertation in 1984 but had to decide whether the economics of religion was a field worth pursuing. As noted, Becker had urged him to narrow his thesis. But to do so, he had orphaned the other part of his idea, the economic analysis of church and sect formation. Now he decided to return to it and see if anyone in economics would take it seriously. In effect, he wanted to see how economic concepts such as rational choice, household production, and club theory could explain so-called irrational behaviors in religion. Why, for example, would rational people join strict sects or cults if there were no obvious economic benefits? In fact, joiners seemed to punish themselves with religious constraints. And then, for all their efforts, society heaped on additional ridicule or persecution. For example, Jehovah's Witnesses not only had gone to jail for their pacifism (they also opposed Hitler, for example) but were beaten on American street corners for handing out heretical literature. Iannaccone had met such people, as would other social scientists, and found them as rational as the next person. So Iannaccone had a choice. Either he could adopt the societal view that individuals who strictly adhere to a religion are irrational and deviant, or he could take the economic view that they are rational calculators of costs and benefits. As an economist, of course, he banked on the latter. "The central puzzle for me was, what makes these apparently irrational groups viable? They impose gratuitous costs on people. And yet we see them flourishing."[25] If he could show that even joining a high-cost, high-risk sect or cult was a rational pursuit of benefits, then explaining mainstream religion would be easy.

To crystallize his theory, Iannaccone wrote up a paper on the cost-benefit mechanism of strict groups and sent it to a number of sociologists of religion. Economists, a secular breed, weren't interested, especially in exotic religions. So, Iannaccone said, he had "nowhere to go except the sociology of religion." As noted, Stark was the only one who responded. Later, in 1986, Iannaccone was in Seattle on business, so he made the "pilgrimage" to Stark's office. Significantly, Stark told him about Roger Finke, who, with Stark, was preparing an article on Adam Smith's views on religious monopoly and competition. Iannaccone began to attend the annual meetings of the American Sociological Association. Then he went to meetings of the Society for the Scientific Study of Religion, where he first met Roger Finke. As Finke recalls, "At these conferences, Larry and I would end up spending two or three hours talking about all the ideas we had. We asked, 'Why hadn't people looked at it this way before?'"[26]

At the University of Chicago, meanwhile, Becker and Coleman had also built a bridge between economics and sociology, and they began holding a regular seminar starting in 1984. Coleman was soon to found a journal as well, *Rationality and Society* (1989). Eventually Becker called up Iannaccone and asked him to present his economic work on religion at the March 1988 seminar, which typically drew senior academics, and which, in this case, had slated the nationally known sociologist Andrew Greeley as a respondent to Iannaccone. It was a bit outlandish, Iannaccone recalls: "I'd not yet published a single thing, but I'm supposed to tell them all about religion and economics!" The seminar met evenings, with Becker and Coleman holding court and the best and brightest ringing a circular seminar table.

Wisely, Iannaccone gave credit to his forebears. Becker had done family. The German sociologist Max Weber and the American theologian H. Richard Niebuhr had done sect and church, and Adam Smith had theorized the marketplace. In forty-five minutes, Iannaccone surveyed his economic models of family, group, and marketplace religion. Greeley was impressed. He admitted his "convert's zeal for rational choice" and concluded that "Professor Iannaccone has made an important contribution not only to rational choice theory but to the sociology of religion." Greeley's discussion paper, in fact, became the last chapter of his 1989 book *Religious Change in America*, published by Harvard University Press. As often happens, Greeley did not note that he had taken the economic scenario from Iannaccone, who at the time was still an unknown quantity. That obscurity would not last long, however.

Iannaccone was meeting other people, such as the sociologist Mark Granovetter. By the mid-1980s, Granovetter's work on strong and weak ties in social groups and how economic actors are embedded in social networks was shaping his field. His concept of embeddedness, applied to rational choices in a culture, was soon to be used in the sociology of religion as well. Naturally, Granovetter was interested in Iannaccone's economic modeling of ties and incentives in strict and lenient religious groups. So he passed the paper on to the editor of the *American Journal of Sociology*, which was planning a special issue on economics in 1988. Published as "A Formal Model of Church and Sect," the article covered the religion niche in the special issue. At last Iannaccone's orphan topic had found a home.

By now, Iannaccone felt he could pursue the topic and still make a living. He even thought it was the start of a "new field," which is the kind of dreaming that proliferates in the modern world of academic overspecialization. In Iannaccone's memory, it was sheer enthusiasm. "You looked at that and, oh my God, you could kind of redo the whole field." This was characteristic of economics, after all, taking a wild theory and testing it relentlessly against reality. "Great economics is done on the brink of absurdity," Iannaccone said. "The trick is not to jump off." Actually, the economics of religion seemed potentially quite a broad field as long as one avoided cliffs, which meant career suicide. Still, a shingle had to be put out, an advertisement posted. That opportunity also came in 1988. The editor of the *Journal of Economic Literature* asked Iannaccone to write a review article, summarizing the field up to the present. "This is your chance to get out of the ghetto," the editor told Iannaccone.[27] So in September 1998, the profession was greeted by a declaration of existence: "Introduction to the Economics of Religion."

By 1990, Iannaccone had begun his prolific output of journal articles, the pent-up results of a decade of research. With mastery of the economic formulas, he relentlessly applied the positive economics approach—taking his theories and measuring them against the reams of sociological data now available on religion in the United States and around the world. In this, Iannaccone was the first to bring theory and data together under the technical rubric of the economics of religion. As he boldly stated, "The best prospects for progress in the scientific study of religion rest in the marriage of economic theory and sociological data." Further, he said, "The economics of religion will eventually bury two myths—that of *Homo economicus* as a cold creature with neither need nor capacity for piety, and that of *Homo religiosus* as a benighted throwback to pre-rational times."[28]

The boldness of the claims was heard unevenly in academia and not at all, at least not yet, in the popular media. That changed a little in 1993 when the well-regarded American sociologist of religion Stephen Warner declared that a "new paradigm" had descended on the field of sociology of religion, which many had believed lost in a maze of contradictory theories. Warner had a few names for the new paradigm, which he characterized mostly as a model that viewed American religion, in comparison to Europe's, as driven by "deregulation." In other words, when government stood back, religions tended to multiply and flourish, an idea that was gaining steam in the 1980s and 1990s. However, Warner also suggested that another name for the paradigm shift was the "economic approach to religion." Indeed, he cited Greeley's 1989 rational-choice book as a major indicator, a book influenced by Iannaccone's coming out at the Chicago seminar.[29]

OLD CLASSICS AND FUTURE PROSPECTS

A good ending point in this story comes in 1994, when a conference was held in Sundance, Idaho, of the friends (mostly) and critics (a few) of full-blown rational-choice theory in religion. The approach taken by Stark, Finke, and Iannaccone—all presenters—was the school of thought at issue. Their colleagues elaborated on the strengths and weaknesses of this work, as well as future possibilities. In one presentation, Stark, now an elder statesman in the field, was compared to Durkheim and Weber, the two greatest names in the sociology of religion. For his part, Stark, who did not relish being thought of as the founder of a sect, warned that labels hurt progress. Labels chained thinkers to turf, ground they could waste a lifetime defending. "We must be very careful not to let our efforts to bring real theories into sociology be compromised by being labeled as the Rational Choice 'approach' or 'perspective,'" Stark said. "For then our work becomes just another one of the field's 'theoretical' sects."[30]

Still, the rational-choice trinity was spinning off considerable influence. Their ideas had both natural allies and some significant converts, not least Andrew Greeley. Among their allies in the late 1980s, for example, was the economist Deepak Lal of University College, London, and the World Bank, who was doing the first economic modeling of Hinduism. He argued that while the "Hindu equilibrium" of India's agricultural economy had provided stability for millennia, the nation's move to a market economy was hampered by Hindu legacies: the caste system, the Brahmin dislike of merchants, and finally the new attempts by "Hindu revivalism" to restore ancient traditions. Around 1990, Lal was among the few top economists who specialized in religion that the vaunted Fundamentalism Project of the American Academy of Arts and Sciences could find when they strained to put together a team of experts to write essays for a project volume.[31]

One day in 1993, the baton was handed to American political science as well. Iannaccone had arrived to speak at UCLA's Economics Department. He also had an appointment with Anthony Gill, a budding political scientist who had had an "aha moment" after reading about the economics of religion in *Rationality and Society*. They sat on the lawn of the campus sculpture garden—with its massive bronzes by Matisse, Moore, Calder, and Rodin—and amid these ominous figures agreed that the economics of religion needed a foothold in political science. From that point, Gill developed the first "political economics of religion." The model analyzed religious change in terms of the shifting cost-benefit incentives of governments and religious institutions. First he applied it to Latin America, where a few years of research persuaded him of the theory's merits: "In Latin America, they definitely use the word *compete*." Next he applied it to the "origin of religious liberty," offering an alternative to the theory that modern freedoms grew out of Enlightenment beliefs about liberty. Such beliefs are fine, Gill argued, but when "competing ideas exist in society, it is often *political interests* that tip the balance." In 2009, the *Review of Politics* said Gill's model did not solve every politics-and-religion puzzle, but it "promises to stimulate useful new research on a wide range of historical and contemporary cases of religious liberty and its absence." The economic approach to religion was also beginning to show up in *American Political Science Review*, the top journal of the field.[32]

Economic models were now being applied to the past and present, from Europe to Asia, but in all cases data were the name of the game—and it is an expensive one to play. In Africa, for example, contemporary survey data are sparse, though a body of it is building. Somewhat less expensive is the retrieval of forgotten data, as seen in the use of a 1931 survey of the Dalit, or untouchable, Christians of India, to test economic models of religion. Where expense is no obstacle, global surveys are now regularly asking citizens in more than a hundred countries the same questions that Lenski asked—about religion, income, values, activities, and so on. In the United States and Europe, some of these surveys have become massive indeed, subjecting between 30,000 and 40,000 individuals to long questionnaires. Sample size is important. In 2009, the first large-scale survey of Buddhism in the United States was launched, since there have never been enough data to speak accurately about this much-publicized American phenomenon. Repositories are also necessary. Kuran, the scholar of Islamic economics, organized a team to compile a coded database of more than 10,000 "pre-modern Islamic court records pertaining to economic life." In turn, Finke founded a massive Internet archive of religion data. Without new and better data, newcomers to the economics of religion will not be able to test their models. Even with data, there's always controversy over what they say.[33]

In 1958, when Lenski did his parochial study of Detroit, he opened it by reviewing the great theoretical sweep of his forebears, Weber and Durkheim. He tested his Detroit data against their theories. By 1973, Glock and his fellow sociologist of religion Phillip E. Hammond were editing a volume on going "beyond the classics"—in other words, the question of whether the scientific study of religion could go beyond and improve upon the work of Marx, Weber, Durkheim, Freud, Niebuhr, and Malinowski, who had made the first modern connections between religion and society, culture, and psychology, but whom no one had questioned in the aftermath. As Hammond wrote later, "It was as if those founders had said it all; by early in the twentieth century the social scientific study of religion had received the model bequeathed by these giants but had not gone importantly beyond it."[34]

In answer to this apparent inertia, the economic approach to religion has tried to transcend the founders, reinventing their golden age, but always doffing the hat as necessary. In its pursuit of being interdisciplinary—overlapping economics, sociology, psychology, and history—the economic approach has tried to improve on, if not usurp, the past. But this is done delicately. It gives a slight bow to Durkheim and his heir Malinowski, but none at all to Marx and Freud. It reserves its most auspicious honors for Weber and Niebuhr, and most of all for Adam Smith, who was not included in the Glock volume of classics. In modern times, the economics of religion is rooted in a period from the 1960s to the 1990s. These decades produced figures worthy of note, as this chapter shows. But these are names still to be tested for their long-term historical contribution. In a hundred years, for example, will a group of thinkers publish a new volume about going beyond the theorists of our day?

For now, the new economics of religion has indeed branched into the world marketplace. It is studying the world and all its religions. In its view, religion is a universal product of human exchanges. The outcomes in religion are determined by the push and pull of the market. The fate of religion turns on winning market share: the ability to present goods and services to a world hungry for rewards, earthly and otherworldly. Now we turn to this larger-scale view of the economic approach to religion. The next chapter begins our look at the marketplace in societies and on continents, the market across history, and what the market says about the global future. To these vast topics we now, in all humility, turn our attention.

CHAPTER 7

Marketplace of the Gods

The paradoxical Henry Ford, who brought the mass-produced automobile to America, was thinking a lot like the leader of a religion when he inaugurated a new industry. Ford was a great believer in monopoly. As an entrepreneur, he was the first to provide the masses with an affordable car, the Model T. Once his innovation was in place, however, Ford brooked no competition. He was generous enough, but he also busted unions and outmaneuvered rivals. Finally, he portrayed his dominance of the market as heaven-sent. "The only monopoly possible is based upon rendering the highest service," he argued in his 1926 book *Today and Tomorrow*. "That sort of monopoly is a benefit."[1]

In the religious economy, religious firms are quite happy to have a monopoly, if they can achieve it.[2] When they do, it, too, is viewed as mandated by the heavens. No monopoly can completely escape the other fact of the marketplace of the gods, however, and that is the reality of competition. In the economic view, this is the dynamic that can explain religion in the past and today: a marketplace where growth toward monopoly is often the motive, but competition is the counterforce. The result, as this chapter will show, is a religious economy in process, filled with niches of consumers being sought by religious suppliers. In this process, religious firms rise and fall, adapt to niches, split, specialize, differentiate products, and try to keep enough market share to survive—or dominate.

For religion, however, this is not just any product. Its main offering is an answer to life, and in each kind of religion that answer can be more "otherworldly" or more "worldly," which can affect its competitive edge in the marketplace.

But we begin with monopoly. The nature of a monopoly is at the heart of both religion and economics. It was Adam Smith's aversion to the monopoly of his day, mercantilism, that gave birth to modern economics' idea of the marketplace: a place where competition shatters monopoly. Smith's idea of dismantling monopoly was modest, of course. But he cast his sights on religion as well. Religious monopoly led to state fanaticism, he believed. And while the

Catholic and Anglican Churches held relative dominance, he welcomed sects as healthy rivals and the Presbyterian system as a democratic way for the grass-roots to keep the head office on its toes. In short, he urged a healthy competition in the religious marketplace.

Ever since Smith, monopoly has been portrayed in both angelic and demonic terms. The political economist John Stuart Mill, a great advocate of individualism, nevertheless espoused what economists today call a "natural monopoly." Mill believed it was most efficient to have only one mail system, for example, or a single railroad line between two cities: a model for today's quasi-governmental firms that provide public goods. Later, Karl Marx demonized monopoly as the final evil fruit of capitalism. He prophesied that the proletariat would overthrow the robber barons, nationalizing industry and setting up a dictatorship of the people. In actuality, these attempts have turned out to be nothing but state monopoly.

In modern economics, the ideal solution is like the golden mean. The best economy operates somewhere between complete monopoly and perfect competition (an ideal state in which no firm dominates, resources are efficiently used, and prices are as low as possible). Few today will oppose the idea that fair competition benefits societies most. For religion, however, this idea of competition has not been easy to accept. While many countries today have separation of church and state, there is hardly fair competition everywhere. In one study, just 72 of 188 countries did *not* have a state religion in 1900. That was changed by the great political upheavals of the twentieth century. In 2000, only 58 nations survived with state religious monopolies, mostly by virtue of a government's political stability and a majority participation in one faith.[3]

But monopoly can occur in more venues than a nation, centered on its political capital city. Monopoly—the lack of a variety of suppliers or lack of religious pluralism—is something that can take place in regions, counties, or towns as well. These smaller units also affect the dynamics of religious economies within nations. Up to about two hundred years ago, the very nature of religion was to have a state monopoly, an idea first dramatically challenged by the U.S. Constitution. Before then, religion generally operated under political powers. Religion was one of many natural monopolies. Governments across history have always found it more cost-effective to have a single subordinate religion that endorses government power, saving it the cost of keeping social order.

With the drafting of the U.S. Constitution, religious monopoly was banned by law, perhaps for the first time. Nevertheless, the Constitution was a national document that could hardly be enforced in every state or locality. In fact, monopoly had been the goal of religion in the earliest American colonies (with the exception of a few years in Maryland and patchy trends in Pennsylvania and Rhode Island) as much as it was in ancient Babylon or medieval Europe—or for Henry Ford in Detroit.

The story of Connecticut is illustrative. In the early 1700s, it was a growing colony. Many of its settlements had broken away from the Massachusetts colony, where religious monopoly was well known. Each new Connecticut town, however, also had its "first church" monopoly. The popular settlement of Woodbury was no different, and its story can tell us much about how the religious marketplace works. Indeed, of all colonial towns, Woodbury has provided perhaps some of the best records of the religious and economic lives of its citizens.[4] Most religion in colonial New England was Puritan, and that meant a doctrine that only "saints"—those with a professed experience of grace—could be members. As it turned out, the saints in each settlement were also typically the chief magistrates and merchants; they had a religious *and* political monopoly.

So dissenters broke away, not to create open markets but to establish their own little monopolies. Such was Woodbury. All the Puritan monopolies faced a dilemma, however. The children of the saints were not declaring experiences of grace. How could they be admitted into the church? Thus was born the "halfway covenant," which for the first time began to expand definitions of membership in the supernatural church. Woodbury adopted the halfway covenant. This allowed it to grow its membership but also diluted the intensity of its following. Woodbury's "first church" was still a monopoly in the mid-1700s, when two new market forces began to break the monopoly apart.

First, an increasingly diverse population passed a law that ended the town's exclusive tax subsidy for Woodbury's first church. About the same time, the so-called First Great Awakening stormed through New England. A key message of its evangelists was to come out of the monopoly churches and start a revival of "true religion." Although some magistrates opposed the evangelists, and colonial assemblies tried to ban them, the American market was essentially open. As a result, America's first colony-wide celebrity was a traveling evangelist, George Whitefield. He landed in America in the hour of its earliest "consumer revolution," according to historians. Whitefield made the most of it with advertising, advance work, media coverage, and a very strong sales pitch. Of the many names his contemporaries gave Whitefield, one was "pedlar in divinity."[5]

In the face of lost subsidies and new rivals, the Woodbury church showed the normal life cycle of a monopoly firm. As it lost market share it settled in with a sufficient constituency to survive, and it had to do what all the other churches were now doing: trying to win popularity contests in order to attract members, which is hardly the way a monopoly operates. In this contest, up and down the colonies, churches split and advertised themselves as "new light" and "old light" providers. Catching the wave of the future, Woodbury went "new light." It adapted to the new consumer environment that had been seeded by the boisterous evangelists. In economic parlance, this is the story of suppliers and consumers meeting in a market niche.

NICHES AND PREFERENCES

The term *niche* first came into use in biology in the early twentieth century, and over the years the idea of a niche came to offer an enduring image: an environment in which an organism has adapted reasonably well in pursuit of survival. For a firm, survival depends on having a sufficiently large clientele in the niche to make a profit. Extending that biological image, the niche is established by a kind of organic give-and-take. In the first step, a niche is a group of consumers with particular preferences. In modern social theory, such a niche is typically produced by demographic similarity: age, sex, race, location, and so on. However, when it comes to religion, niches are clusters of people with similar likes and dislikes in religious content, beliefs, style, demands, and so forth.[6] Once such a grouping exists and can be identified, it can become highly visible when a supplier shows up to provide the religion this group likes most.

On a spectrum of possible niches in religion, people at one end tend to like a more strict and otherworldly faith. On the other end, people tend to like a more lenient, worldly kind of religion. Why believers are inclined this way has no single explanation. It may be upbringing, personal challenges in life, or the need for a social outlet. But the world over, religious consumers show the same pattern—they range across a spectrum of strict to lenient tastes when it comes to the religion they join. In his own day, Adam Smith spoke of "two different schemes or systems of morality," which defined a spectrum between "strict" and "liberal."[7] This spectrum is the demand side of religion. On this spectrum, moreover, these kinds of preferences for religion remain stable. This idea of stable preferences has an echo in the economic theory of Gary Becker, who, as we have noted, argued that when people buy Parisian dresses or Italian sports cars, they are really expressing preferences in terms of more basic goods such as status. When people buy oranges, automobiles, or medical care, says Becker, they are trying to satisfy stable preferences for nutrition, mobility and status, and health.[8]

In this view, and in the economic approach to religious markets, the demand side for religion has its stability as well. There will always be a taste for explanations about the universe. As the philosopher William James suggested, every person is seeking "something more," and that creates the demand for religion. Next, some part of the population will have a taste for strict religion, while others like more lenient religion. At a more superficial level, some may also like more ritual, or more emotion, or more intellectuality in their religious consumption. Given this spectrum, it is easy to imagine how difficult it would be for one religion to establish a monopoly. Such a religion would have to be both strict and lenient, conservative and liberal, focused on the next world but also on this one—an impossibility. We can now see why religions need help to keep a monopoly going: typically, they need government to back them up.

In extreme political cases, for example, there really may not be a choice in religious preferences. If one religion is politically in charge, the consumer options are few—unless it is worth risking life and limb for. During the wars of religion in Europe after the Reformation, French Protestants, or Huguenots, would have liked to stay Protestant. But to do so meant exile or death. In religion, the French market options were constrained, as they were for Japan in that same century. In the early 1600s, the Tokugawa rulers banished or killed a significant number of Christians in the south, seeing this "foreign" religion as a threat to domestic control, much as if it were an imported product dumped in Japan's marketplace as a less expensive rival to the current monopoly.

Clearly, there is a limit to what any single religion can supply to a society, and that is why rival suppliers appear. If the demand side for religion is basically constant, the supply side is dynamic. New suppliers are always trying to break in, just as George Whitefield had done. Even in the most extensive monopoly of a religion—such as the medieval Catholic Church or modern state Shintoism—there are dissenters trying to market something different. And in principle, anybody can supply a new religious product. Religion is the ultimate easy entry business, in other words. As seen in the earlier discussion on credence goods, it is hard to disprove (or prove) the effectiveness of a religious product, so persuasion is important. Like Whitefield, all that a new supplier of religion has to do is start talking and persuading. Firms can monopolize a niche in the beginning, as Henry Ford did with the consumer car market. But soon enough, other suppliers will try to enter that niche—a niche that the Woodbury church could not hold on to forever.

The story of niches in the marketplace is best told by looking at the Western Christian experience, which includes Europe but is especially easy to examine in America, which has an open market principle written into the U.S. Constitution (there is no establishment of religion, but a free exercise thereof). In their study of American religion, sociologists Rodney Stark and Roger Finke speak of a "set of relatively stable niches" that represent six basic kinds of religious consumers the world over: those who like (1) ultrastrict religion, (2) strict religion, (3) conservative religion, (4) moderate religion, (5) liberal religion, or (6) ultraliberal religion.[9] This diversity shows up as overt religious pluralism in cultures where the government allows religious freedom. We would see this full array of niches being served in early America, for example, but we would not see such pluralism in states with political monopolies, such as Catholic France, Tokugawa Japan, and Puritan New England, all in the seventeenth century.

The main point in identifying six kinds of market niches is to create an anchor for a very dynamic situation. There is a great deal of movement across the niches, and there is a flurry of suppliers trying to squeeze into a niche to provide its religious goods and services. This, in short, is the dynamic story of the marketplace. For talking about this dynamic, Mother Nature has provided science with a remarkable tool, and we're not quite sure where it came from. It is the statistical curve. For any large number of objects—people, weather patterns, or atomic particles—the large middle of this famous "bell curve" represents an average characteristic of the entire population. The middle is a very large portion of the total. At each side of the curve (the tails), there are smaller extremes. If the question is human height, for example, the big middle has a worldwide average, while the tails would be smaller extremes of very tall or very short individuals. In religion, the majority of people are in the middle, while smaller segments are at the extremes. Most people want moderate religion, in other words. Smaller segments want it strict or liberal.

This dynamic movement between strict and liberal was observed by social scientists in Europe well before the idea of a statistical normal distribution of large numbers was regularly used. The first to note the dynamic was the German Protestant social historian Ernst Troeltsch when he suggested a distribution in historical Christian forms, primarily between the "church" (moderate to liberal) and the "sect" (moderate to strict) but not excluding a form he called Christian mysticism. His colleague, the German sociologist Max Weber, picked up on the church-sect dynamic as well, but only lightly. Up to this point, they were talking mainly about social class. Upper classes liked more liberal religion (church), while lower classes liked more strict religion (sect). In this view, religious niches were determined by class structures more than individual tastes. At the time, it was a typical sociological view: social class was the most powerful force in shaping people.

Eventually, the American theologian H. Richard Niebuhr elaborated on the church-sect spectrum more fully in his 1929 classic *The Social Sources of Denominationalism*. He, too, focused on the competing social classes between religious niches but revealed a dynamic process by which religious organizations moved across niches. This was the chief insight of Niebuhr: that a particular group, not an individual, can go from strict to liberal. He saw a process taking place, a kind of cycle, in which sects move toward and eventually become churches. Then new sects form—often by splitting off from those churches—to serve the masses who aren't upper-class enough to be in a respectable church. In this dynamic, strict sects arise to serve the interest of the more disinherited masses, while churches form around upper classes. As a sect becomes more church-like, more privileged members of society join, and the less privileged may leave by forming a breakaway sect. In these steps, the very nature of the original church has been altered and a new sect born.

H. Richard Niebuhr has an interesting story himself, one often overshadowed by that of his famous brother, Reinhold. Richard was a product of the immigrant experience in America. His father migrated from Germany as a young man and, after becoming a minister, reared his family in the crucible of German-language immigrants in the Midwest. The boys also came of age in the era of Henry Ford: a time of competition and laissez-faire. Richard preferred socialism to capitalism, at least for a time. He was also scandalized by Protestant denominationalism, which to him represented the infighting of the Christian family. Still, he used the story of America's immigrant churches to show that while many had a "virtual monopoly" in Germany or Scandinavia, for example, they now lived in "an environment of free competition, unprotected and unmolested by state interference."[10]

To prosper, Niebuhr explained, churches emphasized their distinctive doctrine, ethnicity, and even language. These became strong sects, while other churches sought "accommodation" to American culture—a kind of cultural assimilation that made them blander in the marketplace. "The situation, as is the case in other kinds of competition, promoted a high social self-consciousness in the emphasis of the peculiar characteristics of the group," Niebuhr said. "Agreements with competitors were minimized, disagreements were stressed."[11] The economist today would call this branding or product differentiation—whereas common sense explains this equally well.

RELIGION AS TENSION WITH THE WORLD

From what Niebuhr wrote in the 1920s and 1930s, we can jump to the present economic approach to the religious economy, with its emphasis on supply, demand, niches, and distribution curves. There were always problems with the Troeltsch-Weber-Niebuhr analysis, typically because it was suited only to the European church experience. It tended to look at social class as the dividing line between niches. For this reason, the church-sect model was nearly abandoned by historians and social scientists until the 1960s, when it was given a new kind of universal definition. This was offered by the sociologist of religion Benton Johnson. Stripping away issues of class and culture, Johnson said simply that a religion that had little tension with the surrounding society was a church, and a religion in high tension with its environment was a sect.[12] In general, a church was more worldly in where it sought rewards, while a sect was more otherworldly—accounting for its tension with society.

With this tension model, the economic approach to religion had new tools to formulate a full-blown description of a religious economy. Simply, it is a bell curve of niches, and the largest, middle ones—the ones that most believers join—are in moderate tension with society. Then there are two extremes of the curve. At the liberal extreme, a small group of niches serve those who prefer a more secular and agnostic spirituality. In the West, this would include humanist groups, the Ethical Culture Society, many Unitarians, and not a few members of liberal churches where "secular theology" and "religion without God" can find a place. At the other extreme are the sects in high tension with the environment. They include religions with strict supernatural beliefs, those with legalistic moral norms, and communities that separate themselves and their children from society as much as possible.

At this point, sociologists such as Stark have argued that the strict end of the religious economy must be looked at more closely. A sect breaks away from a church. But what do we call a case where an entrepreneur starts a strict religious group from scratch? Whitefield, for example, was an Anglican priest who, in effect, split from his tradition and created a kind of following of "new light" sects. In contrast, Joseph Smith, living in upstate New York in the early nineteenth century, had a revelation and founded his own religion, later known as the Church of Jesus Christ of Latter-day Saints, or Mormons. As suppliers of religion, how are Whitefield and Smith different? In historical and sociological jargon, one galvanized a sect while another founded a cult. A cult is an *innovative* religion in high tension with its environment.[13] Such groups may grow, though most perish. Only the long-lasting ones survive to become a church, as did the Mormons. As is obvious, the terms "sect" and "cult" are contentious in their attempt to suggest a split on one hand and innovation on the other. For example, it could be said that Jesus of Nazareth was a sectarian who broke off from Judaism or that he was a cult leader with an entirely new religion. Similarly, Siddartha Gautama, the Buddha, might be viewed as an innovative cult founder or as someone whose sect was a breakaway from lax, upper-class Hinduism.

We are on controversial ground when we bandy about terms such as "cult," "sect," and "church," but the idea is clear enough: strict groups form to satisfy strict niches, move to the middle as they succeed in growing, and then may dissipate into smaller or shrinking liberal groups in the future—even as, at the same time, new cults or sects are forming on the strict end. The cycle is endless and is limited only by human history. Within certain windows of history, the process is obvious. In colonial times, the Puritans were on the strict end, but today the church of their heirs—the congregational-style United Church of Christ—is perhaps the most liberal of all Christian denominations. Similarly, sects are constantly breaking away from churches, as when the Free Methodists broke from the Methodists in the nineteenth century over both slavery and the middle-class compromises of Methodism.

In this process, churches can straddle niches as well. Some denominations— one thinks of Catholicism and United Methodism in the United States—have both extremely liberal and extremely conservative members. Not without effort, the center holds in these groups, but individuals are always splitting away, left or right. In a case of high pluralism, as in the United States, there are thousands of religious suppliers for all the wide variety of niches. In effect, the market is crowded indeed, and it takes effort for new suppliers, such a new religion or an old church in transition, to gain access to a niche.

In such cases of crowded niches, it is individuals, not organizations, who move from strict to liberal, or liberal to strict—though enough change in the thinking of many individuals who stay loyal to a group can alter that group from within.[14] When an individual moves out of a group, it may be for a variety of reasons, such as personal crisis or a search for social status. Henry Ford made such a move. Reared in conservative midwestern Protestantism, Ford found incentives to shift his tastes, which now included his high rank in the American social class system. He once read the Bible and the conservative McGuffey Readers but began to switch over to Ralph Waldo Emerson, the transcendentalist philosopher and advocate of universalism in religion. Finally, Ford became an Episcopalian. He made a choice to move from one religious niche to another, straddling the old and new for a period in his life. Naturally, Ford wanted to be in less tension with the world. While Ford-like transitions are well known as Americans move up educational or economic ladders, sometimes the opposite happens, as when George W. Bush, reared an upper-class Episcopalian, opted for more populist Methodism to suit his evangelical conversion and interest in a larger political base.

When it comes to individuals moving across niches, there is also generational shifting. The first Puritans in New England, for example, were strict converts seeking to be saints and "purify" the church. Their children, however, were born into such a setting, not converts, and they typically did not want the high-tension life of their parents. So on one hand, they were given church membership by the halfway covenant, and on the other hand, over time they liberalized the church—moving from sect to church and to even more liberal worldly pastures, as the history of New England suggests. The more worldly members of churches, by their own shifts, move entire denominations from sectarian status to the mainstream.

In economic terms, firms move toward monopoly when they capture a larger and larger market share, putting competitors out of business. Firms can move in another direction as well. If a few large firms serve the same market niche, they may become redundant. None of them can make enough profit to survive and grow. Thus we have mergers and acquisitions: one firm gobbles up the others or they enter a cooperative agreement for the sake of everyone's survival in the niche. In 2009, the direction of the U.S. auto industry was just that—toward mergers, if not bankruptcies. Not a few economists have called the historical Roman Catholic Church the "General Motors of religion." But after GM's dramatic loss of customers, rising debt, downsizing, and crash into bankruptcy, the analogy suggests just how fragile and transient commercial monopolies can be compared to religious ones in history.

Either way, these two kinds of movements—attempted monopoly and mergers—can be seen in religion as well. The quest for monopoly is the story of early Christianity in the Roman Empire. A long time ago, there used to be three Roman emperors. Each of them had a different take on Christianity, with Arian belief—that Christ was essentially human—considered the heretical view. Eventually, one Roman emperor took control and made Catholicism the monopoly. Arianism was suppressed. But a total monopoly was not possible. Many of the ancient Christianities in the Near East and Africa became their own local monopolies, resistant to Rome. Later, Rome split with the Eastern bishops on other issues, and hence Eastern Christianity developed its own political and cultural hub.

The mergers are more typical of what happened to the European and North American churches that shifted toward the liberal end of the market niches. At this end, there was less tension with the world and, arguably, fewer reasons to join a church. Low-tension situations are suggested by the popular impression in the United States that the Episcopal Church was once "the Republican Party at prayer," or that the black church is now "the Democratic Party at prayer." But the key point is this: low-tension churches have a hard time showing how their products are different from secular products. On the liberal end, for example, why go to church when you can engage in fellowship at the Rotary Club, get cradle-to-grave welfare from government, and read the *New York Times* for theology? This was the direction of many Western churches, so their branches merged into such generic Protestant forms as the Evangelical Church in Germany and the United Church in Canada. In the 1960s, the more liberal U.S. Protestants also favored the idea of a "superdenomination," but American consumers, liking their niches, torpedoed the project. Still, bilateral merger talks between churches occur quite often, to pool scarce clergy and consolidate dwindling congregations.

There is also activity on the conservative, or strict, end of the market spectrum. As noted above, the very nature of religion dictates that new religions, revivals, and movements mostly arise on the strict end. On one hand, high-tension religions offer a more distinct product, and they evangelize with it more fervently, believing it is the best of all brands, bar none. High-tension religions also operate on the club model, seen in a previous chapter. They don't tolerate free riders, which allows them to organize a dedicated corps of members. Only the club can survive in this early sectarian state—and most don't. Survival is the exception when it comes to thousands of high-tension sects that form and then dissipate. It's much like a kitchen-table entrepreneur trying to beat Microsoft with a software innovation. New software needs a cult following to get started, but even then, Microsoft could swat it like a fly (or buy out the innovation).

Life is tough on the strict end of religion, but high-tension religions do have their advantages. We find strong upstarts that have the potential to rival larger groups. This is the story that church historian Dean Kelley told in his 1972 book *Why Conservative Churches Are Growing*. The publisher chose to use the word *growing* in the title in hopes of selling a how-to book to declining churches. But as Kelley noted later, his preferred title was "Why Strict Churches Are Strong"—conservative or liberal, growing or not. He was pointing to the high-tension nature of sects, and even to what later was called the club model. Kelley echoed Niebuhr, and Stark and Finke echo them both: "Because exclusive religious organizations offer more valuable and apparently less risky rewards, when exclusive firms appear in religious economies dominated by nonexclusive groups, the exclusive firm(s) become dominant."[15]

We can find evidence in Asia, Europe, and America. In all these cases, when religious markets are weak because of so many low-tension or nonexclusive groups, the high-tension religions tend to stand out, attract consumers, and grow. These high-tension groups are able to develop brand-name loyalty, as was the case in Japan with a Buddhist sect called Sōka Gakkai. In Japan, the population does not join religious organizations but rather creates portfolios of various services, whether Buddhist, Taoist, Shintoist, or Confucian. This religious economy has its bell curve extremes, of course, but in Japan, no religion was exclusive—until Sōka Gakkai came along. This Buddhist sect argued that its chanting method alone produced prosperity. It evangelized, and it required members' exclusive loyalty and adherence to rules. It held large revival meetings. It was the little sect that could: it grew from a few thousand households in 1951 to more than 16 million in the 1980s.[16] Eventually it founded a political party. As time passed, Sōka Gakkai inevitably shifted to a lower-tension relationship with society, moving toward the middle on the great religious curve of niches.

Japan experienced its "rush hour of the gods" in the 1950s when the Shinto monopoly was lifted and supplier and consumer began to meet in new religious niches. After a new immigration law was passed in the United States in 1965, that country had its own rush hour of new religions, many from Asia, others proclaiming the Age of Aquarius, and many, many more offering a revival of the alternative spiritualities that had been in the United States, as quiet practices and sects, for a hundred years. In any case, they began to hit the headlines in the 1960s and 1970s, and one puzzle in particular came with the phenomenon. Most of these new religions, even before the 1960s, had headquarters all over the country, but their largest constituencies were in the western United States. Eventually, surveys found that the same was true for Canada.[17] Of course, easterners, southerners, and midwesterners were quick to joke that when North America was tipped sideways, all the "nuts and fruits" rolled westward.

But the religious economy has a more empirical explanation. For a century, the churches on the western side of North America had a much weaker market share. As is well known, the established churches out west were always more liberal. Many of the cowboys, gold miners, pioneers, and leave-us-alone libertarians who settled the region didn't take kindly to churchgoing. As a result, the West has always had the lowest church concentration in North America. The western market was wide open in 1965. In search of consumers, New Age and cult suppliers found many takers in the West but a good deal of competition elsewhere. The Age of Aquarius took hold in the West but not in the South or Northeast, where the religious establishments—Catholic and Baptist, for example—had nominal monopolies on the religious economy.

To be sure, America has a name for being a wild garden of sects, cults, and metaphysical movements. The national marketplace has a wide range of spiritual technologies on offer. However, on a per capita basis, there is even more of this in Europe. How could that be? Like the western side of North America, Europe had a very weak religious market. In Europe, this market was overseen by generic Protestant or Catholic churches sponsored by the government. They had given up trying to evangelize, or sell religious products. Into this weak market flowed hundreds, and eventually thousands, of alternative religious suppliers. Indeed, the proliferation was so great that many European governments—and the European Union itself—began to pass laws against the new groups and penalize citizens who joined them. In market terms, it was as if cults and sects were foods, drugs, or herbs and the U.S. Food and Drug Administration began banning them because they were harmful.[18]

In discussing religious monopoly and weak markets, it is always tempting to return to the days of Adam Smith. He observed that monopoly churches lack zeal, at least compared to sects. As he said, "The clergy, reposing themselves upon their benefices, had neglected to keep up the fervour of faith and devotion of the great body of the people; and having given themselves up to indolence, were incapable of making vigorous exertion in defence even of their own establishment."[19] Personally, Smith preferred that society give up religious superstitions and opt for something more "enlightened." Still, unlike his friend David Hume—who believed that a lazy monopoly religion would kill all fanaticism—Smith believed that the greater the number of sects, the more they would blunt each other and learn to cooperate, a notion implicit in the U.S. Constitution's idea that factions will stop each other from forming tyrannies.

When Smith spoke of sects, he had the early Methodists in mind. They were followers of the Anglican John Wesley, who led a kind of revival, or sectarian breakaway, from established Anglicanism, both in Great Britain and in the United States. Even Wesley commented on the sect-church shift in niches, from otherworldly to worldly. For example, his early sermons warned of how a diligent sectarian Christian who becomes rich easily falls into luxury, laxity, and theological liberalism. "Religion must necessarily produce both industry and frugality, and these cannot but produce riches," Wesley said. "But as riches increase, so will pride, anger, and love of the world in all its branches." In this, Wesley identified how strict sects may move into a moderate-to-liberal niche, where they will lose members who simply prefer the worldly way of life.[20] But Wesley had a solution that is entirely appropriate in the economic view of religion—he innovated and specialized his product to keep a foothold in the stricter niches.

INNOVATION, SPECIALIZATION, PRODUCT DIFFERENTIATION

Wesley's followers were called Methodists because they offered a unique method. It amounted to small group study, strict accountability in local and regional "circuits," and clergy who, without personal wealth, traveled the circuits to encourage strict piety. In the United States, this Methodist innovation and specialization spoke to people on the frontiers. But they had a legendary rival, the Baptists, who also specialized in particular religious products, hellfire colloquial preaching and full-immersion baptism being the most visible. By the early 1800s, Baptists and Methodists had outstripped the former monopoly churches, the Congregationalists, Anglicans, Quakers, and Presbyterians, some of whom operated on state taxes until 1830.

By specializing, a religious group could corner a market, speaking to a niche in a focused way. The innovators in American religion played the supply-side role to maximal effect since the market was so open, especially on the expanding frontiers. In this competitive market, as one firm presents its specialized product, other firms try to differentiate themselves so that their products continue to stand out. Sometimes that ability to differentiate can be immediate—and with dramatic results. In the 1970s, a group of Christian evangelical teenagers in Illinois went door-to-door asking people what they liked and didn't like about church. This began the story of Willow Creek Community Church, which stirred a small marketplace revolution in religion by establishing a new kind of religious firm: the "seeker" church. It began with a market survey to identify a niche of consumers, later to be called the "unchurched Harry." The questionnaire asked about likes and dislikes, and Willow Creek built itself on what was liked. Beginning with a youthful crowd, the congregation expanded exponentially. For a time it achieved the distinction of being the largest congregation in the nation.

Willow Creek specialized from the moment it began. Few religions in history have been so methodical. Nor does the average temple or church typically have the luxury to reinvent itself. By the same token, a religious group—large or small—could *not* exist without a niche. This is something that newspapers, toy companies, cosmetic firms, and clothing stores know all too well. "A religious group will not survive nor be created in the first place if there are no individuals in the group's particular niche," says sociologist Roger Finke. "The probability of a historically African-American denomination existing in an area with no African-Americans is low."[21] And the more niches, the more variation in religious providers. In the case of the black church, for example, niches abound. Entrepreneurial black pastors in the Church of God in Christ are renowned for planting storefront churches in city neighborhoods. In turn, the African Methodist Episcopal Church builds its megacongregations in growing black suburbs.

In this and other cases, it is hard to picture a generalist religion that could address all the variables that create a niche. Attempts to form integrated congregations with black, white, Latino, and Asian members and with many kinds of worship styles have not proved successful in the United States. With no specialty, such a church cannot find enough clientele—a niche—to prosper or expand. From market studies, economists know that when a firm is highly specialized it can hold a niche firmly. No matter how firm its grip, however, other entrepreneurs will try to enter the niche (studies of new members at churches always find that they were formerly members at other churches). Finally, the more heterogeneous the niche, the harder it is for a business to meet all of the individual consumer's needs. It is nearly impossible to unify a diverse group of consumers. In religion, a heterogeneous church is often praised, but it is much harder to maintain than a homogeneous one.[22]

Once again, the strategy of product differentiation becomes important for religions to keep, or gain access to, niches. The story of American religion is simply one long saga of product innovation. In the colonial period, a few European churches controlled the settlements. In 1890, the census identified 143 different religious groups. Today, *Melton's Encyclopedia of American Religion* lists 2,500 different groups, a spectrum that includes variations on all the world's religions.[23] This differentiation was what Niebuhr pointed to when he chronicled a century of immigrant churches arriving in the United States. For example, he said, Methodists specialized in Arminian theology, which said everyone could be saved if they chose to be. "Competition with Arminian Methodists was largely responsible for the change of doctrine in the Baptist Church from Arminianism to Calvinism," which denied free will, Niebuhr argues.[24] Two distinct products were now on offer. Some consumers (the Methodists) wanted to believe that everyone could be saved, but those who became Calvinist Baptists believed only the elect were destined for salvation.

Similarly, when the Anglican Church in the United States faced competition, losing members left and right, Bishop John Henry Hobart asserted Anglican liturgical primacy: only the Anglican sacraments offered salvation. By accentuating this unique feature, the Anglicans specialized, speaking to those whose preference was for high liturgy as the means of getting right with God. This shift toward specialization, however, stirred the famous "Tractarian controversy" and split the Episcopal Church, the U.S. branch of Anglicanism. But despite the split, the Episcopal Church regained its market niche (and also diversified Episcopalians on the religious spectrum). Niebuhr himself believed that such Christian rivalry was un-Christian, but the pattern was there to see: "Competition has affected in comparable manner almost all the churches in America."[25]

COMPETITION AND PLURALISM

In the economic approach to religion, and in describing a religious economy, competition becomes the primary principle. Monopoly, especially when backed by government, blocks competition. But in an open market, competition can only go so far as well. At a certain point, a market is saturated. There are enough suppliers to meet all the niches, from strict to liberal. New suppliers must continue to find new entry points in niches, finer distinctions in the different tastes of religious consumers. Therefore, one principle of the religious economy is that the more pluralistic it is, the more suppliers will specialize—and with more specialized service, more people will consume religion. This, in fact, is the most contested part of the theory of the religious economy.[26] In trying to test the theory, its advocates have said that where there is more pluralism, there *will be* more religious participation, and the opposite will occur where there is monopoly. This does not always turn out to be the case, however. The Mormons, for example, have a virtual monopoly in Utah, but that state nevertheless has the highest rates of Mormon participation as well.[27]

Both sides in this heated debate, which we'll look at more closely in the next chapter, agree that the idea that pluralism causes participation is hard to prove in an absolute way, given the diverse nature of religion on the planet. The problem is to decide at what level monopoly and pluralism are in tension: is it the neighborhood, the town, the county, the region, or the entire country? Without a common agreement on the unit, it is hard to match data perfectly with a theory of the religious economy. For historical reasons, a small town might be entirely Baptist but sit in a dominantly Methodist county, although the largest religious body in the entire state is Roman Catholic—a not unusual mixture of pluralism in parts of the United States. How to define the "most important" unit of pluralism is for the academic economists and sociologists to fight over— as they do with admirable vigor.

But few would dispute that competition is the key element in the theory of a religious economy, and regulation of the market—by religious monopoly or by government—is the key impediment to the increase in religious suppliers. Whether at the level of the town, county, state, or country, any religion that is in competition for market share cannot rest on its laurels. It must try to make its products distinctive. It must try to mobilize organizational resources in ways that reach unserved niches. Even in what seems a religious monopoly, niches and their potential suppliers lie in wait, ready to spring into business. In many countries, Catholicism and Islam seem to have a historical monopoly. On closer inspection, however, competition is hard to suppress. Despite Italy's government-backed Catholic monopoly, there is the "Italian puzzle" of why religious participation is still very high under a so-called single supplier. In fact, however, there are many suppliers catering to many Italian Catholic tastes and preferences. Under the Catholic umbrella, countless different groups, missions, and societies—not just the parish system—speak to various niches and increase consumption of religion.[28]

It would also seem that the Islamic monopoly in Saudi Arabia would create a bland lethargy in popular religion—which is not the case, however. Why is that? Truth be told, there is a great deal of pitched competition in Saudi Islam. According to research by the Center for Studies on New Religions (CESNUR) in Turin, Italy, "State ulamas compete with a vast unregulated private sector, offering all shades of Islam from ultra-fundamentalist to moderately liberal, different interpretations of Wahhabism, and even frank opposition to it, not to mention the presence of both non-Wahhabi Sunni and Shiite minorities."[29] This competition is said to be the real root of Islamic revivals in Saudi Arabia, not the top-down orthodoxy of government-backed clergy.

Turkey is a similar puzzle. Its government has declared itself secular (since 1923), but Islam is still the monopoly. So why is Turkish Islam so lively and active? In Turkey, Islam has always been a world of competing suppliers aiming for a wide variety of niches. Turkish pluralism includes mystical and tolerant Sufism vying with fundamentalist Wahhabism, and modernist Islam doing the same. The strict groups, in turn, vie with each other (not to mention the city with the countryside and Turkish culture with Arabic scriptures). The result is the standard curve of niches. "What appears unique of [the] Turkish religious market is the strength of a conservative-moderate center," says the Italian sociologist Massimo Introvigne of CESNUR. "In this central niche of the religious market at least three different expressions of Turkish Sunni Islam compete." Like Adam Smith and the U.S. Founders, Introvigne argues that a variety of competing suppliers in Turkey produces a large moderate niche in such a way that belligerent "fundamentalism is contained and ultrafundamentalism marginalized."[30]

As these cases suggest, niches can be split to ever finer degrees by more and more specialized suppliers. This may create new niches or simply find people who will participate in several different kinds of religious activities at the same time. For instance, studies of television religion and Internet religion have shown that neither one actually cuts into the church-going population to any appreciable degree.[31] Still, television and the Internet have definitely brought new niches into the market landscape. A certain profile of consumer watches televangelism. Another profile frequents "virtual churches" or clicks its way to religious blogs on a regular basis. What could possibly stop such a proliferation of niches and providers? Consumer preferences can be satiated. At some point no more space can be found for new products, at least until old ones die away or new variations on taste arise.

There are other ways to reverse satiation, or market crowding, and open it up once more. As noted, new sects may split away or try innovation. Even liberal groups can come back from the brink of total accommodation with the world. They can experience revivals and move back toward the stricter niches. This is being seen in the "renewal" movements among liberal Protestant denominations in the West. In the same way, there is a rise in the number of young Catholic priests who are more orthodox than the Second Vatican Council generation of priests before them and are finding a market share among Catholics who like their religion strict and traditional. Their beliefs on salvation, abortion, birth control, and homosexuality create a good deal of tension with modern society. Historically, however, the main brake on diversity in religion has been not market crowding but the coercive power of government. Governments that put strong limits on religious choices have been the rule, not the exception. Latin America and China tell this story.

REGULATION POLITICS: LATIN AMERICA AND CHINA

Not every modern society has the luxury of an open religious marketplace. The closed market is typified by one religion as the natural monopoly, or by the government enforcing the one religion that works best for controlling the society. In the ancient world, kings were sometimes viewed as supernatural agents. When the rulers of ancient Egypt or Babylonia decreed the worship of particular gods, and organized this through official priesthoods and tax systems, we can be sure the public all joined that religion (though dissenters and heretics there surely were, in their own private and undocumented ways). One theory of why the "sun god" monotheism of the Egyptian pharaoh Akhenaton did not survive his rule was that the government's priestly class had a vested interest in state polytheism, since government goods and services were geared to dealing with many gods.[32] The caliph in Islam was Allah's agent on earth. In medieval times, emperors and popes united scepter and sword.

Governments have their own economic reasons when it comes to promoting a religion.[33] Typically, it has been cost-effective for rulers to have a single cooperative metaphysical system. When the masses endow their ruler with sacred status, his job is easier. An official religion can help control populations through belief, symbols, and ethical rules. A police force and taxation also will be necessary. But with religion as a backup, the costs to the royal treasury are less. In short, having an official religion—or no opposition religion—has been a boon to the powers that be for most of history. This government control over religion is always problematic, however, as the cases of Latin America and China will show.

As the founders of Willow Creek Church were conducting their first market surveys, a new voice in the Catholic Church in Latin America was beginning to make headlines. This was the voice of liberation theology, with its opposition to particular political regimes and its "preferential option for the poor." Born in the 1960s and largely exported to the South by intellectuals in Europe, liberation theology was an exciting new gloss on the idea of revolution. But less well known were the economic roots, a half century earlier, of the new interest that Latin American bishops and prelates were showing in ministering to the poor and in openly opposing regimes that had funded and backed the Church for 400 years.

According to the economics of religion, the Catholic monopoly in Latin America was challenged for the first time, ever so slightly, by the arrival of Protestant missionaries in the 1930s. Progress was slow. Laws against open proselytizing had long been in place. After a few hundred years of close church-state cooperation, however, vast parts of the population had been neglected. The Catholic Church mainly served governments and the social elites. The rest of the population was looking for suppliers of religion—and this is what the non-Catholic missionaries (including the YMCA, Bible fundamentalists, Adventists, Mormons, Jehovah's Witnesses, and finally the fast-growing Pentecostals) eventually offered.

In the 1950s, Pope Pius XII had warned of the Protestant threat, and by the 1970s the church was rapidly losing its flock to what even Pope John Paul II in the 1990s called the "ravenous wolves" of sectarian competitors. "The tremendous success of evangelical Protestantism in several Latin American countries provoked many Catholic bishops into reevaluating their own pastoral objectives and methods," writes political scientist Anthony Gill.[34] They first tried to outlaw missionaries, but eventually mimicked Protestant methods, declared the "preferential option for the poor," and in some cases opposed the country's regime to win back popular support.

Biblical justice was at stake, for sure. But there was also a careful cost-benefit analysis. If the church did not openly back the poor, it would lose influence to the Protestants. Eventually it might even have to face Protestant governments, losing its preferential funding and legal status. Indeed, during the 1970s, some bishops dramatically reversed course and opposed their own governments. Others did not. The cost-benefit puzzle would be this: why was opposition a benefit to some bishops but not to others? In Latin America, the Protestants were the dominant competitors at the grassroots, but not the only ones. Marxist theorists moved through the top universities and guerrillas set up jungle camps, while the village marketplace was rife with the indigenous "spiritist" religions of shamans and healers.

As it turns out, where Protestant competition was highest, the bishops were strongest in opposing the government, their former benefactor. In Brazil, Chile, El Salvador, Nicaragua, and Panama, for example, religious competition was high, and it was in these countries that the bishops' anti-regime rhetoric was loudest during the 1970s. Opposition to the regime was especially acute in Brazil and Chile, where Protestant proselytizing at the grassroots was the most aggressive. In countries where bishops remained neutral toward the dictators—Argentina, Bolivia, Honduras, Paraguay, Uruguay—there was little Protestant competition.[35]

In the economic view, noble ideas matter: the great historic documents supporting religious tolerance and freedom have done wonders in Europe, the United States, Latin America, and elsewhere. But what matters more is that governments find a way to stay in power and a cost-effective way to rule the people. In that sense, religions and concepts such as religious liberty are often used quite cynically by governments. In the United States, for example, the idea of religious pluralism helped the new government take the reins of power, as religious factions focused on doctrinal competition rather than marching on the capital, so to speak. In Latin America, Catholicism was tightly woven into the political structure. But at least religion was seen as true and beneficent. In a country such as China, Mao Tse-Tung, the captain of the Communist insurgency, decreed that religion was an opiate of the people and an enemy of the revolution.

But even the god-like Mao had to deal with the marketplace, with its vast human reservoir of preferences and niches. Arguably, his new brand, the Communist Party, filled one niche: that of consumers who were drawn to the idea of a human god. For this key clientele, the state provided Mao statues, icons, mythologies, theater, calendars of "holy" days, and a book of scripture for daily use, the Little Red Book of Mao's sayings. In a vast population such as China's, only a minority joined the Communist Party. The masses stayed in preexisting niches that the government now sought to control. After the revolution of 1949, the Mao regime followed the postwar Soviet model of setting up state-run patriotic associations for a finite number of "normal" religions—Buddhism, Taoism, Islam, Catholicism, Protestantism. "Normal" meant that a group had an approved government leader, gathered only in authorized buildings, and could not teach religion to people under age eighteen.

By 1966, when the great revolution began to lag, Mao declared open expression ("let a thousand flowers bloom"), and once the dissenters were identified, he launched the great Cultural Revolution. The state moved from control of religion to its destruction, tearing down buildings, sending believers to reeducation camps, and killing religious entrepreneurs. When Mao died in 1976, he was succeeded by an economic reformer, Deng Xiaoping. Eventually, places of worship for the five approved religions began to open again, although still nothing could be done outside official buildings or with children. As the early history of China's Communist revolution suggests, a large underground "black market" of religion had developed since the 1950s. This included many Catholics and also the burgeoning "house church" movement of Protestants. Even today, an estimated 80 percent of some 50 million Protestants in China may be underground.

In a society where regulation of religion swings from utter control to utter eradication and then back again, the normal market models of monopoly and laissez-faire are not too helpful, according to sociologist Fenggang Yang. He calls for a triple-market model, with the black market playing its role below ground and the "red market" being those "normal" religions that are tightly controlled by the state. In between, however, exists a vast "gray market" of people in legal religious groups who do "illegal" things and a far larger number who participate in religious practices that are too varied and ambiguous—folk religion, meditation, shamanism, health science, astrology, or other kinds of syncretistic new religious movements—for the government to identify them, let alone regulate them. "When people cannot find satisfaction in the red market and are unwilling to risk black-market penalties, a gray market fills the gap," Yang writes. Moreover, in the gray market, "individual suppliers are not part of the professional clergy or ecclesiastics, but moonlighters."[36]

Yang calls this an invisible marketplace force, but it does make its appearance on occasion—as it did one dramatic day in 1999. On April 25, 10,000 members of the qigong (spiritual exercise) group Falun Gong silently surrounded the Communist headquarters complex in Beijing for a peaceful demonstration—their gracefully regimented exercise—to protest being deregistered as a normal religious group. Since the 1979 thaw, the practice of qigong had flourished, drawing in millions of Chinese and producing a wide array of "masters"—who often claimed lineages and missions from a revered Buddhist or Taoist past. Publicly, the result was a rise in the number of peaceful morning gatherings in parks, where Chinese adherents performed a half hour of morning exercises.

Some leaders in the Communist Party objected. But qigong made its way to "normal" status by arguing the scientific basis of its principles and the patriotic benefits of physical fitness. A few celebrity scientists and party generals even endorsed the practice. So it grew. But it grew too much—and became excessively religious as well. This was especially true of Falun Gong, which arrived on the scene late (1992) but in just seven years had acquired millions of members and missionary branches in the United States and Australia. So the party shut it down. This led to the April 1999 protest, the imprisonment of many Falun Gong members, and the eventual illegalization of all qigong meetings in China (though after 2004, the state physical fitness division allowed a bit of public activity to resurface).

The Falun Gong drama was the most visible proof of the gray market, which is made up of many more varieties of such groups. As Yang summarizes, "The more restrictive and suppressive the regulation, the larger the gray market."[37] When the gray market is obvious enough to be suppressed, as in the Falun Gong case, then the black market will grow. Either way, extreme regulation of massive populations with religious interests seems ultimately unmanageable, Yang concludes. "Heavy regulation of religion will not lead to religious demise, but to complication—it will result in a tripartite religious market." Since no country is without regulations of some sort, then all of them will have gray markets, even the United States.

The nations of Europe do far more to regulate religion, and this is why, Yang argues, there are more new religious movements in Europe than in the United States. The gray market in Europe has grown for lack of free market expression. When scholars study China as a religious marketplace, the scope can be breathtaking. Though statistics are vague, when underground believers and members of government patriotic religions are counted, that leaves a billion Chinese who amount to potential demand for religious suppliers. From what Yang and others can gather from surveys and polls, Chinese are no more irreligious than Americans. But in terms of suppliers, "the U.S. religious market is exceedingly mobilized, whereas the Chinese religious market is seriously underdeveloped."[38]

THE NATURE OF COSTS

The example of China brings us finally to an important puzzle left in the economic approach to religion: what does it mean to pay a cost to grow a religious firm in a religious economy? The story of religious believers in China after 1949 who have died because of their strong desire to practice their religion proves that many human beings will pay the ultimate cost for that human right. The martyrs of religious history signify the extreme of paying the supreme cost for a believed-in benefit, which can be a matter of duty and principle, but also belief in a reward (and justice) after death.

But in the entire sweep of religious economies, there are two other kinds of costs. One is the cost that a government must consider when it wants to regulate religion. If doing so is too expensive or creates a lethal backlash, the government may want to ease up on its regulation, as the U.S. Founders decided to do in adding the Bill of Rights to the Constitution. The second kind of cost at issue in the religious marketplace is what economists call start-up costs. These are usually the reason a small competitor cannot take on a monopoly or oligopoly.

In Henry Ford's day, nobody could afford to build a plant that matched his for low costs, high productivity, and monopoly over consumer tastes and need for an inexpensive car.

According to the economics of religion, deregulation of religion allows easier entry to competitors. When the Woodbury church lost its tax subsidy, for example, the playing field was technically leveled for rival start-up congregations. These rivals could also ask people to give that money to a new church or ministry. At this point, however, a contradiction seems to appear in the interpretation of how costs generate new sects, religions, and movements. As Dean Kelley proposed in 1972, strict churches endure by demanding high commitments from their members. The economic approach to religion extends this by using the club model, which explains why strict religious groups become more efficient. In this view, sectarian groups grow *because* of the high costs (for high religious rewards). As the sect-church curve explains further, religion begins on the strict side, with high demand, and then moves across the niches as tension with the social environment eases. Finally, however, this seems to contradict the mainstream economic idea that a new firm, such as a sect, needs low start-up costs to enter the market.

Today, scholars who debate the economic approach to religion are in perpetual disagreement over when a "cost" is a real cost. Every grand theory has its anomalies, and so the debate on costs may not be resolved easily. There is much diversity in how new religious groups arise. For example, a small rival evangelist in Woodbury in the 1740s, lacking a state salary, would have to work longer hours as a volunteer. With no money (or food), he might burn out before he could start a church. The start-up cost defeats him. Indeed, in the history of business enterprise, it is well known that most new businesses fail—utterly.

But when it comes to religion, another scenario is also possible, as we can imagine back in Woodbury with a rival evangelist. If he has enough "love offerings" to scrape by, his personal energy plus the sacrificial zeal of a few early followers may end up making his ministry competitive. In the first scenario, the start-up costs kill the emerging religious form in its cradle (the religious entrepreneur can't make a living, so he gives up). In the second case, ascetic zeal may be the very thing that persuades people that the religion is authentic (a bona fide credence good). On the economic principle of club formation, a core of devotees join up—sloughing off free riders—and together produce club goods that offer deep satisfaction. With such true believers at the core, a new sect has taken the first step toward getting off the ground.

Of course, some start-up costs are worse than others. The government may kill members of new religious groups or throw them in prison, as was so often seen in the sectarian wars of Europe and early colonial America. As just a sampling, the Massachusetts colony hanged one Quaker woman who kept preaching in public, and it exiled the upstanding citizen Anne Hutchinson, who claimed to have had a personal revelation from God and gathered a devoted following at her home, where she taught other women (and eventually their husbands). If a small Pentecostal group tried to form in the former Soviet Union, its leader and members paid a cost that was not extracted from the Russian Orthodox priest who operated on a state subsidy in the same town.

In the ideal of the economic view, as the government withdraws its regulation (whether persecution or favoritism), start-up costs are lowered everywhere, promoting the rise of more religious groups. However, even in the ideal marketplace, start-up costs are a barrier. With this increase in suppliers, more individuals in the population with unmet religious preferences will start participating in one group or another. Niches become saturated. Black Pentecostal storefront churches can be pretty small in south Chicago, east Los Angeles, or southeast Washington, D.C., but at some point the neighborhood becomes saturated. In the religious marketplace, new openings arise only when small groups shut down or when successful church groups move toward laxity and no longer satisfy the clientele. This is the normal process of church-type groups shrinking, merging, or going out of existence. New niches are opened. When the start-up costs are reasonable, there is potential for a new sect to be born. These kinds of market cycles presumably never end. Human demand for religion persists. Suppliers arise to fill niches whenever they open. The new groups tend to begin on the stricter end of the market spectrum.

When Henry Ford tried to build his monopoly empire, the religious fate of the citizenry was obviously not at stake. Eventually, a few other auto companies began to compete with Ford. In all, more and more Americans began driving cars, and when foreign automakers joined the fray, the competition and variety became even greater. But at this point the analogy of Ford and a religious monopoly breaks down because while cars are objects of transportation and status, religion is a matter of beliefs. As soon as cars were available, Americans liked them. Once there were more kinds of auto companies and more kinds of cars, however, Americans did not get confused and "disbelieve" in cars, although they may have worshiped the Ford Motor Company with less fervor and awe. But according to some, this dramatic shift away from fervor and awe is exactly what happens in the face of religious variety. Once a single religion has lost its monopoly, people became confused by *too* many religions and decide not to believe in any of them. This is the main argument behind secularization theory, which tries to explain the modern-day decline of religion, and in doing so has come to loggerheads with the economic approach to religion—as we'll see in the next chapter.

CHAPTER 8

Debating Secularism

The true identity of Middletown USA remained a mystery for about a decade, at least until a 1937 issue of *Life* magazine declared it was Muncie, Indiana. Through the 1920s, a team of researchers had swarmed over the town of 30,000, gathering data on all aspects of its life. The team's 1929 study was the first such look at an "average" American city, which meant a farm community that had turned into a factory town, had a business class and a working class, and had changed its living styles based on automobiles and radios.

Under the forces of modernity and urbanization, the authors reported, Middletown had also become less religious. A second study, published in 1937, concluded that in the latter years of the Great Depression not much had changed in Middletown, except that there was "further secularization" of the Sabbath and Middletown's other institutions.[1]

Since the 1950s, the fate of Muncie and most of the rest of the world has been called secularization, or the retreat of religion and expansion of worldly (*seculum* in Latin) groups and beliefs. A secular future was being predicted on all fronts for the Western world, in fact, at least until the economic approach to religion began to challenge many of the secular prognostications. In the market, as will be seen, things do change—firms rise and fall and market share shifts—but nothing moves in a single inexorable direction, as the secularization thesis was basically proposing.

In the 1970s, another study was done of Muncie, and indeed the city was still changing here and there—but not as the secularization argument had predicted. By ten different measures, Muncie had rebounded when it came to religion.[2] This finding that religion was holding its own stirred as much debate as the earlier Middletown studies. For this chapter, Middletown can serve as a touchstone for the debate over defining secularism and what the new economic approach to religion offers in this dispute. Had Middletown reversed the process of secularization? Had the process stalled in place? Or was something more complex happening when it came to religion in the modern marketplace? This is the same question being asked in Western culture in general.

On this topic, two rival theories were beginning to clash. The first had roots in the strong Western and modern belief that history progresses inexorably in a single direction. Societies and nations move from agriculture to industry and technology, upsetting old communities and creating fluid and often anonymous societies. By dint of science and technology, both wealth and knowledge increase. Superstition becomes useless in the face of practical knowledge, and hence religion, too, becomes a vestige of a forgotten past. This is the "strong" version of secularization. The sociologist Jeffrey Hadden offers this succinct summary of the strong secularization thesis:

> Once the world was filled with the sacred—in thought, practice, and institutional form. After the Reformation and the Renaissance, the forces of modernization swept across the globe and secularization, a corollary historical process, loosened the dominance of the sacred. In due course, the sacred shall disappear altogether except, possibly, in the private realm.[3]

The first two Middletown studies also suggested this fate for religion. But the town itself turned out to be a bit more complex. Although it did indeed become more secular, wealthy, and modern, the number and variety of religious activities available increased as well. To be sure, religious authority and orthodox beliefs held less sway in modern Middletown. But individuals nevertheless maintained religious beliefs of one kind or another.

The second theory is the market theory, which conceded a weak version of the secularization thesis. In this view, the world indeed progresses toward more complexity and more differentiation between the chief elements in a society, separating religion from government, schools, courts, hospitals, welfare, and businesses. Nevertheless, the world is a marketplace, and therefore secularization will rise and fall, come and go, just as will religion. It is true that religion does not have the imperial voice that it once did in ancient empires, but it still speaks to the hearts of people, and religious groups continue to be powerful vehicles for movements, interest groups, and the building of identity. A form of the weak secularization argument was articulated in 1985 by sociologists Rodney Stark and William Sims Bainbridge:

> While secularization progresses in some parts of a society, a countervailing intensification of religion goes on in other parts. Sometimes the pace of secularization speeds or slows, but the dominant religious organizations in any society are always becoming progressively more worldly, which is to say, more secularized. The result of this trend has never been the end of religion, but merely a shift in

fortunes among religions as faiths that have become too worldly are supplanted by more vigorous and less worldly religions.[4]

Here we see again the "religious economies" argument. Religions that have a high-tension relationship with the world will continue to show up in every culture as religions with low-tension relationships indeed do secularize, becoming more like the world around them and less supernatural in their orientation. In summary, the strong version of secularization sees a linear march into the future, a future in which nobody believes in supernatural things. The weak version, however, sees cycles, and the ebb and flow of religious and secular outcomes.

The loudest debate is over whether religion will indeed die out, which remains an argument in some influential circles. The debate is also sharpened by the entry of economic explanations, now presented in clear enough profile that other parties argue that the very term *secularization* should be abandoned. They argue that the "doctrine" of secularization is a kind of antireligious belief, not a finding about how the real world, with its cyclical markets, actually works. We can begin by asking how the economic approach to religion entered the secularization debate. What does it say about Middletown and the rest of the world? If religion is not bound to wither away, in what shapes and forms will it appear in future social marketplaces?

EUROPE AND AMERICA

These modern-day questions take us back to the 1830s, when Europeans and Americans began to contrast the different ways that religion operated in their societies, which had the same roots but were divided by the Atlantic and history. The most prominent figure in this comparison was a French visitor to the early United States, Alexis de Tocqueville. He toured the country and left behind an insightful list of the ways in which it differed—both good and bad—from his native Europe. The United States tended to have mass bad taste and mob politics, he said. But it also had remarkable religious vitality. Individuals and groups took religion into their own hands, the government stayed out of it, and the American landscape was filled with productive and active voluntary associations.

The story of Tocqueville—or the image of a "European in America"—is really at the heart of how the secularization debate began. It was in Europe, after all, that the great political economists declared that the worldly economics and the machine-like logic of "rationalization" were moving into all corners of life. For better or worse, the modern European thinkers said, as life surrendered to rationality and scientific explanations, religion had little else to offer. Progress was detrimental to religion, and perhaps even fatal.

This was particularly evident in Europe, where religion very often had been an appendage of the state. For centuries, churches were arms of governments, social classes, or political parties. That was still the world of Tocqueville in the 1830s. He lived in the wake of the French Revolution, and it was in this backwash of European history that new governments and parties were founding themselves on the very idea of being antireligious, or at least being enemies of government-backed churches. While the situation in Europe today is more complex than in Tocqueville's simpler times, church and state remain deeply entangled in the nations that make up secular Europe.

That was the situation in Europe in the 1960s when the first European intellectuals presented the secularization thesis. In the words of Bryan Wilson, an eminent British sociologist, secularization is "that process by which religious institutions, actions, and consciousness, lose their social significance." His favorite examples were England and Japan, two modern industrial societies. In England, the churches stood almost empty on Sundays and clergy very nearly played a role like that of museum curators. The same was true of Japan, where "the parish system of Shinto shrines has fallen into decay, while Buddhist temples, used mainly for funeral services, lose their clientele."[5]

In Wilson's England, the archbishop of Canterbury blesses new monarchs. In turn, monarchs choose new archbishops, who promenade to their throne at Canterbury Cathedral as the Prince of Wales looks on. The ceremonial side of European religion continues today. As Wilson and others observe, however, it is clearly vacant of any supernatural beliefs. The ceremony probably still meant something in Tocqueville's day. But today, in secularization theory, it is only ceremony. The behavior in European nations is secular, or what has been called "practical atheism"—despite the persistence of ecclesiastical titles and rich ceremonies.

What Wilson offered was a model of institutional secularization. But the other side of the new set of theories about the decline of religion was the "secularization of consciousness," as the sociologist Peter Berger made the case in his 1967 classic *The Sacred Canopy*: "Put simply, this means that the modern West has produced an increasing number of individuals who look upon the world and their own lives without the benefit of religious interpretation."[6]

This focus on mental secularization was a major contribution of Berger, a native of Germany, a Lutheran, and later in the United States a leading sociologist of religion. Berger, an even more colorful writer than Wilson, came of age when the sociology of knowledge was the great topic, as was the theoretical interest in how people conjured a "real world" by the power of their collective minds—the social construction of reality. In this belief, great truths were invented by human groups, not revealed by a supreme being. Societies created these truths in order to function more smoothly, and religion was a prime example. When one religion dominated a society, it provided a "sacred canopy" under which individuals felt free to believe what everyone else believed. In more technical terms, Berger called this canopy a "plausibility structure" that makes belief believable.

In Europe, for example, the state Catholic and Protestant churches had towered over society. Everyone was a Christian, so it was easy and plausible for citizens to assent to, or conform to, Christian belief. The scourge of modernity, however, was pluralism. This arrival of many different beliefs, from science to non-Christian religions, destroyed the canopies and plausibility structures. That destruction, Berger explained, created a modern crisis of faith and forced individuals to make choices. He called this demand for choice the "heretical imperative," since heresy originally meant choices outside of what was orthodox.[7] In the final secular scenario, this imperative to choose undermined organized religion. As religion fell apart, people retreated into small marginal groups with small canopies. Ultimately, in a secular world, people resorted to individual canopies—privatized religion.

Working in the European tradition, Berger also pointed out the irony of how all this secularization happened. It was Christianity, with its focus on rational beliefs and organizations, that had first tried to dispel superstition and irrationality from the world. Naturally, Christianity also began to secularize its own existence, making the world rational, practical, and a place where economic success was to be applauded. As Berger colorfully said, in terms of rationalizing the world, "Christianity has been its own gravedigger."[8] Even today, people who hold traditional monotheistic beliefs are the most likely to reject metaphysical or paranormal beliefs, suggesting that Christianity continues to demand that people be "rational" in their view of the world.[9]

This European approach to interpreting modernity remained strong both before and after World War II. So American social scientists took up the secularization thesis with aplomb, especially during the 1950s, when many popular media outlets declared a "religious revival" in America, manifest in such colorful rising stars as Billy Graham, Bishop Fulton J. Sheen, Oral Roberts, and Norman Vincent Peale. Many in academia were highly skeptical, however—they saw secularization. The popular theologian Harvey Cox suggested that jettisoning the supernatural was good for religion, as he argued in his best seller *The Secular City*. For some, a secular city was exactly what Middletown (and every other urban setting) was becoming. Modern people were giving up religion, Cox wrote, because the "cosmopolitan confrontations of city living exposed the relativity of the myths and traditions men once thought were unquestionable."[10]

Whatever ordinary city dwellers believed about a secular or religious world, the social scientists and scholars of religion had begun a yeasty debate among themselves, informed by their own personal experiences, their academic loyalties, and a healthy competition between European and American ways of thinking. In the 1970s, Wilson spoke openly of this academic contest, arguing that even the simple man on the street could see what was obscure to professors in the ivory towers. As he put it, "While the decline of religion is taken for granted by the general public, the experts keep the debate alive, marshalling all sorts of arguments and some sorts of evidence, to show that things are not quite what they seem."[11]

SACRED FOOTBALL, GLOBAL REVIVALS

One other important doctrine was at stake in the debate. As seen in earlier chapters, many sociologists worked in the tradition of Emile Durkheim, who said religion was the earliest collective glue to hold primitive societies together. Religion was not so much an individual affair as a collective enthusiasm that, inevitably, individuals became caught up in. This offered a nice model for the secular theorists. Now, they said, the sacred enthusiasm once provided by religion had been replaced by secular alternatives. These could be enthusiasm for a nation-state, for a political party, even for a sports team. When football in Europe and baseball in the United States become all-consuming, in other words, they are the new secular religions, the modern version of the sacred. If the supernatural saints had disappeared, secular analysis suggests, we still have mortal sports stars, whom we collectively immortalize just the same.

We recall that this has been called the functionalist view of religion—it simply functions to glue society together, but in the end, any other glue will do just as well. As we also saw earlier, the economic approach rejected functionalism from the start. The economic approach prefers to work with individuals who are moved by rewards and costs. In the economic view, there is no fabric of society to become secularized, only suppliers and consumers in a complex and fluid marketplace. The differentiation of elements in society would seem logical as humans learn new skills and technologies, but this does not necessarily prove that some kind of invisible "religious collective" had existed in the past but exists no longer. To explore this distinction between the functional view and the marketplace view, let's return to Middletown.

In the functionalist view, we might imagine, Middletown grew out of an agricultural mentality where people were close to nature, bound to small groups, and had no reason to doubt that they could appeal to the gods. Then came technology. Labor became easier, people could leave town if they wanted, and new ideas were coming in, whether through the mobility of people or over the radio. Protestantism was the dominant worldview, but this was being upset by the arrival of Catholics, the growth of sectarianism, and modern ideas that questioned religion. Whereas at one time citizens came out of their homes to worship a similar Protestant God, that was lost; instead, people put their sacred meaning into the civic government, the flag, their public schools, their civic groups, and finally their own possessions.

As the 1929 study reported, the Rotary Club, other civic clubs, and a belief in "magic Middletown" had become "marked sources of religious loyalty and zeal" for many citizens. One man said he traveled to Indianapolis "and shouted myself hoarse for our Bearcats" sports team but would not show that enthusiasm for his church. "No, you bet I wouldn't."[12]

The economic view would interpret the history of Middletown differently. Middletown would be a marketplace. The United States was rapidly urbanizing at the start of the twentieth century, and as people moved from the farm to the city, they found different groups asking for their allegiance. Many of these were churches, but even in urban areas during the Jazz Age, for example, many sects and cults were inviting urbanites to sample their products. From the sacred-canopy point of view, that canopy was torn to shreds by the urban experience, and many people, unsure what to believe and increasingly skeptical of dogmas, priests, and preachers, turned to secular alternatives to fill the void and provide meaning and solidarity in life. In the contrary market view, however, suppliers would always be there to offer the citizens more religious alternatives, keeping religious interest high.

Rather than lose its sacred canopy, Middletown gains new forces of competition and religious advertising. As more and different groups crowd into the city, they compete for members and work to differentiate both religious products and group identities. At the turn of the century in the United States, for example, this was essentially the story of Catholic immigrants meeting Protestants in urban centers. The Catholics and Protestants did not get confused and reject their faiths. Instead, they competed. They mobilized to recruit as many members as possible. In the economic view, pluralism and competition increase religious activity. More products draw more consumers. By the 1980s, for example, Middletown boasted sixty denominations and also "people who practice witchcraft seriously and others who shave their heads and meditate on reincarnation," according a 1983 study. A half century of data on Middletown and religion shows "some fluctuations along the way but never a significant downward trend" in belief and participation. Middletown typifies "the persistence and renewal of religion in a changing society."[13]

While 1960s theologians such as Harvey Cox celebrated a secular religion in the secular city, a group of researchers in the 1970s and 1980s began to think seriously about testing the secularization thesis against data, something that had never been done before. As even Bryan Wilson had argued, secularization was something the man on the street knew better than bickering sociologists. Nevertheless, the new data were hard to ignore. The new study of Middletown was only a start. A few decades earlier, a somewhat exotic and far-off event had taken place in Japan, with the rise of a myriad of new religions. After a dramatic change in U.S. immigration law in 1965, the United States began to have its own bumper crop of sect and cults, some migrating in, many others home-grown.

None of these American new religions proved to be as enduring as, say, the Mormons, who began as a small circle in upstate New York about the time Tocqueville toured America. But they did, for the first time, become an empirical object of study. They were also an apparent contradiction to the secularization thesis. Some of the old guard called the sects and cults a passing fad, not "real" religions. But other empirical events were conspiring as well. The born-again candidate Jimmy Carter won the presidency, the religious right emerged, and the Iranian revolution suggested that entire modern societies could come under the spell of conservative religious movements. Less exciting, but no less empirical, was that American polling had now covered a half century, and both in Europe and across the rest of the world pollsters were beginning to ask people the same questions. Religious belief in the United States had remained stable despite secularization, and while rates of belief were lower in Europe and higher in India, global religion on average certainly had not disappeared under the canopy of the space age.

At this point, the economic approach began to mount its challenge. Historians of the period often cite an address delivered in 1986 by the sociologist Jeffrey Hadden, who argued that secularization is "a *doctrine* more than it is a theory."[14] As noted at the beginning of this chapter, in this view the secularization thesis was essentially an antireligious argument based on the preferences of a century of sociological professionalism. Hadden, too, cited the Hare Krishnas, Jerry Falwell, the Ayatollah Khomeini, and the spread of religio-political conflicts and asked if this was what secularization looked like.

In the United States, the debate was strongly colored by the economic data that Roger Finke stumbled upon in musty libraries in 1982 and 1983. In search of data on crime, juvenile delinquency, and urban trends, Finke scoured the

1906 Census of Religious Bodies, one of the rare times the U.S. government counted religious heads and resources in the country's 150 largest cities. As we've seen, when it dawned on Finke that the data showed that people became more religiously active when they urbanized, he changed the focus of his doctoral studies from criminology to the sociology of religion. Finke and Rodney Stark mined other U.S. census data to try to test a very economic-like theory: urban centers featured pluralism, which led to competition and thus prompted higher rates of religious activity. "Cities, in general, had a higher rate of religious involvement than surrounding towns and hinterlands," they summarized in a paper.[15]

Moving from the abstract to the concrete, they also proposed a mechanism. As Catholic immigrants arrived in urban centers, they hunkered down with parochial schools and other resources. Threatened, the Protestants responded by bringing in revivalists and founding the Sunday school movement. This was a new religious mobilization, the counterforce to secularization, and it was at full pitch among both Catholics and various Protestant groups. The cities became very unsecular, even as they became more modern, educated, and scientific. "Americans in cities always had a much greater range of available choices, and urbanites have always been exposed to more intensive recruitment efforts," they argued. Indeed, "at no time was rural America as religious as urban America."[16] With more religious products offered, more Americans consumed them, and secularization decreased.

Eventually, Stark and Finke took full advantage of the kind of insights that Tocqueville had offered 160 years earlier—mobilized religious sects made the United States more religious, not less. This was the theme of their 1992 book *The Churching of America*. Thanks to mobilization, which had little to do with sacred canopies, American religious affiliation grew from 17 percent in 1776 to 60 percent in 1990. The "holy" commonwealth of Massachusetts in the 1600s, in other words, was actually fairly secular since it was monopolized by Puritans who allowed limited access under their sacred canopy. Today, such monopolies no longer exist in American cities. "Puritan Boston in the time of Cotton Mather had a far lower rate of church membership and attendance than it does today—far lower even than modern Las Vegas or San Francisco."[17]

With their use of historical examples, Stark and Finke laid hold of a great many economic metaphors. They showed that it was a lack of sacred canopies—that is, the monopoly of state church and government regulation—that allowed the "upstart" sects to travel, convert people, and finally outstrip the established East Coast churches in both membership and potential wealth. As we saw in the previous chapter, this was the church-sect competition that had long been the territory of historians of religion—but now it had an economic patina. In the hands of the economic theorists about religion, this theory of religious mobilization—that is, effective and aggressive marketing—also revealed why Europeans spoke of secularization when they actually were pointing to a different process, desacralization.

In the past, many traditional societies were indeed more sacralized. The political and religious ceremonies of old Europe were filled with the message that something sacred was happening when political leaders and priests gathered in ceremonies, parades, and official gatherings. Something supernatural had come down to earth and made the symbols of state and church powerful in themselves. All was sacred—or so it seemed before church and state began to be separated.

Modernity had indeed made this sacred aura lift like the morning mist in the sun. But even if the sacred aura had evaporated, the vast state and ecclesiastical bureaucracies built up over hundreds of years still remained. This applied to Shinto Japan after World War II, and it applies even more to European countries. But even though the bureaucracies have been secularized, the economic view of religion holds that the demand for religion remains constant in the hearts of the masses. Belief in the supernatural lay dormant in the minds of most people. In economic terms, they represented "potential demand" for new religious products and services. The classic case study, of course, was nineteenth-century America, where there were growing numbers of consumers, multitudes of sects and religious entrepreneurs, and very little government regulation stopping them from doing business.

The problem in Europe, according to the economic view of religion, was that after desacralization, government regulation remained in place. Regulations forbade religions to be active, even though people would no doubt consume religious products if they were available in ways that people liked. Hence, "we dispute the claim that any European nation is very secularized," write Stark and economist Laurence Iannaccone.[18] Instead, Europe was simply overregulated, by governments that continued to favor historic religions that people no longer had interest in, and, in turn, forbade new religious activities to enter the marketplace.

MARKETS, MONOPOLY, AND REGULATION

Even a stalwart of the secularization thesis such as Wilson has not denied the marketplace character of religion's struggle to make a showing in the modern world. But Wilson says the market status of modern religious diversity is a testimony to its weakness—its inability to shape an entire culture the way it used to. "The modern world has a supermarket of faiths; received, jazzed-up, homespun, restored, imported and exotic," Wilson says. "But all of them co-exist only because the wider society is so secular, because they are relatively unimportant consumer items."[19] To him, the anemic market is proof of secularization. The supermarket faiths can't possibly shape great events or national destinies.

A second marketplace model, meanwhile, advocates a "neo-secularization" thesis, a kind of weak version that nevertheless declares that progressive secularization is a fact of the modern world.[20] In the modern setting, according to this view, religion is no longer a canopy but just one more interest group lobbying for its concerns. People no longer follow religious authority figures or authoritative sets of doctrine handed down by posterity. Instead, when religion appears in society, it does so in groups that mobilize around special interests or agendas, just as secular groups do. Religion in the modern marketplace is typified by abortion-rights and right-to-life groups, pacifists and national-security enthusiasts, those who want religion accommodated in public settings and those who want it excluded in the name of government neutrality. Religions also mobilize for ethnic rights and interests, such as the perennial property rights clashes in South Asia among Hindus, Sikhs, and Muslims.

In the 1960s, one European thinker who opposed the secularization thesis of his fellows was the sociologist David Martin, an Anglican priest. Eventually, however, he conceded by presenting his own secularization model, which was actually more of a market model based on the political structures of Europe and the United States. It is true, he said, that Christianity brought on its own secularization, but this was dramatically pushed forward by modern industrialization, as well as "crucial events" in the West, especially the Reformation wars and the various revolutions in Europe and the New World. Hence, secularization "patterns" emerged from Russia to America, Latin America to northern Europe, and these patterns—in an economic view—were on "a continuum running from total monopoly to total laissez faire."[21]

The main components in Martin's explanation were Catholic and Protestant, but also monopoly and no monopoly, or the experience of an "internal revolution" or "external revolution." A final factor would become migration, which was essentially unique to the United States. The world looked something like this, according to Martin: First, the turning-point modern events of the Enlightenment and the Reformation left some states dominated by Catholicism. Those states have continued to be culturally Catholic, although some of them experienced a severe antireligious reaction (an internal revolution) such as the French Revolution or the rise of Marxist and socialist political parties. Of these nations, Spain and Portugal have managed to be most monopolistically

Catholic, followed by Italy, Belgium, and France. These are nations with a deep Catholic heritage and a militant political left.

A second kind of system on the spectrum is the "duopoly," in which the nation is partitioned between Catholicism and Protestantism. This mixed pattern is best represented by Germany, the Netherlands, and Switzerland. The next leap toward pluralism on the continuum is England and its former Commonwealth satellites. These are Protestant states, typically with state churches, that also suffered internal revolutions. But this internal clash was between religious sects and was resolved in a modern system of toleration. The English Civil War between the Anglicans and Puritans was typical and became a major launchpad for fleeing Protestant sects to populate the New World.

The fourth pattern is the most pluralistic, typified by America. Here, Protestant migrations led to a system in which there was no state church, but rather several vying factions. Each sect tried to hold various degrees of monopoly. But sectarian splits, increased migration, and mobility across the frontiers undermined every attempt to build a church (or secular) structure to monopolize or regulate religion.

As suggested in Martin's influential overview, the United States escaped some of the intense religious and political upheavals so well known in Europe. When it comes to secularization, therefore, which is normal: Europe or America? Naturally, there has been a good deal of finger-pointing in both directions. In one view, America is an aberration in the world. In the other view, Europe is the planetary oddity: its penchant for statism and secular bureaucracy has regulated public religion to death. Later in his career, Peter Berger—who once argued that the religious canopy was beyond repair—recanted that view and acknowledged that religion had not lost its grip on the global village. But still, something was historically, intellectually, and politically unique about Europe, he said, making it "markedly different from the rest of the world."[22]

Although both economists and sociologists try to look for universal principles in human behavior, this is often difficult to do. And so it may be with the secularization thesis and its opponent, the market thesis. Human beings are the same everywhere. But perhaps the European experience is so radically different from the American experience that it is as if the human beings were different: Europeans, genetically and culturally, are secular, Americans religious. Of course, this may be a preposterous thesis, but it speaks to the difficulty of finding a universal explanation. In recognition of this, the prominent American sociologist Stephen Warner declared in 1993 that there was indeed a "new paradigm" for understanding the survival of religion, and it looked more like a marketplace than a canopy. Still, Warner said, the new paradigm really only worked in the United States.[23] Only in the United States, for example, is there a constitutional deregulation of the religious marketplace, and into this setting came a wave of sects, immigrants, and religious entrepreneurs.

By implication, if America's market is deregulated, then Europe and much of the rest of the world is burdened with regulation, either in rules about religion set by government or by religious monopolies that take all the government's resources, leaving none for smaller groups. Of course, regulation is the nemesis in free market thinking, and so it is in the economics of religion. Modern economics has produced many tools for judging whether a market is efficiently competitive or stifled by monopoly, trusts, collusion, or oligopolies (that is, a few large firms cooperating to keep market control). The tools can be applied to religion as well, as we will see shortly.

Each year at the U.S. Justice Department and at the offices of the European Union, teams of economists and lawyers look at the market shares of various firms that seek to merge. The intent of both governments is to curtail collusion and monopoly, which typically make a market less efficient by raising prices and delivering inferior services. To decide whether mergers will hurt the marketplace, the antitrust bureaucrats pull out a few handy tools for measuring monopolies. The most popular is the Herfindahl Index, quietly invented by Albert O. Hirschman in 1945, and again by Orris C. Herfindahl five years later. (When the index made just one name famous, Hirschman wrote, "Well, it's a cruel world.")[24]

Anyone can use the index. It has become a helpful tool in looking at countries and deciding whether they have healthy competition among religions or inefficient monopolies. The index simply counts the top fifty firms in an industry and then calculates their true dominance. Between 1991 and 1993, three different groups of scholars applied the Herfindahl Index to religion: first in 14 European nations, then in 45 Catholic nations, and finally, in a major sweep, 198 nations. All the studies found a high correlation between monopoly and low levels of church activity—that is, secularization.[25] In the old paradigm, it was pluralism that caused people to lose their beliefs and become secular. In the new findings, it seems that it is monopoly—or overregulation—that suppresses supply of religion, and thus consumers had less of it to go around. The result: society looked secular.

Some social scientists are skeptical of the idea that having more religious firms generates more religious behavior. But they do find sense in the idea that extensive state regulation of religion will increase public secularization. For this, the sociologists Mark Chaves and David E. Cann looked at detailed government regulation of religion in eight Western democracies and concluded that there is a strong tie between "competitiveness and vitality" in religion: in both Catholic and Protestant settings, "subsidized religion" (religion that is supported by the government over alternative religions) does produce less participation in church activity.[26]

In summary, the broadest area of agreement when it comes to a market explanation of secular trends is that overregulation does limit religious choices and suppliers. It also limits competition, which will tend to stifle religious participation. When the government imposes neither favors nor penalties on religions, consumers presumably will feel freer to shop around for a faith that suits their tastes and needs. Suppliers of religion would also face much lower start-up costs to organize the normal fixtures of religion—meeting places, literature, staff—to present consumers with goods and services. For example, in the United States churches are tax exempt, a privilege of not paying taxes while still using public goods; this is regularly contested as an unfair government subsidy.

Looking at America, it can easily seem that the last church monopolies gave way in the sixteenth century, when the medieval Catholic Church lost control of Europe. But even into the 1970s and 1980s, many European countries had laws against meetings by some religious groups or marriages between people of different faiths. Many state churches today continue to exist on public taxes, while other religious groups in Europe may be denied permits to hold meetings. In one way or another, religions still seek privileges under the state.

PAST AGES OF FAITH?

To say that the world is getting more secular is also to say that in the past it was more religious. This interpretation of history has also become a battleground between the strong secularization thesis and those who say the whole idea of secularization should be thrown out in favor of the marketplace principle of change. Historians admit that taking the measure of religiousness in a bygone era is difficult. This can also be a cultural question, for if the test of secularization is church attendance, then the assumption must be that all cultures have had religions requiring Sabbath attendance, and that attendance is proof of the beliefs held by the participants. In fact, there are countries, both East and West, that never had strong attendance-oriented religions; the most popular religions were home-based or even privatized.

Despite such diversity, the secularization thesis has tended to build its argument on the idea of a linear regression of more attendance in the past but less in the present. But it is also assumed that people were more supernatural-minded in the past. "By most criteria, the social significance of religion for the conduct of human life was greater then than it is now," the sociologist Bryan

Wilson says. "If we go back to earlier times, the evidence becomes even more overwhelming."[27]

Nobody doubts that people viewed the world differently in prescientific and then preindustrial times. The question is how to document those past "ages of faith," which are crucial to describe if one wants to show that faith has deteriorated with modernity. Unfortunately, records of religious participation in the past are sketchy at best. Most of the records that survive speak of the social elites. As a result, some historians have become skeptical that the past was an age of faith, at least any more than the present. The British historian R. Martin Goodridge, for example, asked whether past images of religious Europe were "romance or reality," given the paucity of reliable data on people in their everyday lives. As the fact of lost information is faced, said Goodridge, "the concept of 'The Ages of Faith' will lose much, if not all, of its meaning."[28]

European scholars have tended to work in a context that romanticized the splendid past of European Christianity. Furthermore, the Enlightenment figures of France and England described human history in stages. They identified dark ages of faith and bright ages of enlightenment. While there was a kind of cycle—for example, classical Greece and Renaissance Italy were islands of enlightenment—the direction was onward and upward toward a secular religion of enlightenment. The popular 1950s series of books on Western history by Will and Ariel Durant presented this view. The volume on the Middle Ages was *The Age of Faith*. But here again, the Durants tell the story of elites: universities, courts, bureaucrats, librarians, and theologians. There is no mention of how ordinary people lived—they actually lacked meetinghouses, books, and priests. Medieval Christians must have recognized a vast secular world all around them. Hence, the idea of the monastery system was to provide a retreat from the world.

More to the point, there is really no systematic documentation of what preindustrial European individuals actually believed, either in terms of superstition, Christian doctrine, local lore, or merely a peasant's stubborn pragmatism and skepticism. As noted earlier, the secularization idea grew out of the philosophical belief that all religion was a collective euphoria binding society together. However, in the economic view—and perhaps in the facts of history—religion in the past may well have been as privatized, custom-made, and eclectic for each individual as it is today. If that is the case, it would be an almost miraculous feat to document and know the privatized faiths of people in ages past.

For several generations, historians had adopted an evolutionary view of history to organize the data that were available. By definition, evolution goes from primitive to advanced, simple to complex. Accordingly, historians were inclined to hold that beliefs in the past were simpler, and thus prone to superstition. As history moved forward, superstitions were debunked and beliefs, challenged by science, either became more complex or were abandoned. Naturally, therefore, the past was a world of faith and belief. The present is a higher stage in history where belief no longer is credible, mainly because the world has become efficient, rational, and segmented. There no longer is a space where supernatural beings can be active; there no longer are close-knit communities where supernatural beliefs are sustained.

This view of evolutionary "progress" obviously makes sense when technology and medicine are at issue. In the marketplace view, however, it may be possible that religion does not evolve from a lower stage of superstition to a higher stage of disbelief. Rather, such states of belief may go in cycles, appear in various forms, and move across different geographies. Again, the image of the marketplace, not a plane rising upward, easily comes to mind. One concept important in modern sociology, but even more so in economics, is that human societies tend to maintain equilibrium. This market equilibrium can be jostled or operate as multiple equilibriums, but the tendency is to go back to a balance of forces, not lurch in one direction or the other. Neither religious belief nor disbelief goes out of existence. Ages of faith and disbelief seesaw across history, orbiting around each other, growing here, declining there, and diversifying where necessary. This takes place on the material foundations of a world that does march gradually upward, but only in terms of technology, economics, health, education, and communications.

In its most radical vision, the economics of religion proposes that the twenty-first century may turn out to be an age of faith compared to the past. We have already seen mullahs with cell phones, evangelists with global satellite hookups, and the Internet's so-called virtual religion. Modern-day religion may become even more robust and diverse in the future if the right entrepreneurs, products, and innovations catch the consumer tastes of the worldwide public. At any given moment, each generation will look at the secular snapshot of its modern world and conclude it is impossible for it to get "more religious." But snapshots may be deceiving. The great cycles of secularization, regulation, deregulation, and the rise of a new religious pluralism and vitality may be a matter of centuries.

Without a crystal ball, all that the economic view can propose is that societies will have greater or lesser degrees of religious monopoly or competition, and that when there is more competition, more religious options are likely to arise. The cycles may take many generations. That is why, for example, it may seem that in the past three hundred years Europe has gotten very secular. For the present, the bureaucratic states have continued to regulate society without the sacred.

It may take a generation or two for that to change—Europe, for example, may become an openly pluralistic religious market. The Catholic Church has lost its monopoly status in most of Europe and Latin America, yet this "did not immediately create unregulated religious economies filled with eager firms competing for souls," Stark and Iannaccone write.[29] Pluralism in the religious economy will take time to emerge. Even in the United States, it took until the twentieth century to reach a point where more than half of the population attended churches.

BELIEVING, NOT BELONGING

In the 1990s, the British sociologist Grace Davie answered the strong seculari-zation conviction of her European colleagues with a compromise. She called it "believing without belonging," a kind of parallel to the American slogan "spir-itual but not religious." Based on her review of surveys, Davie argued that while church attendance in Britain had indeed plummeted, and Europe was an "exceptional case," individuals in England still held a range of metaphysical and supernatural beliefs. At the least, she said, Europeans had not turned into the scientific skeptics and committed atheists and agnostics that the strong secularization thesis suggested. "The British are far from being—or becom-ing—a secular society in any strict sense of the term," Davie reported.[30] What Davie argued was a common enough assertion in the religious economies approach: overregulation had made monopolies boring and curtailed new sup-pliers, but in their heart of hearts, even Europeans still believed.

The "believing without belonging" theme was favored by some, but the economist David Voas continued to question all such attempts to avert the fact of increasing secularization in Europe. In previous work, he had pointed to the European Values Survey to illustrate three decades of dropping church attendance in all European nations. Now he deployed the massive British Household Panel Survey to show that, despite a good deal of ambiguous spir-ituality among Britons, they were rapidly losing belief as well as attendance. The reports of a "spiritual revolution" were very dubious, but even the preva-lence of experimental and personal spirituality hardly matched their impact in the former "pagan" days of England. As Voas concluded, "'Believing without belonging' was an interesting idea, but it is time for the slogan to enter hon-ourable retirement."[31]

But like so much about retirement, this idea of individual spirituality despite declines in attendance does not want to give up its gainful employment. As

Americans only seem to become more diverse in their choices of individual religion, studies of "secular" Europe and Asia continue to argue that the same goes for people everywhere. In one, Iceland was taken as the epitome of a modern secular society. But on closer inspection, it became evident that Icelanders had never gone to church anyway—the church was the site of seasonal pilgrimages, not Sunday attendance. Pilgrimages and a respectful attitude toward the churches continue. Meanwhile, adults seem to hold the traditional moral (sexual) norms of religion, and an Icelandic carnival of beliefs is maintained by young and old.[32] Similarly, a composite survey of personal beliefs in the United States, Sweden, and Japan continued to show believing without belonging.[33] As is evident at this point, conflicting data—or uses of data—have been marshaled by both sides in this debate. Perhaps the best way to leave it at this point is to cite not data but metaphors. Both the secular theorists and the religious economy theorists offer colorful summaries.

In Scotland, the sociologist Steve Bruce has been an ardent defender of the secularization thesis, though perhaps not its stronger version. His main point is that if people do not participate in religion, their beliefs must certainly not amount to much. Take football (known as soccer across the Atlantic). Even if a football fan rarely goes to a match, he watches it on television, and sales of newspapers with football coverage are brisk, Bruce points out. However, in European religion, "it is very hard to find any similar mark of religious interest among the unchurched." Those who say religion is alive in Europe should consider the football fan who admits, Bruce said, "that he has not been to a game since his father stopped taking him at the age of 5, never watches matches on the television, does not read the football sections of newspapers, does not support any team, does not encourage his son to attend matches, and cannot name any prominent footballer." This is not a football fan. Nor is someone a believer if he admits the same total lack of participation in religion.[34]

The American sociologist William Swatos Jr. prefers a restaurant metaphor to the sports fan illustration. Swatos says religion is prevalent in Europe, though not as a main course served by state churches; rather, it's more as if people picked a variety of selections from a menu at a fine restaurant. "That people are more likely to want their religion à la carte does not necessarily mean that they are 'less religious,'" Swatos argues. To choose à la carte is to be more fastidious than simply ordering meal number three, for example. At the restaurant, the religious consumer is just as likely to choose wisely, composing a rich and balanced meal instead of, say, ordering three desserts and no vegetables. Admittedly, à la carte religion does eliminate the role of chefs and prescribed menus: these would be clergy, doctrinal systems, and ecclesiastical structures. Still, à la carte might be the way of the future, given globalization and the vast number of religious choices offered people.[35]

HOW RELIGIOUS, HOW SECULAR?

We know that football fans can riot over their passion and that people often do overeat. But to shift analogies now, how far can a society go in becoming religious or becoming secular? Putting aside debates on ages of faith in the past, our only contemporary measure is the United States, where some 60 percent of people claim religious affiliation. In addition, between 80 and 90 percent of Americans claim belief in a God or "universal spirit." It would seem, then, that in a global marketplace of religious and secular choices, this may be the maximum religious commitment—of belief and belonging in the human species as a whole. With religion, there is no such thing as a monopoly, just as no market monopoly can be absolute.

What about the other direction—a completely secular world? While Scandinavian countries have often been cited as extreme cases of secularity, the better test is the former Soviet Union, where the government tried to create an absolutely secular monopoly. The Soviet experiment was the first of its kind in history. Once in power, the regime tried to eradicate religion in both supply and demand. To destroy supply, it simply tore down churches, shot or imprisoned priests, and co-opted the church bureaucracy. Under Lenin and Stalin, this was policy up until World War II. In that crisis, Stalin decided to reemploy the church in the patriotic war effort and as a tool of international propaganda. This uneasy alliance continued, but then under Nikita Khrushchev the accommodation policy was reversed, and a lively period of crackdowns, dissidence, samizdat, and human rights agitation began in regard to Soviet religion during the 1970s and 1980s.[36]

The Soviet system also tried to destroy the demand for religion—the desire of people to go to the restaurant of religion and order their spiritual choices. To force Soviet citizens to lose this appetite for religion, the state set up the most comprehensive ideological education system in history. The goal was to reeducate the entire public as a "new man." For such a Herculean task, the Soviets imitated religion at every level. Dialectical materialism was the new metaphysics, Bolsheviks the new saints, and the approved Soviet texts, parades, imagery, and calendars the new catechisms, rituals, symbols, and holy days. The goal, of course, was to eliminate all religious belief, which the Soviet ideology had deemed a "false consciousness," an "opiate of the people," and pure superstition. According to Marxist theory, such ideas could essentially evaporate from human minds and human nature if the social environment was changed.

For the economic approach to religion, the Soviet attack on the supply and demand of religion over the seventy-odd years of an experiment to produce a completely secular society was logical at the start, but futile in the end. As one major study of this strategy shows, the attempt to secularize individuals and groups could not have succeeded.[37] For one thing, both human nature and the culture of Slavic people had been tied to religious ideas so deeply that those ideas were impossible to supplant. It was like trying to eliminate a vast consumer population's taste for automobiles or indoor plumbing—but only harder, since even biologists today puzzle over why religion seems to be hard-wired into the human brain, or at least consonant with how the brain naturally perceives the world. After the fall of the Soviet Union in 1991, fifteen former Soviet republics took the world stage, and in each the historical religious tradition was used as a political base for the new governments.

During the Soviet period, the main branches of world religions—Orthodoxy, Catholicism, Protestantism, Judaism, Islam, and Buddhism—all adapted according to their institutional profiles. In general, the Orthodox Church was so integrated with Russian history—the last czar in 1917 was its head—that there was no alternative but for the Orthodox at first to protest (and be shot, in general) or eventually to go along, as was the practice with the revival of the church by Stalin in the war period. The Muslim and Buddhist enclaves in the empire were similarly co-opted. The Catholic Church, because of its historical rivalry with the Orthodox, had independent structures loyal to Rome already in place, and these simply went underground. The small and informal circles of Protestants and Jews went even deeper into anonymity, sustained by Bibles or Torahs and clandestine rituals.

Once the harsh Soviet regulation was lifted with the fall of the Soviet Union, the inexorable cultural forces of each republic's religious heritage pushed to the forefront once again. Hoping to be elected and to stay in power, political candidates and governments evoked popular religion as any modern government does today—making deals with it, but not quite coming under it in the old version of a sacralized state. Naturally, in most of the fifteen republics the Orthodox Church was the main cultural heritage. Today, it has gained a tacit establishment as the Russian national tradition. The same is true in Islamic countries and the very few that were predominantly Roman Catholic, such as Lithuania and Poland.

In the classic secular view, both Europe and the Soviet Union had secularized as a result of low participation and the decline of church relevance. Modernity did this in Western Europe, whereas the Soviet police did this in Russia and the surrounding states. In either case, the economic view points to the fact that supply was curtailed, while in the population, the potential demand for religion was always there. As the sociologist Paul Froese argues, "The Soviet population showed that widespread religious belief can persist over a seventy-year period, even as religious institutions lose the ability to indoctrinate the young and political forces actively try to undermine faith in the supernatural."[38] The demand is there. What was lacking in the Soviet Union was a supply of religion—preachers, shamans, and gurus hawking their wares. It has been said that the same case prevails in Europe, where the marketplace is overregulated by secular bureaucracy, much the way a government monopoly in telephones and autos, for example, bars alternative providers from opening phone companies or car dealerships. Today, the European nations and the republics of the former Soviet Union closely regulate alternative religions that seek to assemble, own property, acquire permits, or receive state funds—all of which are reserved for a dominant state church.

The resolution to this debate on the true nature of secularism will be resolved only by time. Will Middletown USA become completely secular in another generation? Will Europe and the former Soviet republics be bristling with religious pluralism and participation? In the economic view, at least, the question will hinge on supply, for a period of secularization is a period of low supply to meet public demand for the things of the spirit.

The economic view of religion has answered the claims of secularization by trying to show that individuals—in their minds—have not become secular, despite the fate of religious institutions. Human beings, it is argued, will always seek rewards, and some of these can come only by exchanges with the gods. Generally, the economic approach does not delve into the nature of particular beliefs—any ones will do. But it does acknowledge the psychology of the individual who is seeking rewards and responding to incentives. That is why the economic approach must include one more topic: how religion motivates people in their economic behavior. Perhaps surprisingly, the sacred texts of the world are filled with advice on economic matters. It is no wonder, then, that religion might have something to do with economic outcomes, whether they be successes or failures. That is the topic the German sociologist Max Weber tiptoed into a century ago. He proposed that theology led to a "Protestant ethic," and that led to capitalism. This modest proposal led to a century of debate, as the next chapter will show.

CHAPTER 9

How Religion Shapes Economics

One day in 1907, a copy of the journal *Archive for Social Science and Social Welfare* landed on the desk of the German sociologist Max Weber. Inside its pages, the historian Karl Fischer launched the first public attack on Weber's thesis about religion and economics, published a few years earlier as *The Protestant Ethic and the Spirit of Capitalism*. Fischer accused Weber of going overboard with an "idealist interpretation of history."[1] When Weber read the criticism, he found himself charged with putting the cart before the horse: he attributed capitalism to religious motives in people, not to material causes such as technology.

For much of his career, Weber claimed that he had been misunderstood. But Fischer had a point. Weber indeed had made a bold assertion about religion and economics. In his famous set of essays, Weber argued that the Calvinist belief in predestination had set the psychological stage for a type of person, angst-ridden and highly productive, who collectively produced the "spirit of capitalism." This type of person embarked on a lifelong rational, systematic, and productive business career not for personal enrichment but for the psychological assurance, found in material success, that he was chosen for heaven rather than for damnation. "The God of Calvinism demanded of His believers not single good works, but a life of good works combined into a unified system," Weber said. "The process of sanctifying life could thus almost take on the character of a business enterprise."[2]

By the spirit of capitalism, Weber did not mean simple greed, shrewd commerce, or acquisitiveness. He meant, rather, the frugal bourgeois capitalism incarnated in the ascetic attitudes of John Wesley, or better still, the secular and prudent business success of Benjamin Franklin. In short, Weber had suggested that religious beliefs have economic consequences—even after the religion is gone. Unlike many in his day, Weber did not accept the doctrines of progress and redemption espoused by Romantics, Hegelians, and Marxists. But he did wonder why only the West among the world cultures had developed "rationalized" industry, capitalism, bureaucracy, and the resulting material wealth.

In pursuit of an answer, Weber wrote on economics and Christianity, Islam, Hinduism, and the religions of China. In regard to all religion, he made this kind of reasonable connection between belief and behavior: "The magical and religious forces, and the ethical ideas of duty based upon them, have in the past always been among the most important formative influences on conduct."[3] After Fischer's criticism, Weber offered the rejoinder that his argument was merely suggestive, not absolute. "I emphatically rejected any such 'foolish' thesis that the Reformation created the capitalist spirit on its own," Weber said. He repeated this defense in the final revision of his *Protestant Ethic*. It was "not my aim to substitute for a one-sided materialistic an equally one-sided spiritualistic causal interpretation of culture and of history." Both religious mentalities and material realities shaped economics. "Each is equally possible."[4]

Thus began what some historians wittily call the Hundred Years' War over Weber's ideas. Others had talked about religion and economics well before Weber, of course. In the late Middle Ages, Catholic writers advised monks and laymen about the religious virtues of thrift, diligence, and honesty in the growing money culture of Europe. In eighteenth-century Scotland, Adam Smith looked at how strict religious groups seemed to produce adherents who were more diligent in life. Evangelist Wesley, a contemporary of Smith (and who was looked at closely by Weber), told his followers that diligence would make them wealthy, but at that point they had to fight the temptation of worldly luxury. In Weber's own time, the economic philosophy of the Hegelian idealists was just peaking after a century of saying that spirit, not matter, was the engine of progress.

Like all these predecessors, Weber also wrote in a particular social setting that probably influenced his views. For example, as a Protestant, Weber may have been influenced by the culture war (*Kulturkampf*) between Protestants and Catholics in 1870s Prussia, today's Germany. During its most pitched conflict, the culture war produced an argument about comparing "northern Protestant energy" to "southern Catholic indolence." Since then, there has been an argument for how Catholicism gave birth to modern economics, as seen most recently in theologian Michael Novak's work on the "Catholic ethic" and democratic capitalism. All the same, even Novak offers an amicable summary of Weber's influence. "Weber rightly teaches us that success in economics is largely dependent on the spiritual and moral qualities embodied in the practice of economic agents."[5] In other words, religion can have economic consequences in the lives of individuals.

As may be apparent in this debate so far, all such approaches presume that wealth is a human good. To some human beings, it may be the highest good or the proverbial root of happiness. But to some critics, this assumption at best cannot be proven and at worst is wrongheaded. They would say that human happiness, or ultimate well-being, cannot be measured in terms of wealth. What can be measured, these critics say, and is universally approved, is the project of alleviating protracted, disabling, and perpetual poverty. Religion has been a traditional source of this challenge to economic assumptions about wealth, though this challenge is also seen in economic philosophies such as socialism, where equality, not wealth, is the primary goal. But Weber toiled in the vineyard of his own time. He was struck by the stark differences in economic development in the world, and so we will generally adhere to that topic.

A final criticism of Weber's work has been his lack of empirical data on beliefs, behaviors, and economic aspects of the cultures he wrote about. That is where the modern discussion on religion and economics has picked up from Weber: it is looking for data that can verify or reject the idea that religion influences conduct, and that conduct can produce either economic prosperity or economic underdevelopment. This "belief and development" debate is a slight detour from the main thrust of the economic approach to religion as discussed in this book. The economic approach tries to avoid passing judgment on how religious beliefs—Christian, Jewish, Muslim, Buddhist, Hindu, and so on—may make a life successful or not. Instead, it tries to treat all beliefs equally and ask only how they might motivate cost-benefit behavior or are objects of religious consumption. Still, as this chapter will imply, the economics of religion can jump its normal tracks and ride the railway constructed by the Weberian debate: how do specific beliefs influence economic outcomes, and which outcomes are better?

To some degree, mainstream economists have always been interested in the cultural factors behind economic development. They have asked about the conduct of individuals and societies. In the 1950s, for example, a leading textbook on development stated as an obvious fact that "some religious codes are more compatible with economic growth than others." These codes included thrift, investment, honesty, commerce, experimentation, and risk. A religion that supports these behaviors can "be helpful to growth, whereas in so far as it is hostile to these things, it tends to inhibit growth."[6] In the twenty-first century, research done by the Harvard economist Robert J. Barro has supported a similar claim in regard to entire religious cultures. Even in our modern system of nation-states, Barro said, a "state's religiosity has important influences on its economic performance."[7]

A final difficulty in asking how religion shapes economics is the circular process that is always taking place. What is causing what? Does religion cause economic change, or does economic change alter people's religion? As suggested by Wesley's teaching on wealth, there is one other kind of cyclical problem.

When religious diligence makes people wealthy, they tend to become less religious, mainly because of the worldly comforts and opportunities available to them. As empires past and present suggest, wealth can increase decadence. If that is true, the dilemma is still with us: how will wealthy modern societies rear children with the morals for good conduct (and future wealth)?

These kinds of circular problems, and the long controversy over Weber's thesis about Calvinism, show how difficult generalizations can be. Nevertheless, this chapter will look at four patterns that seem to apply generally. The first pattern is how religion shapes individuals in the market. The second is the necessity of separating the moral bonds of religion from the mechanics of the market. Next we will look at religion's impact on economic prosperity, and then finally at how religion can lead to behaviors that obviously cause economic decline.

QUESTIONS OF CHARACTER

A long history of reflection on the "good life" has resulted in the argument that individuals do not have to practice self-denial to be ethical, moral, or diligent. In commenting on the rise of individualism in the nineteenth century, the French thinker Alexis de Tocqueville spoke of "self-interest rightly understood." This kind of self-interest does not produce "great acts of self-sacrifice," he said after his tours of America in the 1830s. Instead, self-interest "disciplines a number of persons in habits of regularity, temperance, moderation, foresight, self-command; and if it does not lead men straight to virtue by the will, it gradually draws them in that direction by their habits."[8] The modern economist Gary Becker argues that rational self-interest is indeed a basis for moral decisions. "Considerations of price and cost influence ethical and moral choices—such as whether to act honestly—just as they influence choices of personal goods," he argues.[9]

Both economics and religion have emphasized self-interest "rightly understood." Both have identified the extremes of such behavior as well, from avarice in consumption to self-absorption in the pursuit of religious salvation. For the effective performance of an economy, however, it has been universally acknowledged that a workforce made up of individuals with regular habits of temperance, moderation, foresight, and self-control is far better than the opposite. When economic progress fails, according to modern studies, it is more for lack of health, education, and discipline in the workforce than for lack of technology or equipment.[10] As the pioneering British economist Alfred Marshall said: "The most valuable of all capital is that invested in human beings."[11]

Adam Smith also looked at the powerful force of individual self-interest. But in passages of his *Wealth of Nations* that are often overlooked, he spoke of how religion can discipline the lives of individuals. He identified two "schemes or systems of morality" in most societies. The wealthier class, which has wealth enough to adopt "loose" ethics and morals, is nevertheless kept in check by the need to retain reputation and credibility in society. In the lower classes, or in the anonymous setting of urban life, people with fewer resources or no standing in society have little to rely upon. That is the setting in which strict religions provide an "austere" moral system and small groups that pay attention to the behavior of their members. On vices and the "common people," Smith said that "a single week's thoughtlessness and dissipation is often sufficient to undo a poor workman for ever."[12]

Of course, Smith was speaking of the class system of the eighteenth century. But the idea of religion as a system of purpose, discipline, and accountability remains relevant for the lower classes of wealthy societies today, and for entire societies in the developing world. A study of India's onetime untouchable caste, the Dalits, shows that from the time of a socially disruptive "mass movement" of Dalits into Christianity in the 1930s, that underclass began to emerge as a successful entrepreneurial class, now among India's wealthiest and most innovative.[13] Similarly, Pentecostalism and strict Protestant sectarianism in Latin America have also led to the emergence of productive and entrepreneurial sectors. On one hand, this has been achieved simply by suppressing alcohol abuse among the male workforce. On the more positive side of the ledger, sectarian affiliation has inspired the kind of tighter family and social networks that lend themselves to a work ethic, mutual aid, savings, investment, and education.[14]

In overview, self-interest "rightly understood" should prompt most human beings to pursue good habits and responsible living. But one cannot always presume that human beings will develop good character, and it is in this gap that religion plays an important role. It can train young people in good habits and values. It can also reinforce those habits and values throughout life. For individuals who are dealt a harder lot in life—because of poverty, dislocation, or war—the more intense religions often have aided them in mustering the ability to develop strong survival habits and work toward finding greater opportunities. On this the criminologist James Q. Wilson and the Christian ethicist Donald Browning agree: intense religion may not be necessary for society in general, but it can be crucial in helping individual people reverse bad fortune, gain new starts, and find relationships that are essential to well-being.[15]

Today, economists and social scientists are beginning to call this accumulation of character, when provided by religion, a form of human capital.

The dynamics of this kind of human capital—specifically called "religious capital" but now referred to as "spiritual capital" as well—is a topic of growing debate and study. Reference to spiritual capital can often seem too broad, lacking precision. Nevertheless, the term has become helpful in making broader observations, such as those by the Harvard economist Robert Barro. "Spiritual capital includes formal education through organized religion, as well as influences from family and social interactions," he writes. The world over, religion seems to give individuals the traits of honesty, a work ethic, thrift, and openness to strangers. "Thus, the economic effects of organized religion can be seen as operating through the formation of spiritual capital."[16]

TWO SPHERES: RELIGION AND MARKET

In the life of an individual, it is fairly easy to see the links between personal religion, self-interest "rightly understood," and a degree of economic success. When it comes to the larger marketplace, however, the link with religion not only is harder to make out but can seem morally objectionable. After all, Jesus told the rich man to give up his wealth and, more whimsically, said that a camel can squeeze through the eye of a needle more easily than a wealthy man can pry his way into heaven. He went even further, saying, "Those who seek to gain their life will lose it." All of this implies that any sort of personal gain that fuels wider economic success is inimical to religion. So naturally, economists and ethicists who wish to reconcile both gain and morality have tried to explain how this can work, with all due respect to the sayings of Jesus.

Wearing their philosophical hats, economists have responded by making a sharp distinction between personal morality and the impersonal market. They have warned of the bad consequences of confusing the two. As usual, Adam Smith points to this dilemma in his writings, which set up an apparent paradox between self-interest and interest for others. As he said, "It is not from the benevolence of the butcher, the brewer, or the baker, that we expect our dinner, but from their regard to their own interest." This was in *The Wealth of Nations* (1776). But in his earlier work on morals and sympathy, Smith argued that, contrary to self-interest, people develop strong sympathies for the interests of others. "How selfish soever man may be supposed, there are evidently some principles in his nature, which interest him in the fortune of others, and render their happiness necessary to him, though he derives nothing from it except the pleasure of seeing it," Smith says in the opening sentence of *The Theory of Moral Sentiments* (1759).[17]

The founder of modern economics never reconciled these two motives in his writings. What he left behind simply suggests that people live in two realms, one of moral sympathy and the other of impersonal market forces. Indeed, he suggests that self-interest is the highest and most productive virtue in the market. In turn, sympathy and sacrifice for others are natural among family, friends, and close associations. The modern economist Friedrich von Hayek, who won the Nobel Prize in economics in 1974, brought this paradox into sharper focus in his philosophical writings. As part of the so-called Austrian school of economics, he opposed government controls and said the market will self-organize. Similarly, he criticized attempts to impose morality on the market, since morals and markets were two entirely different orders.

We can explore Hayek's view a little more closely. He argued that because no single person—no "directing mind"—could know all the best ways for individuals to make economic exchanges with each other, it was best to leave those decisions to the "man on the spot."[18] This, of course, is a laissez-faire approach to the market, and Hayek argued that, much like Adam Smith's invisible hand, the market takes care of itself by sending a signal called price. Simply put, price is the information that "individuals need to know in order to be able to take the right action," Hayek says. Those actions add up to an organic web of exchanges that organize the market efficiently and fairly. In this view, the market creates a "spontaneous order." No mastermind or dictator—in Hayek's words, no "single central authority"—is capable of doing this, and indeed would do very badly in trying.

As we will see later, the difficulty of imposing a top-down control on the market also arises in attempts to impose the moral system of a religion in market exchanges. But for now, Hayek's insight is this: people live in two "different kinds of orders." They derive their morals from family, religion, and close groups. But in the marketplace, people must relate to each other in impersonal ways that follow rules, perhaps, but are not personal and are morally neutral. A diligent, wise, or clever man may indeed become rich in this impersonal market, but that does not stop him from being charitable and altruistic in his personal, family, and community life. That altruism, however, is not a matter for government or central authorities, who at most would provide rules to referee the market.

In this delicate balance between family and market, a dangerous slide can take place, according to Hayek. One evil is government's attempt to turn the market into a pseudo-family or religion. Another occurs when people turn their families and religions into impersonal markets. In either case, both realms are violated and destroyed. "We must constantly adjust our lives, our thoughts and our emotions, in order to live simultaneously within different kinds of orders according to different rules," Hayek warned. "If we were to apply the unmodified, uncurbed rules of the micro-cosmos (i.e., of the small band or troop, or of, say, our families) to the macro-cosmos (our wider civilization), as our instincts and sentimental yearnings often make us wish to do, *we would destroy it.* Yet if we were to always apply the [competitive] rules of the extended order to our more intimate groupings, *we would crush them.*"[19]

Adam Smith's idea of the invisible hand and Hayek's notion of spontaneous order have been taken by more mathematically inclined thinkers as somewhat "obscure and mystical," says the Nobel Prize–winning economist Vernon Smith, for this reason: "We can never fully understand how this process works in the world because the required information is not given, or available, to any one mind."[20] This failure is a great nuisance to central planners, monopolies, or even moral systems such as Islam that want economic institutions to follow pat rules of behavior in excruciating detail. Nevertheless, most modern societies accept the economic principle that centralized norms must be separate from the market, which runs by its own exchange rules. Where religion helps most, therefore, is in the way its norms shape individuals to be reliable actors in the marketplace.

ISLAM AND WEALTH

But at times, a religion can try to control the marketplace as well, and the most prominent example today is so-called Islamic economics, a new philosophical movement that presents the Quran and its clerical interpreters as the managers of all economic affairs for hundreds of millions of Muslims. Of course, Islamic economics is a very modern invention, arising amid Islamist revivals early in the twentieth century. The way the Muslim religion relates to economics, however, also tells the story of economic development in the Islamic world. As every observer agrees, something happened in the Middle Ages, after which economic development in Islam slowed or declined.

When Weber wrote, the Islamic world had just begun to modernize its financial institutions, but it was far behind the West in economic prosperity. Applying his idea of the Protestant ethic, Weber concluded that although Islam is monotheistic, it did not produce a psychological tension over salvation, as seen in Calvinism. Therefore, Muslims did not work to justify their salvation. Instead, Weber saw Islamic diligence in its military order, which acquired economic success by conquest. Besides being a "national Arabic warrior religion," Weber said, Islam was rooted in two kinds of loyalty: to a prophet and to

Quranic rules of behavior, neither of which motivated capitalist creativity.[21] According to Weber's controversial thesis, the other drag on Muslim economic development was its mysticism, seen in the powerful branch of Sufism. Like mysticism in Hinduism and Catholicism, Weber argued, mysticism in Islam did not produce a worldly capitalist incentive.

We can discuss Weber's view of Islam out of historical curiosity, since few today will support its accuracy. Nevertheless, the mystery of Islam after the Middle Ages continues. According to Islamic tradition, Muhammad's first of many wives, the savvy merchant woman Khadijah, was a business example for all Muslims. So why didn't Islam move toward a modern economic system along with the Western world? One clue in this mystery may be the life of a wealthy Egyptian merchant named Isma'il Abu Taqiyya around the year 1600, when European capitalism began to take off.[22]

Taqiyya lived during the peak of the Ottoman Empire. It was a time when the popularity of coffee in the Middle East had mushroomed. His coffee trade routes extended to Venice, India, and West Africa. In the wake of the coffee craze, the need for sugar also grew. By his diligence and good business manner, Taqiyya soon became a chief supplier of sugar in the eastern Mediterranean. In a modern biography of Taqiyya, he is portrayed as taking full advantage of the Islamic legal codes regarding trade, working with brokers and agents, and making all his oral deals in the Islamic courts. Based on the Quran, the courts forbade charging interest. But more important for Taqiyya's booming business, Islamic law also required that each negotiation be a personal, face-to-face deal. Taqiyya's life was preoccupied with hundreds, if not thousands, of oral agreements, some of which survive in court records.

In his lifetime, Taqiyya became rich. His Cairo home was opulent and his wives and children many. In all, he could be a Muslim, follow Islamic norms, and still be a smashing business success. Given the time in which Taqiyya lived, we can compare his success to an apparent business failure taking place in the West, across the world in England. There, the king of England was approving a new style of corporation called the joint stock company, in which investors put up the funding and reaped both the benefits and risks of a large and long-term business enterprise. One of these joint company exploits, in 1607, was the founding of Jamestown Colony in what is now Virginia. The declared mission of the Jamestown joint stock venture was to spread Christianity. But unlike Taqiyya's venture under Islamic courts, the Jamestown investors operated on purely secular, pragmatic, and flexible agreements.

The short-term results in Jamestown and in Cairo could not have been more different. Taqiyya became rich. The Jamestown venture, however, produced no profit. So after seventeen years, it was taken over by the royal government. But in the economic long run, the Jamestown model was to vastly supersede what even Taqiyya accomplished in Cairo. During his lifetime, Taqiyya could not expand his venture further because Islamic law required face-to-face deals. He could not pool money, use intermediaries, or form what today—and in England at the time of the Jamestown venture—is called a corporation. Finally, under Islamic law, at Taqiyya's death his wealth had to be broken up and dispersed equally among the members of a very large family. "Inheritance law also played a role in the fragmentation of the Abu Taqiyya fortune," writes his biographer.[23] In effect, after being in business forty-five years (1580 to 1625), Taqiyya's coffee and sugar operation collapsed.

In contrast, the Jamestown venture lived on. It made its state wealthy in the world tobacco trade, and many similar joint stock companies brought wealth and long-term development to both the New World and Europe. Not only did the corporation emerge in Europe, allowing impersonal investing and exchanges, but family companies that did well could stay intact for generations. If inheritance was a question, Europe had its laws of primogeniture, which passed on an entire business firm to the eldest son. There was nothing in the Bible that necessarily dictated the European model, but in the Middle East, the holy Quran is what decided how Muslims would do business. In fact, Christians and Jews who were business agents in Islamic lands were able to grow wealthier because of more flexibility in arranging business partnerships. The point, if we return to Hayek's argument about "two orders," is that Islam did not keep the religious order and the market order separate.

A leading student of this history is the economist Timur Kuran, who has explained in detail all the ways that Islamic culture missed out on the economic revolution that eventually separated the West from the Middle East. "Certain elements of Islamic law blocked evolutionary paths that might have generated a modern financial system," Kuran writes.[24] As noted, these obstacles included Islamic rules on deal making, interest, private ownership, and inheritance, but also a tradition of allowing rich people to avoid taxes by setting up a *waqf*—a public service such as a waterworks, mosque, or school—and also a welfare tax system, *zakat*, that was centrally organized and subject to the normal politics of centralized controls. As Kuran explains, many of these ideas are said to come directly from the Quran, although like any sacred text, its verses have always been open to varied interpretations. Furthermore, advocates of modern-day Islamic economics say that these principles produced a golden age in seventh-century Arabia, when the Prophet Muhammad and his righteous successor caliphs ruled for forty years.

The dilemma, of course, is that imposing seventh-century principles on modern times can block economic flexibility. Those medieval traditions were

strongly in place in Taqiyya's day, and that, according to hist
Kuran, explains why the Middle East fell behind in economic deve
lesson of Islam, however, applies to all religious cultures. "The c
every society faces, and not only Islam, is to undertake institutional
so that society can move from personal exchange to impersonal
Kuran says. "Most of the exchanges in the advanced economy today, and even
in the semi-advanced, are impersonal." The recent movement of Islamic economics, with its revival of ancient norms, tries to fuse a familial system with a
market system, which bodes failure in one or the other. "The problem with
'Islamic economics' in general is that it tries to apply institutions that were very
well suited to an economy where the norm was personal exchange. It seeks to
apply those, because they are part of the religious heritage, to the modern
world, and of course it does not work."[25]

As with all religious cultures, Islam hopes that devout Muslims will follow
the teachings of the Quran and the mullahs to be good people, be honest, and
be devout. Unfortunately, such a virtuous citizenry has been elusive across history. Many Islamic countries have imposed strict rules on private behavior, for
example, but "there is no evidence that such measures have brought about the
behavioral changes envisioned in Islamic texts," Kuran says. "Nor is there evidence from any other country that the promotion of Islamic morality has
altered work patterns or business relations."[26]

What is needed, in the modern economic view, is a moral system for families and close communities in Islam, but a market system that is impersonal
and operates on rules of fairness, open and honest business exchange, and the
incentives of making a profit. In many cases, Islamic law has worked against
such incentives. The symbol of this mismatch, according to Kuran, is the rise of
"Islamic banking," which purports to follow the Quran's ban on charging
interest. In Islamic interpretation, a lender must share both risk and profit with
the borrower. If the loan is a total loss, that is the burden of the bank—as written, it is said, in holy texts. Historically, however, the ban on interest began in
the Quran as the Prophet's rejection of *riba*, an ancient desert law that default-
ing debtors must pay twice the interest, and then twice again on the next
default. In Muhammad's day, *riba* was used to enslave debtors, and so he called
for an end to the practice.

But *riba* is not the same as normal interest, says Kuran, even though Islamists trying to make an ideological point since the 1930s have said all interest is
against the Quran. This aspect of Islamic economics was formalized by Muslim
writers in India in the 1960s, and by 1975 the first Islamic banks began to
appear in nations such as Pakistan, Saudi Arabia, and Iran. They now operate
in at least sixteen countries, but not without the normal struggle of matching

Islamic norms to modern economics. These banks do not charge interest, but they survive by charging borrowers "bank fees," "financial commissions," and "service charges"—a kind of back-door interest. In one example of the mechanism, a bank may "lend" money by directly paying for a shipment of steel to Iran, or a piece of machinery destined for Pakistan, and then transferring ownership to the borrower and charging a large service fee. Technically, the bank has shared the risk—if only for a few seconds—but in the end has garnered a nice profit and may also be insured against loss of the steel or machinery, or default by the borrower.

Still, Islamic banks do not speak to the normal economic incentives of the modern world, and therefore they tend to draw high-risk borrowers and cannot compete with secular banks in the same cities or abroad. "Islamic banking defies the separation between economics and religion," writes Kuran. "It invokes religious authority in a domain that modern civilization has secularized." As a result, it has a religious form but in reality charges extra fees to stay in business. One Malaysian observer said of Islamic banking, "The only difference is whether the man behind the counter is wearing a religious hat or a bow tie." Islamic banking, in other words, is what Hayek might call an improper mixing of family morals (sharing) and market incentives (business exchange and profit). This is a story for all religions, but Islam is under the modern spotlight. "The communalist economic morality of Islam has had, of course, its counterparts in other religions, including Christianity," Kuran summarizes. "But in the centuries leading up to the industrial revolution, expanding segments of Christendom moved away from communalism and toward individualism."[27]

RELIGION AS SOCIAL CAPITAL

Religion's impact on economic prosperity, if not imposed from a papal throne or by an ayatollah in Iran, can nevertheless bubble up from the society itself. This is being spoken of today as the social capital that is generated by a given society. The World Bank defines social capital as "the norms and social relations embedded in social structures that enable people to coordinate action to achieve desired goals."[28] While social capital does not control the economic marketplace, it creates a situation in which people generally have healthy networks, social norms, and enough trust to cooperate and coordinate for everyone's mutual benefit. The opposite, of course, would be a society of distrustful factions, or a society in which the people are completely cynical about the government and, while not revolting against it, circumvent all its rules through corruption and black markets. With social capital spread around, a given society can openly cooperate.

This idea of social capital has a colorful history. The British economist Alfred Marshall wrote a good deal on the social dimension of capital, looking at the rearing of children or the collective resources of a society. But the contemporary use of the term entered the lexicon in the setting of Appalachia in West Virginia in the 1920s, where educator, religious activist, and social reformer L. Judson Hanifan was trying to determine how a community could advance its health, security, and productivity. The key, Hanifan said, is for people to be connected: isolation led to many human problems. "In the use of the phrase social capital I make no reference to the usual acceptation of the term capital, except in a figurative sense," Hanifan wrote. "I do not refer to real estate, or to personal property or to cold cash, but rather to that in life which tends to make these tangible substances count for most in the daily lives of people: namely good will, fellowship, sympathy, and social intercourse among the individuals and families who make up a social unit."[29]

As Harvard sociologist Robert Putnam observes, Hanifan's definition anticipated all the new work being done on this topic beginning in the 1970s. By the next decade it was a main feature of discussions about the economic advancement of minorities and inevitably of the debate about why some social classes and some cultures slide into dysfunction, while others support economic advancement. In its simplest terms, Putnam explains, social capital means membership in a group. That membership creates networks through which people can learn about trust and reciprocity, seek aid in need, and have a social identity as they walk into the impersonal world of the economic marketplace.

When the social unit is a religion, then this accumulation of benefits has been called religious social capital by economists since the 1970s. One definition of individual religious capital, for example, includes the social dimension: friendships with fellow worshipers. Some versions of spiritual capital focus on social connections, as in sociologist Peter Berger's definition: "a subspecies of social capital, referring to the power, influence, knowledge, and dispositions created by participation in a particular religious tradition."[30] Let us begin by looking at case studies of how religious capital may be having an impact on economic development. As noted earlier, the search for happiness in the world based on economics is fraught with peril, and world surveys often show that industrialized nations experience more unhappiness than poorer countries. Nevertheless, we are here to test whether religion can be shown to produce a wealthier society. That is the question asked by a series of recent studies on income, entrepreneurship, and trade.

INCOME, ENTREPRENEURSHIP, AND TRADE

When Harvard economist Robert Barro and his wife and academic colleague, Rachel McCleary, set out to measure how religion and economics relate in nearly sixty countries, they faced the same challenges as Weber had: obtaining comparative data. Fortunately, in the twenty-first century researchers can draw upon a range of international surveys, including the periodic World Values Surveys, the International Social Survey Program, and the Gallup Millennium Survey. To discover the attitudes, beliefs, and religious behaviors of citizens in each country, Barro and McCleary ran the data from these surveys though sophisticated computer comparisons with wealth and incomes in the same nations.

The puzzle they discovered was this: Nations with increased religious participation, such as church attendance, had lower levels of economic development. At the same time, however, nations whose citizens had high rates of belief in the consequences of religion—such as belief in hell—showed higher economic performance. The findings suggest, according to the authors, that national workforces make a trade-off in their use of time between work and leisure, or religion. At the same time, nations whose workers felt that there were consequences to their beliefs and behaviors were more productive. Religion produces an economic contradiction: more participation leads to less productivity, but more belief in the afterlife raises output. "If people spend too much time in religious activities, there is a negative effect on economic growth," McCleary says. On the other hand, prosperity blooms where there is moderate to low attendance but extra-high belief in the afterlife, heaven or hell. "To put it another way, the main [economic] growth effect that we find is a positive response to an increase in believing relative to belonging."[31]

The findings point to the circular problem of not only how religion and economics influence each other but also how nations can keep the best balance. The most productive workers, it seems, hold authentic beliefs but do not waste too much time going to the church or mosque. The question for a society then becomes how to cultivate belief yet keep generating wealth. As seen in chapter 8, a central argument of modern times is that increased wealth in the world has promoted secularization. If a society entirely eschews religion, how will it pass on moral behaviors to children and enforce them in adults? McCleary describes this dilemma as the vicious cycle of wealth undermining morals, but then compares that to a "virtuous cycle" in which a society finds a balance that takes full economic advantage of believing and belonging.[32]

Another study of the sixty-six nations covered by the World Values Survey also found a correlation between religion and upbeat economic activity. The survey asked about economic attitudes toward cooperation, government, working women, legal rules, thriftiness, and the market economy. There did not seem to be a clash between religious people and basic market economics, the study concluded. "On average, religious beliefs are associated with 'good' economic attitudes, where 'good' is defined as conducive to higher per capita income and growth." As we will explore later, however, religion also creates enclaves rather than openness to markets. The one deleterious finding in this sixty-six-nation survey, for example, is that religious people are more prejudiced against outsiders. They are also more likely to oppose women leaving the home for the workplace. Religions differed on these and other topics, but overall, "Christian religions are more positively associated with attitudes conducive to economic growth."[33]

Now we look at entrepreneurship. For many economists, all economic development requires a certain kind of person, whatever his or her religion may be: the entrepreneur. Historically, comments on religion and the work ethic typically have presented the picture of men and women who show up at the factory or office and do their duty. To spark an economy, however, it takes an entrepreneur with the distinct personality traits of being motivated, creative, and comfortable with risk taking. Arguably, every religion has had successful entrepreneurs, namely, their founders or chief disciples and missionaries. In the marketplace, the successful entrepreneur needs both the inclination and the best possible social environment, and that is where a personal religious commitment may play a role, according to one study of 90,000 workers in India, most of whom were salaried employees but others of whom were self-employed.[34]

The study tested the proposition that, given the need for motivation in entrepreneurship, extra inspiration may be required. Therefore, it asked whether "religions with great transformative potential may facilitate entrepreneurial behavior." According to the patterns in India, different religions and social settings define who strikes out on their own as business owners. "While India is rich with diverse religions, some of them, such as Islam and Christianity, are conducive to entrepreneurship," the authors said. "By contrast, others, and in particular Hinduism, inhibit entrepreneurship." For example, Hindus are more likely than Christians or Muslims to be salaried employees. Hindus in the lowest caste, which is especially reliant on government, are least entrepreneurial of all.

The two factors in Hinduism that may be at play are the religion's traditional deemphasis of earthly pursuits and its support of a caste system. The Hindu tradition of asceticism and belief that the world is an illusion may be theological ideas with an economic impact. Similarly, the Hindu metaphysics about reincarnation has justified the ancient caste system, which, like social class in England, lingers into modern times. What causes what is always a hard problem to solve, according to the study. But clues can be found by looking more closely at the social circumstances.

In India, for example, transplanted faiths such as Islam and Christianity encourage entrepreneurial practices, even though they too are subject to strong class stratifications and economic roles. Christians and Muslims are not entirely free of the caste system. But their beliefs may prompt a more self-reliant and worldly attitude toward business success. Entrepreneurship may be an easier option in marginalized minority groups or in ethnic and religious subcultures that offer their own network of clients. This seems to work for Hindus doing business abroad. As immigrants, according to other studies, they are far more likely to be self-employed or take the risks necessary for innovation. It is also possible, of course, that the Hindus who migrate abroad have entrepreneurial temperaments, explaining why they left their home country for one with an open market. Whatever the case, religious beliefs do tend to shape concepts of economic activity, and these in turn are shaped by different environments.

Environments determine the minority status of religions as well, and it is clear to historians that this influences business choices. European Jews, for example, who had to be mobile, excelled in "portable" businesses. Historians and social scientists also have long debated whether the "mentality" of various religious sects is what prompted them to develop certain industries, or whether those sects just happened to live in parts of a country where, given its resources, that industry was inevitable. The study of India faces the same questions, but its most evident conclusion for now is that the Hindu mind does not emphasize entrepreneurship, which is characterized by risk, creativity, and desire for advancement in wealth: "At least in the case of India, Max Weber's insight is found to hold—religion is an important influence on economic behavior."

International trade is a final area where the religious capital of nations is likely to have an impact. When Islamic terrorists hit the United States in 2001, one of their targets was the World Trade Center. For many, this act symbolizes radical religion's threat to world trade and a global economy. Ethnic, religious, and communal strife has demonstrably hurt business in the countries where that strife is most prevalent. Foreign investment will flee a nation that erupts in ethnic or religious conflict. That has been the story, for example, in Northern Ireland, parts of the former Soviet Union, and, for a moment, in India's financial capital, Mumbai (formerly known as Bombay), after the al-Qaeda attacks of 2008.

In regard to international trade, the other significant question about helping or hurting an economy involves the network effect. Networks are made up of friendly and cooperative actors in different countries or parts of an economy. Networks based on nationality and language are classic cases. In business, networks can decrease the cost of gaining information and establishing reputations. Immigrant populations doing business with contacts "back home" are a common grounding of the kinds of networks that have shaped history. If networks are strongly based on ethnic or religious ties, however, the benefits might be limited. Once a closed religious network is operating, it may never expand. It may never do business with nonbelievers, so to speak. Such inward-looking networks will not be able to take advantage of new market opportunities.

Networks can also involve entire nations. They might have natural religious ties that grease the wheels of commerce. Examples might be trade between Egypt and Indonesia, two large Muslim countries. England and Scandinavia form a similar Protestant network, and Spain and Poland, or a Latin American nation, might represent a Catholic network. This is the kind of detail that a study of eighty-four countries revealed: "The sharing of religious beliefs by adherents of the same religion living in different countries can create networks of trust and familiarity that facilitate complex international economic transactions."[35] But as might be expected, the eight religions—Buddhism, Catholicism, Confucianism, Hinduism, Judaism, Islam, Eastern Orthodoxy, and Protestantism—showed different patterns in regard to trade.

Some countries showed high volumes of trade with others of their religious tradition, while this affinity made no difference or had a negative effect in other countries. "The more [that] Buddhists, Confucians, Hindus, Eastern Orthodox . . . , or Protestants share their particular religious cultures with people in another country, [with] all other things equal, the greater is bilateral trade between those countries," says the study.[36] But the more that two countries share a Catholic culture, the lower its bilateral trade. In the case of countries with an Islamic or Jewish culture, there is no significant improvement or loss in comparison to other countries in general. Based on other global surveys, the authors speculate that the Catholic distinctiveness may arise from national cultures with high rates of "contractual defaults" and corruption, such as the common use of bribes. This problem of defaults and bribe requirements may also suggest why trade between Muslim nations does not seem to benefit from their affinity of religious outlook.

Any theological probing of why this happens invariably goes back down Weber's controversial and somewhat psychological pathway—that beliefs affect mentalities of entire cultures. For example, some economists have suggested that Catholic and Islamic ideas of forgiveness and penance have made those cultures less scrupulous in business dealings: their people will be forgiven by God anyway. Along the same lines, the World Values Surveys consistently find higher rates of distrust in predominantly Catholic societies and aversion to market economics in Muslim societies. In other international measures, Catholic and Muslim societies, perhaps due to hierarchical traditions, have ranked higher in business and government corruption. If this experience makes a difference in world trade, business leaders in Catholic or Muslim countries may feel no advantage in trading with nations of similar religious heritage.

Nevertheless, the sharing of religious cultures has defined trade in the past and mostly shows that this benefit continues. On closer inspection, religion could turn out to be a resource alongside other international institutions, such as trade blocs, trade courts, and multinational businesses, to make the world economy operate more effectively. In this view, religion does not have to be an obstacle to globalization, despite the horrifying symbolism of the World Trade Center's burning towers. But each religion has a different effect on trade, so the future will depend on "the relative growth rates of the world's different religions," concludes this study.

Some of these shifts might be unexpected. For example, the growth and innovation in religion in the twenty-first century are happening mostly in the developing world—Africa, Latin America, and Asia.[37] The future question for the economics of religion is whether this religious ferment will help accelerate economic productivity or retard it. Will it improve the standard of living in the poorest nations? Or will religions mobilize the dispossessed to attack the nations and agents of the industrialized world?

RELIGION, ECONOMICS, AND BAD BEHAVIOR

We have seen how, in general, an economy can suffer from undue family and communal controls, even though that same economy can prosper only when enough moral individuals follow rules and trust that other people will do likewise. But a more daunting problem can be open violence between groups vying over economic disparities.

When this happens, the warring factions are often held together, and galvanized, by their common social capital, which includes their common religious convictions. Economist Kuran notes that when economic disparities grow too great, religion can become a rallying point for conflict, creating the kind of violence that undermines everyone's economic progress. "Intercommunal struggles can throw property rights into jeopardy, discourage local investment, and cause capital flight, thus impair[ing] any economic growth," he writes.[38] Even in trade, religion can turn out to be prohibitive of cooperation if religious networks are too balkanized.

In all these cases, the accumulation of social capital and the production of club goods can strengthen a group's bonds based on religion. This accumulation can mobilize religious aggression, on one hand, or move religious groups into isolation, on the other, both of which hurt a marketplace's openness, fair play, and adherence to rules. The fact that social capital and club goods, seemingly so valuable to society, can also reinforce bad behavior shows how economic dynamics often produce unexpected by-products. As Putnam says, "If there is one enduring lesson from the early social capital debates, it is that we cannot assume that social capital is everywhere and always a good thing; virtuous forms can have unintended consequences that are not socially desirable."[39]

Economists call these by-products and unintended consequences "negative externalities," or effects that are harmful to others while beneficial to some. Smog is a good example: factories provide jobs and make products, but they also produce smog that hurts neighbors. The same applies to strong groups. One can cite the Ku Klux Klan, the Mafia, the Taliban, or the Black Panthers for their strong bonds of social capital, but also for the obvious downside. Another dilemma of social capital is that while the poor would benefit from it most, it is typically the better-off in society who can gather it up. The wealthy classes can be bound closely together by their shared experience. But these tight bonds can throw up barriers against less wealthy people who seek to enter the higher social classes, where the doors to opportunity are fiercely guarded.

The solution, of course, is to have just the right amount of social capital and the right amount of openness to other kinds of civic markets and associations. In this light, sociologist Mark Granovetter has spoken of the importance of weak ties as well as strong ties. For example, strong ties bind a group of people together through constant contact by way of class, religion, or ethnicity but do not provide links to other social opportunities. By contrast, those opportunities often come via weak ties. Weak ties allow for interaction between tight groups that might otherwise balkanize society. Weak ties allow for casual communication and cooperation and often the best tips on job opportunities. Says Granovetter: "Weak ties provide people with access to information and resources beyond those available in their own social circle; but strong ties have greater motivation to be of assistance and are typically more easily available." In sum, there is a "utility of ties of different strength."[40] Closed groups lack weak ties. This handicaps them in the marketplace or in broader political action. Unfortunately, it is primarily the poor, or the truly alienated, who rely on strong ties alone.

Following Granovetter, Putnam speaks of social capital as the ability to create both ties that bind groups internally and ties that bridge different groups. "This is not to say that bonding groups are necessarily bad; indeed, evidence suggests that most of us get our social support from bonding rather than bridging social ties," says Putnam. "It is true, however, that without the natural restraints imposed by members' crosscutting allegiances and diverse perspectives, tightly knit and homogeneous groups can rather easily combine for sinister ends. In other words, bonding without bridging equals Bosnia."[41] He cites studies showing that violence between Hindus and Muslims in India is reduced when other kinds of civic associations bridge members of the rival groups. When Putnam speaks of sinister ends, however, the easiest example that comes to mind is terrorist groups, especially those bound by religion—a topic that economists are probing as well.

The early debate on the formation of terrorist groups usually revolved around the question of whether they were motivated by poverty and ignorance or by shrewd ideological planning. The general conclusion, based on the number of Islamic terrorists who were from the middle class and college-educated, is that ideological convictions or religious beliefs are the chief cause, rather than poverty.[42] From the point of view of social ties and social capital, terrorist organizations have lost weak ties with broader social resources and turned instead for identity and material needs to narrower, and perhaps more desperate, strong ties.

The economist naturally would look for other economic factors to explain why a terrorist organization would form and why its members, presumed to be making cost-benefit choices just like any other human being, would be willing to die in a suicide bombing. This is the question that economist Eli Berman has approached with the club and club goods theory in economics.[43] In this view, the secular terrorist (i.e., Tamil Tiger) or religious terrorist (i.e., al-Qaeda or Hamas member) does indeed calculate costs and benefits when joining the group. In the club model, the group is organized strictly enough to slough off free riders who want to join but not pay the price. The group also demands that members take high risks, such as stigma and sacrifice, and this further separates them from the world outside. For this cost, however, the terrorist has to ask, what benefits are there?

The benefits are the club goods that the group produces and that only the members can have access to. As Berman has shown, there are many such goods that can motivate terrorist acts. One can be the intensity of religious belief generated in a tightly bound group, such as the belief in rewards in the afterlife for a terrorist "martyr." But the material and social rewards are the strongest incentives and most effective means of control in the group, he argues in his book *Radical, Religious, and Violent: The New Economics of Terrorism*.[44] The individual knows that membership in such a group means that the others will fight for his preservation, much as any U.S. Marine will cover his buddy in combat. It is well known that Muslim terrorist cells promise financial support to the family of a terrorist volunteer. Indeed, the Muslim Brotherhood in Egypt, which was the seedbed of wider radical Islamic movements in the early twentieth century, built its strength on a vast social welfare system.

In the extreme terrorist club, according to Berman, the dynamic of excluding free riders and enhancing the production of club goods for members' consumption helps explain the effective intensity of the terrorist cell. The economist assumes that the cell is acting rationally, even though its goal is to wreak death and destruction on society. Apart from the specific goal, the intensity of a religious club can be a universal thing. In the history of most religious sects, the social environment was not debilitating. In comparison, terrorist groups evoke the dark side because they arise in dysfunctional societies or failed states, Berman says. The negative activity of violence, meanwhile, reinforces the compliance and loyalty of members to the group. For society, this cohesion is a very negative outcome indeed. But for adherents of the group, the violence is tied to a positive payoff: the group's promise that it will reward its most dedicated members, and their families, with financial and social benefits.[45]

The way to intervene in such negative religious club formation, Berman says, is to pursue both ideological and material strategies. For one, the religious beliefs that justify suicide bombings can be openly challenged. But also, the environment of a failed state must be addressed. At the same time, material opportunities should be extended to the typical terrorist recruit: a young man who may feel thwarted in his ability to make a living or succeed.

The way religious beliefs and organizations influence economic and political developments is likely to remain a pressing topic for the future. Looking back, the so-called Hundred Years' War over Weber's thesis has not ended because the basic questions are still so fascinating to us. When it comes to policy, religion may also be a useful tool: it may be a factor in nudging nations toward economic health and stability. Finding a workable relationship between diverse religions, state regulations, and free markets may also help avoid a religious "clash of civilizations," which some are predicting or even advocating.

In the economic view, these kinds of clashes are best avoided by working toward freedom of religion.[46] But just as important is the ability of a market system to operate free of ideological controls by one religion or another. Freedom of religion and a nonideological market are two concerns we will return to in the final chapter.

CHAPTER 10

The Merits of Mammon

There are many reasons to climb a mountain. "Because it is there!" is among the most famous. In this book, we have navigated the slopes and switchbacks of economics, religion, and history with the goal of gaining a view from the summit. Now that we've reached the top, we can take in a panorama of the economic approach to religion. For some it is a revelation. For others it may not be a very pretty picture.

Down in the valley lives *Homo economicus*. For many, these inhabitants make up a rather one-dimensional portrait of humanity. We calculate, consume, and compete, always trying to maximize our satisfaction. In short, the classic economic image of the human being seems the very antithesis of what religion is all about. Theologians have noticed this, of course, and the result is a good deal of polemic against self-interest, capitalism, and the whole market mentality. But as this book has tried to show, the economic approach to religion is hardly as grim a vista as that. Among the many possible approaches to human behavior, the rational costs-and-benefits one offers insights but hardly a silver bullet. There are always constraints in life. Things of great value have a high cost indeed, as the aspirations of religion have regularly shown.

To consider the merits of the economic approach, we can begin by sampling some of the criticisms against mixing religious motives with economic models. Second, we can look at alternative "altruistic" systems of human behavior and assess their plausibility. After this, we can conclude with some of the helpful aspects of our economic view over the valley below.

THE MARKET CRITICS

We began this book by noting that the economic approach tries to avoid the black boxes of biology and of culture. Rather than explore how genes, the brain, and the nervous system control human behavior, or look for a myriad of cultural influences, the economic approach has presumed that people act rationally in their self-interest, able to roughly calculate their own preferences. In a broader sense, this is the basis of the social contract, not just the stock exchange or the commodities market. Nevertheless, the economic approach may seem reductionist—reducing human life to an extremely simple, even shallow, principle. For many critics of the economic approach to religion, it lacks depth. It also puts economists in a position to claim that somehow they alone, among all social scientists, philosophers, and visionaries, truly understand the human being.

The popular theologian Harvey Cox, for example, has written humorously about reducing life to buying and selling and ultimately making the market into a god. This vision of the new God is offered to us not by theologians, he says, but rather by "econologians"—the university experts, business columnists, and talking heads who displaced the gods from Olympus and endowed the market with divine-like powers. Now, says Cox, "this celestial pinnacle is occupied by The Market, which I capitalize to signify both the mystery that enshrouds it and the reverence it inspires in business folk." For him the serious point is that, when The Market is God, nothing is sacred, for all things can be bought and sold. "Since the earliest stages of human history, of course, there have been bazaars, rialtos, and trading posts—all markets. But The Market was never God, because there were other centers of value and meaning, other 'gods.' The Market operated within a plethora of other institutions that restrained it."[1]

From inside the field itself, economist Robert Nelson has offered a similar view of the role of economists as only the latest group of social experts who have aspired to be the priesthood of the twentieth century. Like theologians, they too have created a system of thought that teaches a redemption narrative, a story of the human fall into poverty followed by the path to salvation via economic efficiency. This sacred narrative is no longer written in Latin or Sanskrit; now it comes in the form of mathematics. With these tools, which are less science than theology, Nelson argues, the economists have aspired to be "the priesthood of a modern secular religion of economic progress."[2] That pursuit is likely to fail, however, since total efficiency in human nature and society is elusive. Economists would not be the first experts, Nelson suggests, to try to impose scientific order on human beings, which is just as likely to cramp human freedom and misconstrue reality.

Fortunately, the economic approach to religion surveyed in this book is a far more modest proposal. It does not presume to say much about the material well-being of humanity. It does not offer a platform for policies related to taxes, inflation, unions, products, technology, and business cycles. Instead, it simply looks closely at how people make the most of life when it comes to ultimate beliefs and participating in groups that have organized around those beliefs. It looks at principles rather than policy, and, on the topic of religion, it certainly leaves open the question of powers higher than The Market offering incentives to human beings.

Like the economic approach, some biological interpretations of human behavior have also been called reductionist. Some biologists have reduced all human behavior to genetics. The "selfish gene" has been proposed as the central actor. However, when it comes to explaining religion, the evolutionary biologist David Sloan Wilson feels that the focus on genetics misses the broader and richer interpretation of evolutionary biology. That does not mean, though, that Wilson thinks the economic approach is any better. He has taken on the economic approach to religion by offering an alternative. For a start, he concedes that the economic or rational-choice approach to religion is one of the most cohesive and dynamic in social science. But he believes that by using the biological concept of adaptation, religion is better explained as a characteristic of a group that increases the group's fitness and opportunities for survival.

Human beings can gain more resources simply by "the *coordinated action* of individuals," Wilson says, so groups will trump individuals in the historical process of social evolution. Religion holds groups together. And religious groups in particular are incomparably fascinating for how they have evolved a vast array of beliefs, norms, and customs that create group solidarity. "Must we really attribute all adaptive features of a religion to a psychological process of cost-benefit reasoning?" asks Wilson. "Isn't a process of blind variation and selective retention possible? After all, thousands of religions are born and die without notice because they never attract more than a few members. . . . Perhaps the adaptive features of the few that survive are like random mutations rather than the product of rational choice."[3]

In taking this view, Wilson says that biology is trying to become a social science by reviving a sociological theory that, as we have noted, is called functionalism. In this, religion functions as a means to produce social action. Unlike past evolutionary theory, which focused on the striving of individuals, the approach espoused by Wilson sees groups as the central adaptive unit in human social evolution. And for holding groups together, religion has served quite well, as the French thinker Emile Durkheim explained so long ago. If economics and early evolutionary biology focused excessively on the individual, says Wilson, that is no longer going to help social science: "Those days are over."

As we saw in previous chapters, processes of evolution and religious economies are very similar when viewed on the surface: many religions adapt well and go through life cycles, competing with their environments in the process. The evolutionary and economic approaches also share similar insights on the origin of altruism, or acting in the interest of others. Of course, this is the gospel of religion: do unto others, and even sacrifice self-interest for another's well-being.

In a supernatural religion, altruism is classically attributed to either commands by God or the practice of love. Biology has its own two solutions. More narrowly, genetic theory has explained altruism simply as an organism sacrificing for related others so that its genes survive into the future. This is the behavior of ants, a superbly unselfish species. In this view, moreover, a mother loves the child because, in effect, the child represents the mother's own genetic survival. More broadly, Wilson sidelines genes to focus on the "superorganism," or social group, that all individuals must be part of. Here individuals learn that it is to everyone's benefit to coordinate with others. Rewards, and even survival, come by being other-oriented. A more cooperative species evolves because the noncooperators don't survive as well.

The economic approach, however, finally falls back on something that Adam Smith tried to do a few centuries ago. As a moral philosopher, he said human beings show sympathy toward others, especially family and close associates. By development of this trait, Smith believed human beings could look at a larger system and agree to its social rules, rules that seemed beneficial but that were enforced by laws and social sanctions as well. Once these "moral sentiments" were all in place, Smith said, people could be entirely self-interested in the marketplace, which allowed the generation of wealth and profit by every player in the market. Economists such as Gary Becker, for example, have argued that the biological explanation is not necessary because it is clear enough that through constant social exchanges, individuals and groups learn to cooperate—there is mutual benefit, often achieved by sacrifice or compromise.[4] The same is found in game theory, which is a mathematical model of economic calculations of risk, cost, and benefit.

One final appeal for this economic approach can be made to sacred scriptures themselves. For all the urging about love and charity, scriptures such as the Bible, the Quran, or the Buddhist texts speak regularly to individual self-interest: lose your life to gain your life. In scriptures, the moral exhortation is about the wisdom necessary to gain your life successfully, not a call to self-immolation for the sake of others. To the contrary, religion speaks to the basic hope for life, success, and fulfillment—always with costs attached to the gains.

ALTERNATIVE ALTRUISTIC SYSTEMS

One of the chief economic alternatives offered by religion is a world in which human beings are basically unselfish. This has been called a "gift culture," a "redemptive economy," and by socialist idealists "nonselfish economics." This focus on human generosity is hard to turn down. In a gift culture, individuals and groups produce things to give them to other people. No return is expected. We have a variety of examples from history, many of which continue to resonate today.

In the Old Testament, for instance, a jubilee year was prescribed every seven years, and also every fifty years. During the jubilee year of the short cycle, fields were left fallow, work suspended, and resources handed around freely. In the fifty-year cycle, during the jubilee year the Israelites were told to return all lands to their ancestral owners, presumably to keep kin systems intact. This was to be done in a process of fair dealing, the freeing of slaves, and giving aid to the poor. Historians are uncertain whether this ever took place, but if it had, according to a census by King David, it would have been a project for a society as large as 3 million men, women, and children.

The New Testament also offers such a utopian vision of the economic life. As the first church gathered, the book of Acts tells us, it was like a beneficent commune. Everything was put in a common pot and shared equally. The early believers "were together and had all things in common; they would sell their possessions and goods and distribute the proceeds to all, as any had need" (Acts 2:43). Even Karl Marx referred to this part of the Bible in his argument for economic collectivism with a communist party at the top, managing the equality. Islam has an equally ideal vision of the economic life. This was the golden age of the seventh-century Arabian desert, where for forty years the mandates of God and the wisdom of the Prophet and the righteous caliphs guided an unselfish society in which wealth and resources were distributed equally.

Later, in the much larger medieval society of the West, the Catholic philosopher Thomas Aquinas spoke of a way of life in which resources were to be viewed as gifts given to humanity by God, and given to each other by the same token. As some historians have noted, however, not even in the full intellectual life of the medieval thinkers had the idea of a neutral market been conceived, and certainly not analyzed. The communal economics of old even held some appeal for Thomas Jefferson. He was so repulsed by the inheritance of wealth passed down by the aristocracy of his era that he once drew up a plan— like the jubilee year, or like the French Revolution—under which family inheritances would be confiscated every few decades and redistributed into society. For better or worse, however, communal economics has not become the dominant pattern in the modern world, although it certainly can survive in smaller settings. As Cox has lamented, market economics has indeed become omnipresent, if not deified.

The economic approach to religion recognizes the pervasive fact of market exchange and has drawn upon its insights to explain human behavior. But unlike the prescriptive economics surveyed above—economic systems that prescribe how material resources should be distributed—the economic approach to religion has nothing to say on that matter. Instead, it sees religion as an exchange system in the lives of individuals and groups that operates parallel to, but distinct from, secular economics. As history shows, political freedom is tightly connected to economic freedom, and so any economic system will determine how much freedom there is in the religious marketplace. But in principle, the vision offered at our mountain summit is of two realms. In one, there is religious belief and behavior. The other realm covers the dynamics of the labor force, taxation, and monetary policy. It is not easy to bridge the two, but typically, when religion has its say, the bridging is done by charity and philanthropy.

In other words, the economic approach to religion applauds religion's push for altruism. Once religions are organized, in fact, they typically offer altruistic services. They also use their moral voices to urge governments and citizens to do the same. But the heart of the economic model is to look for incentives of benefit over cost, and that would include what motivates religion to be altruistic. The incentive for losing one's life, after all, is to gain one's life, as even Jesus explained.

GOODS, SERVICES, AND RATIONALITY

There are merits in all of these criticisms of the economic approach to religion. But in such discussions, there are never absolute answers. We are talking about some of the best possible ways to explain the world around us. In that light, the economic approach to religion can openly talk about goods and services that religions have provided humankind. Consider a list of five such offerings drawn up by the economists Brooks Hull and Frederick Bold.[5]

First of all, it is easy enough to recognize that religions have produced some of the longest-standing codes of conduct. As institutions with norms, religions have reduced the cost of human living across history by one simple mechanism: the protection of property rights. As we noted earlier, large portions— even dominant portions—of religious texts are about what belongs to whom and how that is regulated. Of course, it all belongs to the deities. But after that, property is apportioned among finite human beings. Religion offers the additional sanction of supernatural punishment (or reward) when the secular authorities are unable to find out who is malevolently greedy, cheating, or stealing.

All these elements in religion have provided a firm basis for property rights, which speaks to the essential human trait of incentive: to have what one works for and to seek happiness with that resource. As the economist would say, in providing these norms, religion has produced public goods that can be consumed by everyone. Today, religions generally do not govern modern nation-states. But without doubt, in the past they were guarantors of property rights. Arguably, their divinely sanctioned rules of behavior have persuaded the secular world to follow such ideals as the Ten Commandments, the Golden Rule, and even the Sermon on the Mount. Religion has also attached its wisdom to the economic principle of making trade-offs, as illustrated by the story of two people who arrive at a door, both self-interested in getting through it. Unless one defers to the other, neither can succeed. Game theorists call this the game of chicken—who will lose nerve first? If both are saints, however, they will insist that the other goes first, so the problem continues. Finally the two people must turn to rules of thumb—ladies first or elders first, for example. Religion is often a source of these respectful norms, which can turn self-interest into practical altruism.

Saving humanity the costs of enforcing property rights is only the first of five important goods and services produced by religion. Second is the thing that most characterizes religion, and something that it alone offers: a plausible answer about the afterlife. All human beings die. Every person calculates incentives in life either in an eighty-or-so-year range or with an added lifetime after that. Neither theology nor science can prove or disprove the afterlife. So no matter how modern the world becomes, the second lifetime is part of the great human wager. Religion also produces explanations on this topic. By all accounts, it continues to be a product consumed in vast amounts by the human race.

In the economic view, it would be naive to think that even the major religious organizations can provide an unending stream of free public goods—such as property rights and cosmic explanations—without trying to regain resources in the process. To the chagrin of many, religions do hawk their wares. Sometimes religions do seem like big business. They are sellers in the marketplace. One of the products that they market is an explanation of the universe, and often a cost is required to receive a regular supply of this explanation. But on balance, there is really nothing humanly wrong with that. Even religion must pay the bills. It must work to keep membership commitment. Religion, too, should be a productive member of society, not just a ward of the state. At minimum, it must stay in business. At maximum, its growth and productivity will determine how many private and public goods it can offer to the population.

After property rights and the afterlife, religion has produced three other kinds of goods: social welfare, entertainment, and insurance against the hazards of life. The first and second of these are well known. In providing social welfare and group enjoyment, religion, like any family, club, or association, works separately from the impersonal marketplace to provide well-being to its members. That is one reason people join groups. As studies show, there still seems to be no better place for parents to rear children than in the context of an organized faith. Entertainment also makes life less dull, even providing a quality that Hull calls "temporal bliss." In countless ways, one can point to religious gatherings, worship services, or the great forms of art, music, and architecture that have characterized all religions across history. These fill the human senses. They inspire amid the humdrum.

The final product of religion bears a closer look, for it, too, is something perhaps that only religion can provide: daily assurances to help people deal with loss, sickness, emotional distress, or the need to find calm in the storm of a tumultuous mind or amid human conflict. These tools—products and services, that is—include prayer, rituals, and evocation of the gods, among many others. In summary, even in a marketplace driven by self-interest, cost and benefit, and the desire to maximize, religion offers a range of explanations and products that can lead people to behave well and seek what is good. The economic approach does not question the sacrifice of martyrs or great acts of loving courage. But these are the exceptions in human experience, while the daily acts of self-interested altruism make up the healthy fabric of the world.

Now comes an entirely different benefit of the economic approach: its tendency to see religious people as rational. Human beings have the basic gift of rationality. In light of our modern understanding of mental health, brain disease, and chemical imbalance, the slogan of the British utilitarian Jeremy Bentham—that even a madman calculates—may be going too far. But not by much, at least in the economic view. As cognitive psychology has shown, the human brain can miscalculate, both in physical perceptions (like seeing a mirage in the desert) and in statistical predictions and patterns. People can be unsure about many things, such as which flavor of ice cream they like most and which flavor they will like a year from now.

Nevertheless, even the proponents of cognitive bias are not saying humans are irrational. And while religion has often been denigrated as an irrational fantasy, it continues to stand in the estimable league of possible rational explanations of many things about life that even scientists and Nobel Prize winners will never really be able to explain. One telling example is a science book published in the twenty-first century in which scientists disclose a wide variety of things that they believe "but cannot prove."[6] In science as in religion, human beings usually have good reason for what they believe, even if final proof is elusive.

Religions tend to come in coherent systems of theology, which admittedly will always contain elements of contradiction and appeals to mystery. After all, humans are finite and the gods are infinite. But more than rational systems, religion is also a rational wager. We recall that in seventeenth-century France, the mathematical genius Blaise Pascal held a rather strict view of Roman Catholicism, and hence he believed the only choice was for one God or none, and after that, either heaven or hell. Rationally, Pascal was correct in identifying the best bet—to believe, since the winnings could be immense but any loss would be small. The modern world, while it has been a spawning ground for new and strict fundamentalisms, mostly presents people with a wide variety of beliefs to consider. In the economic view, people pick and choose, investing in portfolios or in one main stock when it comes to ultimate things. And while this is often done under the constraints of tradition, peer group pressures, or laziness, to the degree that religious commitment and assent is a choice, it seems to be a rational enough choice. It is a calculation of cost and benefit. Hence, in the positive column, religion may seem fantastic to some. But all in all, it is a rational enterprise. The economic approach offers this seal of approval to the world of religion.

THE SUPPLY SIDE AND FREEDOM

The economic approach to religion has emphasized the supply side of the human marketplace. This does not mean that the demand side is absent or lacking in dynamism. The challenge in all economic theory is to understand these two moving parts of the market machine: supply and demand. Human beings want certain things, and this can shift and change. Firms and businesses—and individuals and families—try to supply them, moving as gingerly as possible in the shifting trends of the marketplace.

The economic approach to religion offers its own kind of model for how this takes place. It says that the basic human demand for religion is mostly constant. As the American psychologist William James said, every human being seems to be in pursuit of "something more" at some point in their lives. People everywhere and in all times have wanted the basic products of religion: explanations about life, and various public goods that have to do with families, groups, and cultures. With this consumer demand constant, it is the supply of religion that will become the key to understanding changes in human religious behavior, the rise and fall of religions, and why certain niches in religion—ranging from strict to liberal—seem to be evident in all human cultures and societies.[7]

Not every student of the economic approach to religion gives the supply side pride of place. For some, religion is equal parts supply and demand. Nevertheless, the supply-side approach has tried to correct the demand-side prejudice of the past. It has also tried to put an emphasis on the principle of freedom. In the past, great religious changes often have been attributed to great psychological crises or shifts in the population. The historian of religion William G. McLoughlin, for example, was prepared to put the 1960s into a category along with other great religious awakenings in American history. For any such American event, the touchstone is the First Great Awakening of the 1730s and 1740s. Like later episodes, this one has been attributed to a great psychological transformation in the collective mind. Such awakenings "begin in periods of cultural distortion and grave personal stress, when we lose faith in the legitimacy of our norms, the viability of our institutions, and the authority of our leaders in church and state," McLoughlin wrote in 1978.[8] This is not an untypical view of religion in general—that people turn to it only in a time of dramatic crisis or psychological change. In short, this is the demand-side version of religion.

To correct that overemphasis, the new economic approach to religion tries to show how supply-side explanations may go even further in explaining why so many people turned to religion during the various great awakenings and even the 1960s, or in the modern revivals of fundamentalism. In the supply-side view, the sales forces of religion have moved into the market and persuaded people to inspect, sample, and finally consume the great variety of religious products on offer. Suppliers responded to the opportunity of an open market, unregulated by government. While phrases such as "successful marketing campaign" can sound like a crass alternative to "awakening" or "new consciousness," sociologists have offered more elevated terms for the same thing, such as "religious mobilization" and "resource allocation." If the colonial marketplace had not been disestablished, ending government control of religion, then scores of revivalists and evangelists would not have made the First Great Awakening the event that it seems to have been, though for sure its impact can easily be exaggerated.

A more empirical example of such a great upheaval in religion is Japan's "rush hour of the gods," which we touched on at the opening of this book. The rush hour came after the end of World War II, and Japan, as a defeated nation, had certainly gone through a great deal of social stress, especially among ordinary people. In the classic study of Japan's postwar new religions, the search for the cause focused on the demand side: the new popular religions were a haven for the dispossessed, a vehicle for social expression, and even an alternative to a tightly controlled nationalism that had been imposed on the Japanese psyche for a few generations. The popular religions were "a hospitable refuge in time of crises," H. Neill McFarland wrote in 1967. "These religious movements offer one of the few opportunities in Japanese society for the distressed individual to be identified with a community."[9]

But in the economic approach, the supply side should first be explored before delving into human psyches—and McFarland recognizes this as well. He notes that when the imperial state system was deregulated, Japan entered a time of laissez-faire religion unlike any period before. Also, as befits a competitive market, those with the strongest feelings against the new religions were the leaders of the established religious groups. To many, the rush hour of popular religious groups seemed like so much grasping for benefits. But this utilitarian motivation, McFarland says, is what made the groups so purposeful and gave them the energy to last long enough to mature in their beliefs and evolve toward more mainstream social contributions. The postwar constitution created an open marketplace. The supply of religion rushed in. As McFarland concludes, "Unless the social conditions are propitious, a proselytizing movement has no chance of prospering."[10] A free market seemed propitious indeed.

Again, to explain an awakening, the supply-side emphasis will first look for how deregulated a religion market is and how many suppliers there are. In the 1970s, I was a college student in the San Francisco Bay area, my native turf, and I still cherish the idea—suggested by McLoughlin and others—that my peers and I had suddenly given rise to a new consciousness, full-blown, as when Athena sprang from the head of Zeus. Perhaps it was a new great awakening, a time of psychological crisis and demand for "something more." But looking back, while the idea of my generation being a vanguard for a new consciousness is quite romantic, the economic explanation is just as plausible. In California, for example, a host of spiritual and cultural entrepreneurs were selling the new consciousness (not to mention drugs and alternative lifestyles to affluent young people who could pay for them). To say the least, the market was wide open. In the economic explanation, this demand for something more is always there. Demand for meaning is constant, but the supply—new products, new enthusiasm, new efforts, new immediacy, a new "high"—is what comes and goes and brings new life to the marketplace of the gods.

What made the supply-side revolution possible in colonial America, postwar Japan, and California in the 1960s and 1970s was the freedom of the marketplace. No government threw the entrepreneurs into jail. There was no established church backed with public taxes, regulations, or police. In America in particular, the relative freedom of the religious marketplace has allowed the supply of religion to grow in greater and greater variety. The economic approach to religion does not doubt the role of demand: people's tastes change with age, mobility, marriage, and life crises. But the freedom of individuals to have religious products presented to them, and to move across the spectrum of choice looking for the best fit, is where the idea of supply intersects with the principle of freedom. As an equation, the supply of religion plus the freedom available to market it adds up to an explanation for why religion is diverse and vibrant in some parts of the world but monotone, underground, or seemingly evaporated like the morning mist in other parts.

The economics of religion also sees freedom as an antidote to religious violence, which is today a front-burner topic and one reason religion can indeed seem irrational. During the 1980s, when urban crime was on the rise, the neoconservative philosopher Irving Kristol famously said that if he were met in a dark alley one night by a group of young people, he would hope it would be a group returning home from a fundamentalist Bible church or a Pentecostal meeting. Religion, even if unscientific, seemed very safe. A few decades later, after the rise of Islamic terrorism, the atheist commentator Christopher Hitchens turned Kristol's analogy on its head. Hitchens said that in the Middle East, if he were walking home late at night, he would much rather meet a gang of secular teenagers in a dark alley. In the duel of rhetoric—both pro-religion and anti-religion—there are points to be made about how religion can make a given society amicable or subject to violence.

The economic view recognizes both, but it also takes a stand on what is most likely to promote the violence: the overregulation of religion by its chief secular competitor, the government. One study of violent events in the world's nations found that, second only to a war, government clampdowns on religion—especially of minority groups—are the best predictor of whether that country has riots, killings, ethnic grudges, and terrorism.[11] No society can be completely unregulated. As we saw in a previous chapter, government has every interest in being endorsed by a single religion, and then using that religion to enforce social order and keep the government leaders in power with as little cost as possible. Nevertheless, in the economic view, governments should learn that allowing a high degree of religious freedom is far more likely to improve social peace, productivity, and dynamism. It is also more likely to marginalize extremists, who have a much harder time recruiting in open markets with many acceptable options. In short, the economic approach recommends freedom of religion.

This book opened by offering a mountain climb to a new vista, a broad theory about religion. It promised that no one had to believe in the economic approach, but only consider the new insights it can offer. This is not a utopian vision, either. But it does have a structure that is worth sketching in brief. In this, the world is made up of families and groups in cultures, bound together by religions that people are born into or, at some stage in life, adhere to by choice. This religious marketplace is a world of families and social bonds. It is also a world of moral evaluations. It is indeed like a bazaar, rialto, or trading post, but the religious marketplace has a personal side that the economic marketplace never will. The religious market has gods but is not God. The religious and secular markets intersect, but they are different. The religious market, as it should, jealously guards its independence from the trading floor of the commodities exchange and from the tentacles of government. We may hope that self-interested governments will find it in their interest to allow religious freedom.

This book has no interest in making Adam Smith a saint, but as in so much else in economic theory, he offered broad and flexible insights on markets and human morality. Smith, and Friedrich von Hayek after him, pointed to two realms, a set of parallel universes, one moral, the other impersonal and based on exchange. Nobody, including the economic approach to religion, has a perfect solution for how to balance the two. But seeing them for what they are is a great help. The marketplace of Wall Street, the auto industry, the Internet, and international trade make up one reality. The marketplace of the gods is another. The first market is entirely impersonal. And in its quest for money, this marketplace may indeed be like God. The second market, however, is personal. It can't be God because the marketplace of religion is a vehicle to the gods, and as tradition has it, the gods don't need mammon. They only need the attention of human beings looking for "something more."

ACKNOWLEDGMENTS

This book returns me to topics that caught my interest long ago. In the 1980s there was a good deal of discussion about theology and economic policy and, as a Washington, D.C., reporter, I followed this closely. In the previous decade, I had also begun to follow the sociology of religion, beginning with H. Richard Niebuhr, Peter Berger, and Dean M. Kelley, later catching up with the work of Rodney Stark and William Sims Bainbridge, and, later still, Stark and Roger Finke. Then around 2006 I began to notice a good deal of hoopla in the book market about economic explanations for just about everything—books that were best sellers. So the idea for this book percolated. Once persuaded, I went up a steep slope of reading for a year and then was ready to go. My thanks to Cynthia Read at Oxford University Press for accepting the proposal. As a lay reader on this topic, I owe a debt to the many technical writers who probe these issues for a living. Without reading the abundant work of Laurence R. Iannaccone, Robert Ekelund, and others, I would not have had the slightest orientation for my own layman's approach. Many experts on this topic graciously agreed to be interviewed as well: Iannaccone, Finke, Ronald Ehrenberg, Vernon Smith, William Sims Bainbridge, Brooks Hull, Steven J. Brams, Timur Kuran, Eli Berman, and Anthony Gill. Some were kind enough to read all or part of the draft manuscript. Michael McBride offered good suggestions for the glossary. Any shortcomings in the book, however, arise from my judgments alone. I was also fortunate to attend two conferences (2007, 2009) of the Association for the Study of Religion, Culture, and Economics, and to hear many papers on the economics of religion and the debates that followed. Thanks to all.

GLOSSARY

advertising Any firm's gamble that spending on information can change public preferences. The investment may also prove to the public that a product is reliable because of the *sunk cost*, or irretrievable loss, of providing free information. Successful advertising increases *brand loyalty* and *product differentiation*. It also solves problems of *asymmetric information* between buyer and seller. These principles apply to religion in the marketplace as well.

afterlife In the economics of religion, a place where eternal happiness, peace, and communion with God can be consumed. Acquiring these products is based on fulfilling certain duties in life as prescribed by a religion. Belief in a good afterlife can also be consumed in the present.

agency costs The cost of controlling a delegated agent whose interests and incentives may be different from the goals of the owner or head office. This is called the *principal-agent problem*. It is a management challenge for both business firms and large religious organizations.

ages of faith Periods in history when people took religion more seriously, although the authenticity of these past ages is difficult to document.

aggregate The idea that group behaviors are made up of individual behaviors, as if adding up many individuals. This contrasts with the belief that groups produce their own special behaviors separate from those of individuals.

altruism Behavior that is unselfish, cooperative, or sacrificial. In both economics and religion, the origin of altruism is considered a puzzle since organisms are geared toward self-preservation. In some economic models, helping others provides a self-satisfying *utility* or future benefit, while other models simply reject the self-interest premise and presume individuals at times will act altruistically, even against their self-interest.

Arminianism The Protestant belief that human beings have free will in their choice of salvation. This is opposite to a main tenet of Calvinism.

asymmetric information The lack of the same information available to all the economic players in a transaction. Shared information between a buyer and seller should produce the clearest incentives and the most *efficiency*, but this is often hard to obtain, as seen between a used car salesperson and a buyer. *Game theory* presumes that people negotiate with such *imperfect information.*

Austrian economics An economic philosophy that emphasized free individuals in markets and in moral groups and rejected centralized government management of the economy. It defined economics as pursuit of ends with scarce means and said timing and *opportunity costs* are main features of economic analysis. A humanistic tradition that did not emphasize mathematics, it was espoused by Ludwig von Mises, Joseph Schumpeter, and Friedrich von Hayek. Schumpeter highlighted the role of *innovation, entrepreneurs,* and *creative destruction.*

bargain What two parties do in pursuit of the least cost in a transaction. In religion, human beings do this with supernatural beings based on rules set down by theology and religion.

behavioral economics The study of consumer behavior, habits, and choices based on the assumption of *cognitive bias,* or common mistaken judgments by ordinary people. Behavioral economics is skeptical about the notion of a rational *economic man.* A component is *prospect theory*, which suggests that when individuals face uncertainty they are chiefly motivated to avoid losses and stay with familiar habits. Whether this is a rational or non-rational behavior is much debated.

believing without belonging A slogan that suggests people are religious even if they do not attend institutions. A synonym is "spiritual but not religious."

bell curve A statistical pattern that shows how any set of *large numbers* in nature (the heights of all Americans, for example) tends to follow a *normal distribution* in which the average number makes up the largest area of the curve, while the two extremes grow smaller. This curve has been used to describe a range of human preferences in religion, with the greatest number of people preferring moderate religion. Those with liberal or strict preferences are a smaller number on the extremes.

bounded rationality The limited ability of an organism to gather all information and calculate all possibilities. The term was coined by Herbert Simon, a Nobel laureate in economics.

brand loyalty The loyalty producers seek in their customers through reliable products, a good image, and intangible affections. Religions seek this loyalty to retain members.

caliphs The spiritual and political leaders who were successors to the Prophet Muhammad.

Calvinism The Protestant teachings of John Calvin, who argued that God "elects" only some people for salvation. In the economics of religion, worry about whether one is chosen may motivate diligent behavior, such as the work ethic.

capital Resources for production that are man-made, such as money, assets, or skills. Capital is not for consumption but for further production.

capitalism An economic system based on the ability of people to accumulate capital and use it to make larger expenditures or investments that can reduce costs or increase profits. Unlike *socialism*, under capitalism, the return on capital investments is owned and consumed privately, not publicly.

caste system A rigid and stratified social system in India that is based on a belief that reincarnation has put each individual in a given social rank.

Chicago school The laissez-faire economic philosophy that grew from the University of Chicago, espoused by figures such as Frank Knight and Milton Friedman. Differs from the Austrian school by its more technical theory and mathematical methodology.

church-sect model The idea that history has produced two kinds of religious groups, one lenient (church) and the other strict (sect). These have tended to align with social classes (rich and poor) as well. The model is a product of European observation of Christianity but has been broadened into the concept that all religious groups can be in either low tension or high tension with their secular environments, leading to strict or lenient behavior in the marketplace.

clash of civilizations The concept that different religions have so deeply defined different civilizations that they will inevitably clash as their borders meet. As an alternative, the *religious economies* model argues that religious conflict and violence arise from overregulation or suppression of religion.

club The economic model of a limited-size group that requires high investments of commitment by members to benefit from *club goods*, products of the club that those outside the club are excluded from consuming.

cognitive bias The experimental finding that the physical brain misperceives and misjudges perceptions in fairly consistent patterns among most people. People compensate by adopting habitual *decision rules*, or best guesses.

competition The preferred market situation, in which prices are just above production costs and no monopolies prevail. In theory, *perfect competition* means no barriers between buyers and sellers, full knowledge of choices and prices, the success of quality and innovation, and the failure of inefficiency.

confession The religious practices of divulging sins and being assured of forgiveness. The practice is significant in all religions and influences risk and behavior.

constraints Limits on all choices and goals in life set by available resources, both physical and mental.

conversion The act of changing from belief in one religion to belief in another. According to the economic view, it typically happens at younger ages before habits and preferences (also called *human religious capital*) are strongly formed.

cost-benefit analysis Judging the total benefit and cost of an action, which may include side effects or the loss of other alternatives, called an *opportunity cost*. The economic view of religion assumes that human beings seek benefits and avoid costs in the net effect of all choices.

creative destruction An economic theory proposed by Joseph Schumpeter that says when monopolies freeze out healthy competition, only entrepreneurs and innovators can break up that stagnation. This shows up in cycles driven by *creative responses* to staid monopolies.

credence goods Products whose quality cannot be verified before or after consumption, so they are trusted only on the "credence," or integrity, of the producer. They differ from *search goods*, which can be validated by information, or *experience goods*, which are verified by at least one use. Theological beliefs are the ultimate credence good. Many of the goods of religion are so utterly impossible to evaluate in this life that they have also been called *meta-credence goods* and require a consumer's total faith.

crowding out When the expansion of government services discourages private-sector efforts. This is seen in the way state welfare crowds out charity or self-help. This can also discourage the role of religion as a social service.

cults and sects Cults are strict and young religions that are new innovations, while sects are strict groups that have split away from older religions. Very few cults in history have become full-scale religions; sects are far more likely to expand and become church-like institutions. Both cults and sects can be interpreted as operating on the *club* model.

cultural embeddedness The belief that individual choices are controlled by the given options of a culture, making it impossible to choose outside, or against, cultural norms. In *rational choice* theory, culture is the framework in which rational (that is, consistent) choices are made. Some cultural theorists argue that culture is so strong that it prohibits real choices.

deregulation Lifting government restrictions on market activity, such as regulation of competition, price, or type of business. It is at the heart of the laissez-faire assumption that on-the-spot judgment and freedom is most efficient in satisfying human needs and producing wealth. In the *religious economies* model, deregulation means the end of subsidies to some religions and the elimination of restrictions on others so that any religion can organize and proselytize.

decision theory The study of how an individual, with limited information, calculates how to achieve a goal, or best outcome, in a given circumstance. Decisions that are strategic and pitted against rivals are studied by *game theory*.

deism Belief in a supreme being who is a creator and designer of the universe but who is otherwise not involved in human affairs.

demand side The side of the marketplace where consumers desire certain kinds of products, typically based on necessity but also on preferences, tastes, risk tolerance, or income. In religion, the demand side is the desire for products that provide meaning or salvation, sometime called *salvation goods, salvation consumption,* or *afterlife consumption.*

desacralization The process of a state or nation ending the ceremonial religious trappings that used to accompany government functions or public festivals. Before this happens, a nation would be called *sacralized*, its state activities made sacred by the presence of symbols, priests, and religious language.

differentiation The historical process of religion separating from government, law, education, and other social services. This growing autonomy of each realm is interpreted as the basic force behind *secularization*, or the end of religion's overall influence.

disestablishment The ending of the establishment of one or a few religions by direct government funding or restrictions on nonestablished religions. It is the prelude to religious liberty.

diversified stock portfolio The idea that holding several stocks will protect an investor from any great loss, even if some of the stocks fall. In religion, this is seen in people who practice many different faiths, suggesting a lack of complete confidence in one single stock, or faith.

division of labor The practice of individuals focusing on specialized tasks, making overall production more efficient. This is seen in factory assembly lines, households, and religious organizations. Free trade theory sees nations as offering this division of specialized purposes.

duopoly When two major firms dominate a market. This describes the dual dominance of Catholic and Protestant state churches in various European nations after the Reformation. Buddhism is often part of a duopoly in Asia, complementing Hinduism, Christianity, or Islam.

Eastern religions Hinduism, Buddhism, Taoism, Sikhism, and Confucianism. These faiths are typically seen as being ethical or spiritual-natural, but not monotheistic. However, a God or gods and supernatural powers do play a role in Hinduism, Buddhism, and Sikhism.

economic view of life The view that individuals seek benefits and avoid costs based on knowing their own preferences, having certain resource constraints, and thinking about the future.

economic rationality A technical and mathematical concept that says people will seek the best cost-benefit status and then will continue that behavior.

economics of religion The application of economic principles, formulas, and insights to the behaviors, history, and beliefs of the world religions. It differs from the *theology of economics*, which asks about the godly nature of economics systems such as capitalism, socialism, or the corporation, as well as from *religious economics*, which studies financial support of religion and teaching the morality of charity and giving.

economy of scale A firm's ability to make profits by producing on a large scale, thus reducing costs and increasing efficiency. This may apply to a very large religion or church, such as Catholicism.

economy of scope A firm's ability to provide many different but related services and thus draw a larger number of varied consumers. Megachurches, with many ministries, or malls, with many shops, have economies of scope, making each service less costly than if it were run separately.

efficiency The ability to obtain a goal by the smallest possible use of resources, either in material or in effort. *Inefficiency* is failure to achieve the most cost-effective goal possible.

Enlightenment The period of the sixteenth and seventeenth centuries when science, and then secular reason, became central to Western culture. The Enlightenment gave rise to modern economics.

entrepreneur A person who innovates in a product, invention, or service without the resources of an already existing firm. Many founders of religions have entrepreneurial temperaments.

entry costs and barriers The cost or restrictions faced by a producer trying to enter a particular market to offer competing products and services. New businesses and new religious enterprises face these costs, and most fail as a result. There is always an incumbent advantage, as when larger firms already control resources and can operate with economies of scale.

equilibrium In nature, society, and the marketplace, the idea that countervailing forces, such as supply and demand, will generally balance out, despite regular disturbances.

eschatology The study of beliefs about the end of the world and the afterlife. Every religion has an eschatology, which is a unique product of religion alone.

evangelical Relating to the branch of Protestantism that emphasizes a personal conversion experience, conservative moral rules, and spreading an exclusive faith to others.

exchange theory The theory that all complex social relations begin with two people, and then small groups, making exchanges in pursuit of material, social, or psychological rewards. Exchange theory is also the basis for the political concept of the *social contract*, which two parties enter voluntarily with guarantees of mutual compliance.

expected utility The mathematical representation of the idea that people, when faced by the normal uncertainty of the future, try to make consistent choices to maximize their utility, or benefit. The idea remains in economic textbooks but has proven questionable. A similar idea is *rational expectation*, the belief of some economic theories that people, on the whole, can think accurately about the future.

experimental economics The laboratory study of how subjects play competitive and cooperative games with others, usually anonymously, in pursuit of the best cost-benefit outcomes. This is also the laboratory study of game theory.

externality The side effects of an economic transaction that are not being considered in the transaction or behavior of the parties involved. Smog from a profitable factory is a *negative externality*, while workforce productivity caused by public health measures is a *positive externality*. In theory, the true profit of something must include these side effects. Externalities also have an impact on business: a war is a negative externality to trade, while good weather is a positive externality to farming.

firm Any organization that takes in inputs to produce outputs, has internal personnel as well as outside contracts, and exists to seek profits.

First Great Awakening A religious event from the 1730s to 1760s in the American colonies that emphasized revivals and experiential religion. Historians say it coincided with the rise of the first consumer culture in the United States.

free rider problem The natural tendency of the public to take benefits without contributing. This is presumed to be unavoidable with *public goods*, but free riding is a menace in the context of *private goods* and *club goods*.

functionalism The sociological theory that religion came into existence primarily to create group solidarity in society. This solidarity is a function that secular groups and ideologies can also serve, as they are believed to be doing after the rise of modernity and the reported decline of religion.

game theory The mathematical study of interpersonal decision making. A game is a strategic setting, from chess to nuclear war. In some games, individuals' attempts to achieve their best outcome may lead to mutual cooperation, but in other settings they may lead to mutual disadvantage. In the latter situation, repeated interaction can help foster better cooperation.

gift culture The idea taught by some religions and idealistic forms of socialism that the distribution of resources can be done unselfishly as people give each other what they need.

goods Economic theory speaks of *public, private,* and *club* goods. Each is produced at a particular kind of cost to serve a particular consumer. Some goods are competed over, while others are for exclusive use. Public goods are provided by nature, paid for by taxes, or offered by charitable and nonprofit groups and, less frequently, by private firms, such as in broadcast television. These goods are also subject to *free rider* problems. Private goods are obtained for personal consumption. Club goods are shared by members of voluntary organizations. These all apply to religion—public benefit, personal consumption, and exclusive group consumption.

gratuitous costs Sacrifices that people make that seem to produce no benefit, typified in religious groups by moral constraints, dress codes, loss of time, or burnt offerings. In the economics of religion, these costs serve a useful purpose: they signal commitments that make groups more productive.

gray market In societies that suppress or overregulate religion, such as communist states, this market is neither underground (black market) nor state-controlled (red market) but rather is informal, entrepreneurial, vast, and hard for governments to control.

habit A learned behavior that is repeated, usually for a person's well-being, but also as a detriment (e.g., addiction). In economic theory, habit is based on accumulation of experience (*human capital*), making the habit stronger, easier, and more satisfying—and thus rational. Some economists have called this *rational addiction*. Religious practice can become a habit that increases satisfaction.

heresy A belief outside of orthodoxy. In religion, heresy typically means a distortion of an orthodox belief, not an entirely new or foreign idea. Heresy often becomes orthodoxy as history proceeds.

high gods In the history of religion, supernatural beings with broader powers and explanations, known best in the evolution of henotheism (a council of chief gods) to monotheism (a single God).

high-risk religions Religions that teach ultimate consequences after death, such as heaven and hell. Adherents of these faiths try to live in ways that assuage uncertainty or reduce the risk of hell.

household production The idea that a household, typically of parents and children, is like a small factory that brings in resources and produces products, both material and spiritual, that the family itself consumes.

human capital The lifetime experiences, training, and skills that a person accumulates that may be invested, or profited from, as life unfolds. Education is the classic example of human capital in terms of producing a good job and earnings.

human religious capital The knowledge, experience, skills, attachments, and social connections that a person accumulates by being reared in, and staying active in, a particular religion. This is a profitable investment that leads to greater satisfaction as a religious believer. Some theorists have focused specifically on *social religious capital*, which is the purely social, network, and moral advantage of belonging to a religious organization, in contrast to other kinds of organizations.

immediate gratification The human tendency to want gratification without delay, a trait that business sales and advertising capitalize on. The opposite is *delayed gratification*, a human temperament that prefers restraint and denial now in order to reap greater benefits in the future.

incentives Rewards that motivate people to action. Incentives can be material, social, or psychological and spiritual. Disincentives, which can also be used strategically, threaten costs or punishments for certain behaviors.

indulgences The medieval Roman Catholic Church teaching that financial donations earn merit for individuals so that in the afterlife they are not stuck in purgatory but can move into heaven, with higher donations related to quicker results. This collection of money was one cause of the Reformation.

information cost The recognition that consumers pay a cost in time or money to find good information about the prices and quality of goods and services. This cost is decreased by being part of an *information network*—a social or interest group—that eases information gathering. This is also related to *search cost*, a consumer's expense for finding what is wanted. Technology, knowledge, and networks decrease search costs. Overall, an economy is most efficient when information is inexpensive, accurate, and comprehensive. Religions claim to offer such information about life.

insurance A mechanism that transfers risk to a third party, as when a person buys auto insurance so someone else will pay for an expensive car accident if it takes place. Religion offers a variety of kinds of insurance, from belief itself to various practices that put major life risks, such as personal loss or death, in the hands of supernatural beings.

interest A sum that compensates a lender for giving up consumption of the loaned object and for the *risk* taken in making the loan. Historically, interest taking was condemned by Greek and Roman philosophers and by the Roman Catholic Church as *usury* and by Islam as *riba*. However, interest is the only real incentive to providing loans, so it has become basic to modern economies, usually with legal ceilings on sums charged.

invisible hand Adam Smith used the phrase only twice in his writings but it came to mean the self-regulating power of a free, competitive market. Heirs of Smith use synonyms such as *spontaneous order*.

Islamic banking A new movement espoused by Islamists to make all banks used by Muslims free of *interest*. This view says the Quran requires lenders to share in the risk and possible profit but accept total losses since no interest is charged. In practice, however, Islamic banks charge other fees as their incentive to lend.

Islamic economics An ideological movement that began among Islamists in India in the mid-twentieth century to revive ancient economic rules found in the Quran. They include a ban on interest (*riba*), the use of *zakat*, a charity tax, and the *waqf*, public works or services paid for by wealthy Muslims.

Keynesian economics Named for the British economist John Maynard Keynes, a school of macroeconomics that advocates government intervention, spending, and taxation. During a recession, Keynesian methods are prescribed to stimulate an economy's productivity, demand, and employment.

laissez-faire A word from French economics (meaning "let do") that was elaborated into a formal model by British classical economics: a free, open, and competitive market with no government controls.

law of supply and demand The rule that if the price of a good rises, then its *supply* will increase, but also, as the price rises, consumers will buy, or *demand*, less quantities of the good. The two—supply and demand—interact dynamically around a balancing point called *equilibrium* in the market.

liberation theology A theological movement of the 1970s that combined Marxism and biblical interpretation to say that revolution and the redistribution of wealth lead to the kingdom of God. It was created in Europe but practiced mostly in Latin America.

macroeconomics The study of the largest economic forces, such as growth, competition, and trade among nations. *Microeconomics* looks at individuals, households, and firms.

magic The use of a spiritual technology such as a chant, potion, or ritual to provide consumers with a benefit, such as health or good fortune. In sociology, magic differs from religion by being a one-time service, not an organization of people who worship gods and satisfy social needs. Magic, as compared to religious belief, is easily disproved by its lack of immediate results.

Mahayana A form of Buddhism that appeals to the wider population, offering devotional practices and a number of gods and spirits who help people in life. It rose in competition to the more elite, and atheistic, Theravada (or Hinayana) Buddhism.

marginal A value judgment on the cost or usefulness of one more unit of something, suggested in the terms *marginal price* and *marginal utility*. For a thirsty man, deciding the value of one more cup of water is the *marginal value*. For a firm deciding whether to produce one more unit of output, this is the *marginal cost*. In economics—and life in general—most decisions are made at the margin.

megachurch Churches with more than 2,000 members. Large churches are common in history, but since the 1990s in the United States they have become a replicated organizational trend.

mergers and acquisitions The action taken when competing firms begin to lose market share because of saturation or loss of consumers. Competing religious organizations also merge when the consumer base shrinks.

metaphysics The study of the nonmaterial, or spiritual, principles by which the universe operates. It differs from theology by trying to harmonize general theological beliefs, such as God, with the logical operations of the physical and mental worlds.

methodological individualism An approach in social science that begins with individuals as the primary actors. This contrasts with sociological and anthropological approaches that look at groups and social forces as the primary explanations. Economics has typically followed methodological individualism.

Middle Way A way of life taught by Buddha that avoids the extremes of self-denial and self-indulgence. It prescribes physical moderation, detachment from desires, and right thinking.

Middletown The fictitious name for Muncie, Indiana, when it was studied as an average American town in 1929, 1937, and 1983. The Middletown study looked closely at religion and is the classic sociological case study in America.

monasticism The institution that allows religious people to withdraw from the world as monks following daily disciplines. It is seen in all religions, but in medieval Christianity it was so prevalent that it shaped the economic and political development of Europe. Tibet is today's strongest example of *mass monasticism.*

monopoly When one firm is the sole supplier in a market—the exact opposite of *perfect competition.* Somewhere in between is *monopolistic competition.* In a *franchise monopoly,* firms find it more efficient to monopolize by using outside contractors rather than expanding their *vertically integrated* divisions. A *natural monopoly,* such as mail delivery or distribution of water, is seen as efficient and not opportunistic. However, no monopoly—in business or in religion—is absolute because it is hard to meet all consumer needs. In the view of history, dominant religions have tended toward monopoly, especially with government support, but religious pluralism is also a strong market tendency.

monotheism Belief in a single god. This differs from henotheism, in which there is a supreme god among a few other gods. Pure monotheism is best seen in Judaism and Islam, since Christianity has a Trinity and many religions have other gods or spirits, such as angels of devils. The opposite is *polytheism.*

moral hazard The behavioral problem that arises when people are insured, since they may behave badly or take excessive risks because of that insurance. It is a basic problem of human incentives in economics and religion.

moral philosophy The logical study of how human beings behave rightly in their personal lives and in relationship to others. Moral philosophy does not need religion but often uses religious assumptions. Modern economics grew out of Enlightenment moral philosophy, which looked at right behavior and also the creation of wealth, trust, and efficiency in society.

multidimensional firm A hierarchical structure common in large corporations: a head office delegates various production duties to subordinate divisions, each with its own management. The divisions send revenue back up the chain. The exemplar in business was General Motors and in religion the medieval Roman Catholic Church.

neoclassical economics A revision of the *classical economics* developed by Adam Smith. Neoclassical economics is far more mathematical, free-market-oriented, and ideological in its application. In practice, it analyzes how firms can maximize their efficiency and productivity in an economy that is theoretically coordinated by price and keeps an *equilibrium* of supply and demand.

networks Patterns of relationship between individuals that allow them to collect information and benefits. Human networks are said to have ties that are strong (with intimates) and weak (with acquaintances), which provide different human contacts and opportunities. Networks provide a successful consumer base for a business or a religion. In either, the *network effect* makes a service more valuable as more people use it, as with software, a best-selling book, or a large religious organization.

new religions A term first used in Japan for new Buddhist sects arising in the 1950s and later modified to *new religious movements* (NRMs) to describe developments in America after the 1960s. These have also been called cults, a pejorative term used in the popular media.

niche A biological concept that explains how an organism adapts to a changing environment. The concept of niche has been adopted by sociology and economics as well to speak of how individuals and groups occupy specific demographic or market niches, which suppliers target with goods and services. In the sociology of religion, the niche has been used to devise a *bell curve* that represents a society's range of strict to liberal preferences in religion.

nirvana Escape from the repeated cycles of reincarnation believed in by some Eastern religions. Nirvana is akin to heaven by being escape from all desire, which is said to be the root of unhappiness.

oligopoly Dominance of the market by a few firms. In business, this can approach a monopoly if the firms cooperate. Religion in many countries operates as an oligopoly of two or three dominant faiths with large institutions and government support.

opportunity costs The cost of making a choice because that choice means giving up the value of the next best alternative choice. In other words, the true cost of anything must include what is lost as well. This says that values are determined by comparison. Economists try to calculate this cost with mathematics.

optimize To make the most favorable or best use of something. This differs slightly from *maximize*, which suggests a maximum limit to which something can be increased. Economics commonly speaks of optimizing and *maximizing utility*, or benefit. Optimum can be measured only if there is a defined goal and defined *constraints*.

positive economics The view that economics is about how the world is, not how it should be (*normative economics*). In modern use, the term represents a 1953 elaboration by Milton Friedman who, seeking to go beyond mere *quantitative economics* (statistics), argued that economists are free to propose creative theories (or hypotheses) as long as they test them against data. This makes positive economics a deductive science.

potential demand The fact that consumers have a deep potential to desire more products, even if that consumption is temporarily suppressed because of the lack of product variety or innovation. This is a key concept in supply-side economics and the *religious economies* model.

preferences The choices that motivate consumer behavior. Economic theory presumes *stable preferences* in human beings, who may change their *tastes* in consumption but are consistent in seeking basic goods such as health and status. Economists speak of *hidden preferences* and *revealed preferences*, meaning that consumer behavior is more telling than what consumers simply say: actions speak louder than words. The *economics of religion* also presumes that human beings have stable preferences for basic religious answers or experiences but make a range of choices in types of religion. As in all economic theory, economists use stable preference as a methodological assumption but not a strong claim about the real world.

price discrimination Charging different people different prices for the same thing based on what they are willing to pay in different circumstances. This is typically a practice of monopolies and is ideal for maximizing profit and reducing surplus. In religion, the medieval Catholic Church offered different prices for penance depending on the wealth or poverty of the constituents.

privatized religion The development of a religious belief or outlook that is held only by one person and is idiosyncratic enough that it finds no parallel in a religious group or institution. Privatized religion is said to be the outcome of modernity, when there is no longer public agreement on a uniform religion. To avoid conflict or embarrassment, individuals keep their beliefs private.

product differentiation The effort to make a product slightly different from another product that is so similar that consumers can *substitute* one for the other.

property rights A circumstance of law and order in which proper ownership of goods, both physical and intellectual, is clearly defined and protected. Clear ownership makes trade possible and motivates owners to maintain the quality of possessions. Property rights law was important in developing advanced and free societies, and in the early stages of human societies, religion provided important sanctions against theft and harm.

proselytizing The act of trying to convert people to a particular religion, either as a personal appeal or in organized *religious mobilizations*, which have been evident in Christianity, Islam, and Hinduism in particular, but only rarely in Judaism or Buddhism.

Protestant ethic The German sociologist Max Weber's theory that Calvinism, with its psychological concern over salvation, produces individuals with a diligent and thrifty work ethic, producing wealth and stimulating the *spirit of capitalism*.

Protestant Reformation The sixteenth-century protest against the Roman Catholic Church that led to rejection of the papacy in favor of belief in the Bible alone and the *priesthood of believers*.

public choice The theory that governments and institutions are as self-interested in their incentives and choices as are individuals. It challenges the claim made by bureaucracies—either secular or religious—that public servants have only the public interest in mind.

purgatory The doctrine of a middle ground between heaven and hell where the sins of an individual can be purged for possible entry into heaven. In the Middle Ages, *indulgences* were paid so that individuals could move from purgatory to heaven.

rationality The idea that human beings can calculate logical relationships, see contradictions, and discover the most efficient means to achieve a goal. Social scientists speak of *objective rationality*, measured by achieving goals, and *subjective rationality*, which amounts at best to good reasons for actions. Rationality is an important assumption in economic behavior, and it is one of the ideas underlying religions' claims that theological beliefs have good reasons behind them.

rational choice A school of thought in economics and sociology that presumes individuals are rational agents whose behaviors reflect this regularity of rational choosing. Rational choice does not make claims about the content of people's beliefs. It looks only for consistency in choice.

reductionism The scientific method of reducing natural and social phenomena to their simplest parts. In biology this would be atoms and molecules, for example, and in sociology it would be self-interested individuals. Reductionism is criticized for oversimplifying complex phenomena.

reincarnation The religious belief that human souls return to earth in different life forms depending on their spiritual progress in the previous life. The idea was held by ancient Greeks and is common in Asian religions. The release from rebirth in the world (*nirvana*) is the goal of spiritual discipline.

religion Traditionally, the human effort to have a beneficial relationship to supernatural beings guided by the theology, rules, and rituals of a religious tradition. In another view, called *functionalism*, religion is any belief or ideology that unites people by way of a shared meaning, solidarity, or ultimate explanation of life, which may not include supernatural forces.

religious human capital The skills and experiences gained in a particular religion, which include knowledge, familiarity with ritual and doctrine, and social friendships. In addition to cognitive mastery of a tradition and helpful social opportunities, religious capital also includes an increasingly satisfying emotional attachment to a religious culture. It is also called *spiritual capital* to avoid implying institutional membership while still focusing on skills, integrity, and work ethic.

religious economy All religious activity going on in a society. As in any market, this economy includes current and potential adherents and can be made up of as few as two organizations, but however many there are, they seek to attract and maintain adherents by presenting unique religious cultures. In theory, a religious economy has relatively *stable niches* of consumers, ranging from strict to liberal. When unregulated, a religious economy produces a greater variety of religions, or *religious pluralism*, due to the easy entry of religious suppliers and potential for increased variation in the tastes of consumers. The primary historical dynamic in a religious economy is the gradual rise of dominant religions and competition from new sectarian ones, which may, in turn, become dominant.

rent A term that entered economics from the early nineteenth century that means making a profit by having an exclusive advantage in the market, such as the only available property. *Rent seeking* refers to the ways firms manipulate markets or government rules to gain profits without making extra investments or innovations.

revelation Divine intervention in the world in the form of God revealing himself, offering transcendent knowledge or an otherworldly experience. Most religions are founded on revelation, both directly to founders and in the form of texts, such as the Bible or the Quran.

risk Risk is a calculable degree of potential loss in the future. It differs from uncertainty, which offers no variable to calculate the future. *Risk analysis* is the mathematical calculation of variables that may predict chances of loss. Risk management is any effort to calculate how to make losses less either by precautions, *diversification*, or *insurance*.

risk aversion A part of human nature that seeks to avoid loss in the future. It may be stronger or weaker in different individuals as manifest in behaviors, precautions, and choices about religion, which deals with future possibilities. *Risk takers*, in business or religion, do not have the same aversion to risk as others.

sacred canopy A concept used to explain why at times in history most people held strong religious beliefs: human society seemed to have a sacred covering, making it easier for everyone to believe. A technical synonym is *plausibility structure*, or a structure of common belief that makes holding religious views very plausible. Without the structure of many people agreeing, religious belief becomes implausible, or difficult to hold.

sacrifice and stigma Two kinds of costs that members of strict religions, or religious clubs, are willing to pay to hold membership and consume *club goods*. Both also repel *free riders*, who are unwilling to make the sacrifice or to be stigmatized by following various religious practices, dress, or codes.

satisfice The idea that organisms will be motivated to achieve satisfaction of a desire or aspiration and will not take extra steps to maximize their benefit: settling for good enough rather than the best possible. The idea was proposed by Herbert Simon as an alternative to the economic notion of *utility maximization*.

scarcity The basic assumption of economic theory: that there is never enough to fulfill all human needs and longings. This is also called the *budget constraint* in each particular case. Scarcity does not mean poverty, however. In the psychology of religion, it is believed that human beings with worldly scarcity seek otherworldly alternatives (some call them *compensators*), which is the logic behind the use of *deprivation theory* in psychology and sociology. Illness and death are the ultimate scarcity for all humans and thus spur the human propensity to seek eternal resources.

scriptures The texts found in all organized religions, viewed as either divine revelation or great wisdom. The core texts are the Torah for Judaism, the Bible for Christianity, the Quran for Islam, the Analects for Confucianism, and the sutras for Buddhism. Auxiliary and interpretative texts range in the thousands as well.

sect A religious group that breaks away from a larger established religion, usually to restore an original strictness in belief and practice. Sects are in *higher tension* with their secular environments than are mainstream religions, making them smaller and more intense, thus with potential to grow.

secularization The separation of religion from other social institutions and its declining importance in public events and in personal lives. The secularization thesis says that this process is inevitable as the world become modern, possibly leading to the end of religion. This idea is rejected by the *religious economies* model and interpretation of history. *Neosecularization* theory argues that religions can remain vital and active as interest groups but not worldviews for a society.

self-interest The observed psychological and biological fact that all organisms must act for self-benefit to survive. In one view, economics presumes that *all* human behavior is self-interested. In another view, economics is the study of consistency in human choices, whether they are self-interested or altruistic. Either way, self-interest can be defined as both a sin and a virtue, the first being neglect of others, the second being personal discipline and integrity.

signal The information or cue that allows people to see the hidden intentions, values, and commitments of others in the marketplace. On one hand, *price* signals the value of something among all buyers and sellers. Signaling is also a way to verify the quality of something, and so these kinds of signals work only if they impose a cost on the sender, which guarantees the signal is not a cheap lie. In religion the costly signals of dress, rituals, or rules convey a group's validity and indicate who is committed and trustworthy.

social capital Human capital that is specifically accumulated in relationships with others by means of membership in a group. It provides community trust, opportunity, and support in times of need. This has been further described as encompassing both the *strong ties* of close groups and the *weak ties* of many casual acquaintances. Some economists question whether social capital is necessary for an efficient economy (as in the United States), although it may certainly help other countries or specific social groups.

socialism An economic system in which a central government owns the means of production and redistributes wealth, from each according to his ability to each according to his need. Its moderate forms exist around the world, and its extreme experiments have been implemented in communist nations.

sociology The scientific study of groups as the major components of a society. Rather than focus on individuals, sociology looks for *social action*, social roles, and systems operating within systems. Historically it is one of the most secular social sciences since it views religion as a primitive social force.

start-up costs The high cost of entering a competitive market where other entities already have an advantage. Typically these consist of money spent to organize, but they can also result from restrictive regulations that require fees or limit activities. These costs guarantee that most new businesses fail, as do most attempts to start new religions.

statistical sampling A form of survey perfected after the 1940s in which a *random sample* of the population is polled and then conclusions are drawn about patterns in the entire population. Typically, a random poll of 1,000 people can accurately predict future behavior, such as elections, but surveys of tens of thousands are typical today in the U.S. census and major social science studies, including those on religion.

substitution The economic principle that consumers will substitute one product for another if the products are too similar, which leads producers to try to differentiate their products enough so that they have no substitutes. Religion does this also in developing finer and finer distinctions in theology between one group and another.

supernatural punishment hypothesis The theory that cultures and societies with a high god who acts as judge tend to behave better, leading to cooperation and more elaborate rules of fairness.

superstar effect The economic theory that explains why only a few top experts in each field take in most of the income, despite a larger number of similarly talented people. More generally, it suggests that fame and public response multiply exponentially, since groups of people act like herds: also known as the *rich get richer* or the *best-seller effect*. It can apply to success in religious movements and groups as well.

supply side The side of the economic marketplace in which producers provide varieties of products. When the supply side is emphasized in policy, it proposes limited regulation, taxation, or government intervention so that producers can reduce their costs and supply more kinds of products.

survivor technique A method proposed by the economist George Stigler to evaluate the necessary sizes of firms when they gain the dominant market share. It parallels the Darwinian idea that an organism that survives does so at its optimal size and adaptation. Religious organizations, like firms, operate at various sizes to achieve a survivable market share.

switching Moving from one religious affiliation to another. Switching is most likely to take place at a younger age, with a geographical move, or with marriage. However, most people do not switch, and when they do, according to *human religious capital* theory, it tends to be to a tradition similar to their former one.

time preference The human choice between wanting something now or later, often rooted in individual temperaments. Economists use the *rate of time preference* to capture how much an individual prefers consumption today relative to a future date. Many people *discount* the future, meaning they put less value on things that are further away in time.

transaction cost The fact that every exchange includes extra costs (of time and money) in addition to the price. This cost is like friction in a transaction. In theory, firms came into existence to reduce such costs by having internal production as well as external contracts.

two orders of exchange A concept found in Adam Smith and Friedrich von Hayek that the moral and *sympathetic bonds* of families and intimate groups are of a separate order from the *impersonal exchanges* in the marketplace. Life is a challenge to balance these two orders and not confuse them.

two systems of morality Adam Smith's observation that wealthy people prefer a more liberal moral order while the poor need a stricter one to make up for risks presented by poverty. The wealthy can more easily save themselves from moral mistakes than the poor.

utilitarian Characterizing the nineteenth-century British school of thinking that said human behavior can be understood as finding *means* to ends. The value of a thing is its *usefulness*, or utility, in achieving a goal, not its morality as a means. In politics it means achieving the greatest happiness of the greatest number.

utility The measure of benefit a consumer gains from consuming goods or services, often expressed in mathematical form as a *utility function*. The more utility a consumer gets from an item, the less value an extra unit of that item will have, which is called diminishing *marginal utility*. In the past, utility meant *hedonistic* satisfaction (pain or pleasure), but it now refers to any kind of perceived benefit.

utility maximization The classic economic assumption that all individuals will want to increase their perceived benefit all the time and in every choice.

vertical integration When a single firm includes several stages of production, usually provided by separate firms. Vertical integration can increase the power of monopolies, as can *horizontal integration*, when two similar firms *merge* to become a larger entity, though without the control of supply chains seen in vertical systems.

NOTES

Chapter 1

1. H. Neill McFarland, *The Rush Hour of the Gods: A Study of the New Religious Movements in Japan* (New York: Harper and Row, 1967).

2. Jonathan Gruber and Daniel M. Hungerman, "The Church vs. the Mall: What Happens When Religion Faces Increased Secular Competition?" NBER Working Paper 12410, National Bureau of Economic Research, August 2006.

3. Anthony Gill, *Rendering unto Caesar: The Catholic Church and the State in Latin America* (Chicago: University of Chicago Press, 1998).

4. Laurence R. Iannaccone, "Skewness Explained: A Rational Choice Model of Religious Giving," *Journal for the Scientific Study of Religion* 36 (1997): 141–57. See also Dean R. Hoge, "Introduction: The Problem of Understanding Church Giving," *Review of Religious Research* 36 (December 1994): 101–10.

5. Timur Kuran, *Islam and Mammon: The Economic Predicament of Islamism* (Princeton, NJ: Princeton University Press, 2004).

6. For the first summary of the "economics of religion" field, see Laurence R. Iannaccone, "Introduction to the Economics of Religion," *Journal of Economic Literature* 36 (September 1998): 1465–96.

7. Milton Friedman, "The Methodology of Positive Economics," in Milton Friedman, *Essays in Positive Economics* (Chicago: University of Chicago Press, 1953), 39, 43.

8. Mark J. Machina, "States of the World and the State of Decision Theory," in *The Economics of Risk*, ed. Donald J. Meyer (Kalamazoo, MI: W. E. Upjohn Institute for Employment Research, 2003), 22.

9. Robert Wuthnow, *After the Baby Boomers* (Princeton, NJ: Princeton University Press, 2008), 256.

10. Interview with Vernon Smith, August 19, 2008.

11. J. S. Dusenberry, "Comment on 'An Economic Analysis of Fertility,'" in *Demographic and Economic Change in Developed Countries* (Princeton, NJ: Princeton University Press, 1960), 233.

12. Shelly Lundberg and Robert Pollak, "Bargaining and Distribution in Marriage," *Journal of Economic Perspectives* 10 (1996): 139–58.

13. Stephen R. Warner, "Work in Progress Toward a New Paradigm for the Sociological Study of Religion in the United States," *American Journal of Sociology* 98 (1993): 1044–93.

Chapter 2

1. Kenneth Arrow, "Risk Perception in Psychology and Economics," *Economic Inquiry* 20 (January 1982): 1.

2. Herbert A. Simon, "Rationality in Psychology and Economics," in *Rational Choice: The Contrast Between Economics and Psychology*, ed. Robin M. Hogarth and Melvin W. Reder (Chicago: University of Chicago Press, 1986), 25.

3. Herbert Simon, "A Comparison of Game Theory and Learning Theory," *Psychometrika* 21 (September 1956): 267–72.

4. See also Lucien Lévy-Bruhl, *How Natives Think* (Princeton, NJ: Princeton University Press, 1985 [1910]).

5. Edward Evans-Pritchard, *Nuer Religion* (Oxford: Oxford University Press, 1956), 16.

6. Edward Evans-Pritchard, "Lévy-Bruhl's Theory of Primitive Mentality," *Bulletin of the Faculty of Arts*, University of Egypt, 1934. Cited in Bryan R. Wilson, ed., *Rationality* (Oxford: Basil Blackwell, 1974), 79, 80n1.

7. Evans-Pritchard, *Nuer Religion*, 224.

8. E. E. Evans-Pritchard, *Theories of Primitive Religion* (Oxford: Clarendon Press, 1965), 108, 67.

9. Herbert A. Simon, "Rational Choice and the Structure of the Environment," in *Economics, Bounded Rationality and the Cognitive Revolution*, ed. Massimo Egidi, Robin Marris, and Riccardo Viale (Aldershot: Edward Elgar, 1992), 39.

10. Herbert A. Simon, "Introductory Comment," in *Economics, Bounded Rationality and the Cognitive Revolution*, 3; Herbert A. Simon, "Rational Decision-Making in Business Organizations," Nobel Memorial Lecture, December 8, 1978, 357 (at http://nobelprize.org/nobel_prizes/economics/laureates/1978/simon-lecture.pdf).

11. Daniel Kahneman, "Maps of Bounded Rationality: A Perspective on Intuitive Judgement and Choice," Nobel Memorial Lecture, December 8, 2002, 451–52 (at http://nobelprize.org/nobel_prizes/economics/laureates/2002/kahnemann-lecture.pdf).

12. Dan Ariely, *Predictably Irrational: The Hidden Forces That Shape Our Decisions* (New York: Harper, 2008), 232.

13. Karl-Gustaf Löfgren and Anne-Sophie Crepi, "Interview with the 2002 Laureates in Economics, Daniel Kahneman and Vernon L. Smith," December 12, 2002, video, 29 min. (at http://nobelprize.org/nobel_prizes/economics/laureates/2002/kahneman-interview.html).

14. Bentham excerpted in John Troyer, ed., *The Classic Utilitarians: Bentham and Mill* (Indianapolis: Hackett, 2003), 37.

15. Mark A. Lutz, *Economics for the Common Good: Two Centuries of Social Economic Thought in the Humanistic Tradition* (London: Routledge, 1999), 150, 152.

16. Interview with Vernon Smith, August 19, 2008. All Smith quotes from this interview.

17. For a history of methodological individualism, see Lars Udehn, *Methodological Individualism: Background, History, and Meaning* (London: Routledge, 2001). James S. Coleman quoted from Coleman, "Collective Decisions," *Social Inquiry* 34 (1964): 167.

18. Interview with Steven Brams, December 21, 2008. All quotes from this interview.

19. The Royal Swedish Academy of Sciences, "This Year's Laureate Has Extended the Sphere of Economic Analysis to New Areas of Human Behavior and Relations," Bank of Sweden [Nobel] Prize in Economic Sciences press release, October 13, 1992; Gary S. Becker, *The Economic Approach to Human Behavior* (Chicago: University of Chicago Press, 1976), 4. See also Gary S. Becker, "The Economic Way of Looking at Life," Nobel Memorial Lecture, December 9, 1992 (at http://nobelprize.org/nobel_prizes/economics/laureates/1992/becker-lecture.pdf).

20. Becker, *The Economic Approach to Human Behavior*, 8; Jack Hirshfleifer, "The Expanding Domain of Economics," *American Economic Review* 75 (December 1985): 53.

21. Douglas Clement, "Interview with Gary Becker," *The Region* 16 (June 2002): 16–25 (at www.minneapolisfed.org/publications_papers/pub_display.cfm?id=3407).

22. Emile Durkheim, *The Elementary Forms of Religious Life*, trans. Karen E. Fields (New York: Free Press, 1995), 426.

23. Raymond Boudon, "The 'Cognitivist Model': A Generalized 'Rational-Choice Model,'" *Rationality and Society* 8 (1996): 146–47.

24. Raymond Boudon, "Subjective Rationality and the Explanation of Social Behavior," *Rationality and Society* 1 (October 1989): 175.

25. Richard Zeckhauser, "Comments: Behavioral Versus Rational Economics," in *Rational Choice: The Contrast Between Economics and Psychology*, 258.

26. Raymond Boudon, "Beyond Rational Choice Theory," *Annual Review of Sociology* 29 (2003): 13.

27. James A. Beckford, "Choosing Rationality," in *Research in the Social Scientific Study of Religion*, ed. David O. Moberg and Ralph L. Piedmont (Leiden: Brill, 2001), 12:3.

28. James V. Spickard, "Rethinking Religious Social Action: What Is 'Rational' About Rational-Choice Theory?" *Sociology of Religion* 59 (1998): 110.

29. Robert Wuthnow, *After the Baby Boomers* (Princeton, NJ: Princeton University Press, 2008), 256; Christopher G. Ellison, "Rational Choice Explanations of Individual Religious Behavior: Notes on the Problem of Social Embeddedness," *Journal for the Scientific Study of Religion* 34 (1995): 90.

30. Laurence R. Iannaccone, "Rational Choice: Framework for the Scientific Study of Religion," in *Rational Choice Theory and Religion: Summary and Assessment*, ed. Lawrence A. Young (New York: Routledge, 1997), 26.

31. Rodney Stark and Roger Finke, *Acts of Faith: Explaining the Human Side of Religion* (Berkeley: University of California Press, 2000), 37.

32. Ibid. 38, 41.

33. Laurence R. Iannaccone, Rodney Stark, and Roger Finke, "Rationality and the 'Religious Mind,'" *Economic Inquiry* 36 (July 1998): 384, 387.

Chapter 3

1. Pew Forum on Religion and Public Life, "Changes in Americans' Religious Affiliation," *U.S. Religious Landscape Survey* (Washington, D.C., 2008), 33 (at http://religions.pewforum.org/reports).

2. David Voas and Alasdair Crockett, "Religion in Britain: Neither Believing nor Belonging," *Sociology* 39 (February 2005): 11–28.

3. In analyzing the "bargaining" between husband and wife, some economists recommend using "game theory," which looks at how rival, or competitive, spousal interests work toward a best-possible equilibrium. See Shelly Lundberg and Robert Pollak, "Bargaining and Distribution in Marriage," *Journal of Economic Perspectives* 10 (1996): 139–58.

4. See J. Stolz, "Salvation Goods and Religious Markets," *Social Compass* 53 (March 1, 2006): 13–32; Andrew M. Greeley, *Religious Change in America* (Cambridge, MA: Harvard University Press, 1989), 123.

5. Alfred Marshall, *Principles of Economics*, vol. 1, 3rd ed. (London: Macmillan, 1895), 643.

6. George J. Stigler and Gary S. Becker, "De Gustibus Non Est Disputandum," *American Economic Review* 67 (1977): 76–90.

7. Mark J. Machina, "States of the World and the State of Decision Theory," in *The Economics of Risk*, ed. Donald J. Meyer (Kalamazoo, MI: W. E. Upjohn Institute for Employment Research, 2003), 20–21.

8. Laurence R. Iannaccone, "Religious Practice: A Human Capital Approach," *Journal for the Scientific Study of Religion* 29 (1990): 299; Rodney Stark and Roger Finke, *Acts of Faith: Explaining the Human Side of Religion* (Berkeley: University of California Press, 2000), 120.

9. Gary S. Becker, "The Economic Way of Looking at Life," Nobel Memorial Lecture, December 9, 1992, 43 (at http://nobelprize.org/nobel_prizes/economics/laureates/1992/becker-lecture.pdf); Gary S. Becker, "A Theory of the Allocation of Time," *Economic Journal* 75 (1965): 493–517.

10. E-mail interview with Ronald Ehrenberg, March 19, 2008.

11. Corry Azzi and Ronald Ehrenberg, "Household Allocation of Time and Church Attendance," *Journal of Political Economy* 84 (1975): 27–56.

12. Interview with Laurence R. Iannaccone, May 5, 2008; Iannaccone, "Religious Practice," 297–314.

13. Douglas J. Davies and Mathew Guest, *Bishops, Wives, and Children: Spiritual Capital Across the Generations* (Aldershot: Ashgate, 2007), 147–48.

14. Marie Wachline, *Bible Literacy Report* (Front Royal, VA: Bible Literacy Project, 2005), 33 (at http://www.bibleliteracy.org/Secure/Documents/BibleLiteracyReport2005.pdf).

15. U.S. Department of Transportation, *Summary of Travel Trends: 2001 National Household Travel Survey*, December 2004 (at http://nhts.ornl.gov/2001/pub/STT.pdf).

16. Tuhin K. Das and Ishita Datta Ray, "Market of Religion in West Bengal," in *West Bengal Economy: Some Contemporary Issues*, ed. A Raychaudhuri and T. K. Das (New Delhi: Allied, 2005), 470–500.

17. Masamichi Sasaki and Tatsuzo Suzuki, "Changes in Religious Commitment in the United States, Holland, and Japan," *American Journal of Sociology* 92 (1987): 1073; Alan S. Miller, "Why Japanese Religions Look Different: the Social Role of Religious Organizations in Japan," *Review of Religious Research* 39 (June 1998): 362.

18. Dean R. Hoge, "Introduction: The Problem of Understanding Church Giving," *Review of Religious Research* 36 (December, 1994): 103.

19. Eli Berman, Laurence R. Iannaccone, and Giuseppe Ragusa, "From Empty Pews to Empty Cradles: Fertility Decline Among European Catholics," May 2007 (at http://econ.ucsd.edu/~elib/pews.pdf).

20. Eli Berman, "Sect, Subsidy and Sacrifice: An Economist's View of Ultra-Orthodox Jews," *Quarterly Journal of Economics* 115 (2000): 905–53; Arland Thornton, "Religion and Fertility: The Case of the Mormons," *Journal of Marriage and Family* 41 (1979): 131–42; Tim B. Heaton, "How Does Religion Influence Fertility? The Case of the Mormons," *Journal for the Scientific Study of Religion* 25 (1986): 248–58; Lester E. Bush, "Birth Control among the Mormons: Introduction to an Insistent Question," *Dialogue* 10 (1976): 12–44.

21. Laurence R. Iannaccone and Sean F. Everton, "Never on Sun(ny) Days: Lessons from Church Attendance Counts," *Journal for the Scientific Study of Religion* 43 (2004): 191–207.

22. C. Kirk Hadaway and Penny Long Marler, "All in the Family: Religious Mobility in America," *Review of Religious Research* 35 (1993): 97.

23. William Samuelson and Richard Zeckhauser, "Status Quo Bias in Decision Making," *Journal of Risk and Uncertainty* 1 (1988): 7–59.

24. Samuel A. Mueller, "Dimensions of Interdenominational Mobility in the United States," *Journal for the Scientific Study of Religion* 10 (1971): 76–84.

25. Andrew M. Greeley, *Religious Change in America* (Cambridge, MA: Harvard University Press, 1989), 123, 122.

26. Pew Forum, *U.S. Religious Landscape Survey*, 5.

27. Ibid., 27.

28. Richard N. Ostling, "The Generation that Forgot God," *Time*, April 5, 1993, 44–45.

29. Iannaccone, "Religious Practice," 301.

30. Darren E. Sherkat, "Tracking the Restructuring of American Religion: Religious Affiliation and Patterns of Religious Mobility, 1973–1978," *Social Forces* 79 (June 2001): 1485.

31. Harry Travis, "Religious In-Marriage and Intermarriage in Canada 1934–1969: A Methodological and Empirical Investigation." Working Paper 76-36. University of Wisconsin Center for Demography and Ecology, 1976; Thomas P. Monahan, "The

Extent of Interdenominational Marriage in the United States," *Journal for the Scientific Study of Religion* 10 (summer 1971): 90. See also Andrew Greeley, "Religious Intermarriage in a Denominational Society," American Journal of Sociology 75 (May 1970): 949–52. He reports that "denominational homogeneity exists for at least three-quarters of the [membership of the] major religious denominations."

32. Pew Forum, *U.S. Religious Landscape Survey*, 34.

33. Cokie Roberts and Steven V. Roberts, *From This Day Forward* (New York: William Morrow, 2000), 20.

34. Iannaccone quoted from his longer first draft for, "Religious Practice," 301–2.

35. Roberts, *From This Day Forward*, 352.

36. Cynthia Woolever and Deborah Bruce, *A Field Guide to U.S. Congregations: Who's Going Where and Why* (Louisville, KY: Westminster John Knox, 2002), 13, 14.

37. Rodney Stark, "Age and Faith: A Changing Outlook or an Old Process?" *Sociological Analysis* 29 (1968): 10.

38. Das, "Market of Religion in West Bengal," 470–500. Alan S. Miller, "Conventional Religious Behavior in Modern Japan: A Service Industry Approach," *Journal for the Scientific Study of Religion* 31 (1992): 213.

Chapter 4

1. Laurence R. Iannaccone, "Introduction to the Economics of Religion," *Journal of Economic Literature* 36 (September 1998): 1491.

2. Brian J. Osoba, "Risk, Discounting, and Religious Choice: Evidence from Panel Data," paper presented at the annual meeting of the Association for the Study of Religion, Economics, and Culture, October 22, 2004 (at www.religionomics.com/old/erel/S2-Archives/REC04/Osoba%20-%20Risk%20and%20Religious%20Choice.pdf).

3. Ibid.

4. John T. Durkin Jr. and Andrew M. Greeley, "A Model of Religious Choice Under Uncertainty," *Rationality and Society* 3 (April 1991): 178.

5. Ibid., 179.

6. Ulrich Blum and Leonard Dudley, "Religion and Economic Growth: Was Weber Right?" *Journal of Evaluative Economics* 11 (2001): 207–30.

7. Mary Douglas and A. Wildavsky, *Risk and Culture: An Essay on the Selection of Technological and Environmental Dangers* (Berkeley: University of California Press, 1982), 8.

8. Laurence R. Iannaccone, "Risk, Rationality, and Religious Portfolios," *Economic Inquiry* 33 (April 1995): 288.

9. James R. Lewis and J. Gordon Melton, eds. *Perspectives on the New Age* (Albany, NY: State University of New York Press, 1992).

10. M. R. Darby and E. Karni, "Free Competition and the Optimal Amount of Fraud," *Journal of Law and Economics* 16 (April 1973): 67–88. The authors note that consumers usually deal with potential fraud in the marketplace by "search" and

"experience" consumption, but the authors add "credence" goods as a type that needs extra verification of reliability (68).

11. Robert B. Ekelund Jr., Robert F. Hebert, and Robert D. Tollison, *The Market-place of Christianity* (Cambridge, MA: MIT Press, 2006), 28.

12. Brooks B. Hull and Frederick Bold, "Towards an Economic Theory of the Church," *International Journal of Social Economics* 16 (1989): 11.

13. P. Nelson, "Information and Consumer Behavior," *Journal of Political Economy* 78 (March/April 1970): 311–29; P. Nelson, "Advertising as Information," *Journal of Political Economy* 82 (July/August 1974): 729–54.

14. B. Klein and K. B. Leffler, "The Role of Market Forces in Assuring Contractual Performance," *Journal of Political Economy* 89 (August 1981): 615–42.

15. Hull and Bold, "Towards an Economic Theory of the Church," 11.

16. Dahlenburg quoted in James Mellado, "Willow Creek Community Church (A)," Harvard Business School case study, February 23, 1999, 9.

17. Sherwin Rosen, "The Economics of Superstars," *American Economic Review* 71 (1981): 845.

18. Melford E. Spiro, "Religion and the Irrational," in *Symposium on New Approaches to the Study of Religion*, ed. June Helm (Seattle: University of Washington Press, 1964), 105.

19. Steven J. Brams, *Superior Beings: If They Exist, How Would We Know?* (New York: Springer-Verlag, 1983), 164.

20. Rodney Stark and Roger Finke, *Acts of Faith: Explaining the Human Side of Religion* (Berkeley: University of California Press, 2000), 107.

21. Rodney Stark and William Sims Bainbridge, *A Theory of Religion* (New York: Peter Lang, 1987), 85.

22. Alan S. Miller, "Going to Hell in Asia: The Relationship Between Risk and Religion in a Cross Cultural Setting," *Review of Religious Research* 42 (2000): 5–18.

23. Eric Y. Liu, "Are Risk-Taking Persons Less Religious? Risk-Preference, Religious Affiliation, and Religious Participation in Taiwan," paper presented at the annual meeting of the Association for the Study of Religion, Economics, and Culture, April 3–5, 2009 (at www.religionomics.com/asrec/ASREC09_Papers/Liu%20-%20Risk%20-%20ASREC09.doc).

24. Brian Davies and Gillian Evans, eds., *Anselm of Canterbury: Major Works* (Oxford: Oxford University Press, 1998), 77.

25. Tetzel quoted in Diarmaid MacCulloch, *The Reformation: A History* (New York: Viking Penguin, 2004), 123. Another Tetzel doggerel is: "When clinking coin the cash-bell rings; The soul from purging fires springs." Quoted in Robert Herndon Fife, *The Revolt of Martin Luther* (New York: Columbia University Press, 1957), 255.

26. Dominic D. P. Johnson, "God's Punishment and Public Goods: A Test of the Supernatural Punishment Hypothesis in 186 World Cultures," *Human Nature* 16 (Winter 2005): 426.

27. Brooks B. Hull and Frederick Bold, "Hell, Religion, and Cultural Change," *Journal of Institutional and Theoretical Economics* 150 (1994): 453.

28. Ibid., 454.

29. Ibid.

30. Stephen R. Prothero, *American Jesus: How the Son of God Became a National Icon* (New York: Farrar, Straus, and Giroux, 2003).

Chapter 5

1. Ronald H. Coase, "The Nature of the Firm," *Economica* 4 (November 1937): 386–405.

2. James M. Buchanan, "An Economic Theory of Clubs," *Economica* 32 (1965): 1–14.

3. For this history I have relied upon Damien Keown, *Buddhism: A Very Short Introduction* (Oxford: Oxford University Press, 1996), and Charles S. Prebish, ed., *Buddhism: A Modern Perspective* (University Park: Pennsylvania State University Press, 1994). See also Ian Mabbett, "The Beginnings of Buddhism," *History Today* 52 (January 2002): 24.

4. Houston Smith, *The World's Religions* (San Francisco: HarperSanFrancisco, 1991), 92.

5. Laurence R. Iannaccone, "Sacrifice and Stigma: Reducing Free-Riding in Cults, Communes, and Other Collectives," *Journal of Political Economy* 100 (1992): 271, 272.

6. Daniel L. Chen, "Club Goods and Group Identity: Evidence from Islamic Resurgence During the Indonesian Financial Crisis," *Journal of Political Economy* (forthcoming).

7. Smith, *The World's Religions,* 125.

8. Adam Smith, *The Wealth of Nations, Books IV–V* (London: Penguin Books, 1999 [1776]), 385.

9. Smith, *The World's Religions*, 92–93.

10. Emile Durkheim, *The Elementary Forms of Religious Life*, trans. Karen E. Fields (New York: Free Press, 1995), 41, 42.

11. Laurence R. Iannaccone, "Introduction to the Economics of Religion," *Journal of Economic Literature* 36 (September 1998): 1491.

12. Robert B. Ekelund Jr., Robert F. Hebert, and Robert D. Tollison, *The Marketplace of Christianity* (Cambridge, MA: MIT Press, 2006), 64, 27. See also Robert B. Ekelund Jr. et. al, *Sacred Trust: The Medieval Church as an Economic Firm* (New York: Oxford University Press, 1996). On property rights, see also Douglas Allen, "Border in the Church: A Property Rights Approach," *Journal of Economic Behavior* 27 (1990): 97–117.

13. Ekelund, *The Marketplace of Christianity*, 62.

14. Tim Harford, *The Undercover Economist: Exposing Why the Rich Are Rich, the Poor Are Poor—and Why You Can Never Buy a Decent Used Car!* (New York: Oxford University Press, 2006), 5–29.

15. Ekelund, *The Marketplace of Christianity*, 58.

16. Rachel M. McCleary and Leonard W. J. van der Kuijp, "The Formation of the Tibetan State Religion: The Geluk School 1419–1642." Center for International Development Working Paper no. 154, Harvard University, December 2007 (rev. January 2008), ii, 1 (at http://www.cid.harvard.edu/cidwp/pdf/154.pdf).

17. McCleary, "The Formation of the Tibetan State Religion," 1.

18. See Iannaccone, "Sacrifice and Stigma."

19. Barak D. Richman, "How Community Institutions Create Economic Advantage: Jewish Diamond Merchants in New York," *Law and Social Inquiry* 31 (Spring 2006): 413. Richman's discussion with the diamond cutter is quoted in an early version of his study.

20. George J. Stigler, "The Economies of Scale," *Journal of Law and Economics* 1 (1958): 54–71.

21. Robert J. Stonebraker, "Optimal Church Size: The Bigger the Better?" *Journal for the Scientific Study of Religion* 32 (1993): 231–41; Stephanie M. Brewer, James J. Jozefowicz, and Robert J. Stonebraker, "Religious Free Riders: The Impact of Market Share," *Journal for the Scientific Study of Religion* 45 (September 2006): 389–96.

22. Kenneth G. Elzinga and Colin T. Page, "Congregational Economies of Scale and the Megachurch: An Application of the Stigler Survivor Technique," paper presented at the annual meeting of the Association for the Study of Religion, Economics, and Culture, April 4, 2009.

23. Joseph A. Schumpeter, "The Creative Response in Economic History," *Journal of Economic History* 7 (1947): 149–59; Joseph A. Schumpeter, "The Process of Creative Destruction," in Schumpeter, *Capitalism, Socialism and Democracy* (New York: Harper, 1942), 81–106.

24. Peter Drucker, "What Business Can Learn from Nonprofits," *Harvard Business Review*, July-August 1989, 88–93.

25. Bill Hybels, *Courageous Leadership* (Grand Rapids, MI: Zondervan, 2002), 70, 71.

26. Osteen quoted in "Interview with Joel Osteen," *Larry King Live*, CNN, June 20, 2005. The financial figures come from "Joel Osteen Answers His Critics," *CBS* "60 Minutes," December 23, 2007 (author's transcripts).

27. Scott Thumma, "The Business of Megachurches," paper presented at the annual meeting of the Association for the Study of Religion, Economics, and Culture, October 2006.

28. See James Mellado, "Willow Creek Community Church (A)," Harvard Business School case study, February 23, 1999.

29. Scott Thumma, "The View from the Comfy Padded Pew: New Data on Megachurch Attendees," paper presented at the annual meeting of the Association for the Study of Religion, Economics, and Culture, April 4, 2009.

30. Thumma, "The Business of Megachurches."

31. Darren Sherkat, "Embedding Religious Choices: Integrating Preferences and Social Constraints into Rational Choice Theories of Religious Behavior," in *Rational Choice Theory and Religion: Summary and Assessment*, ed. Lawrence A. Young (New York: Routledge, 1997), 68.

Chapter 6

1. In his *Wealth of Nations*, Adam Smith presents most of his economic concepts of religion in a section on public funding and education. See *Wealth of Nations*, book 5, part 3, articles 2–3.

2. Themistius quoted in Peter Heather and David Moncur, ed. and trans., *Politics, Philosophy, and Empire in the Fourth Century: Select Orations of Themistius* (Liverpool: Liverpool University Press, 2001), 168.

3. Theodore Caplow et al., *All Faithful People: Change and Continuity in Middletown's Religion* (Minneapolis: University of Minnesota Press, 1983), 20. See pp. 20–30 for Caplow's inventory of religion surveys from 1924 to the 1970s.

4. Gerhard Lenski, *The Religious Factor: A Sociological Study of Religion's Impact on Politics, Economics, and Family Life* (Garden City, NY: Doubleday, 1961), 15–16, 289–97.

5. Charles Y. Glock, "The Religious Revival in America?" in *Religion and the Face of America*, ed. Jane Zahn (Berkeley: University of California Extension, 1959), 41. For a history of this period, see also Jeffrey K. Hadden, "Toward Desacralizing Secularization Theory," *Social Forces* (1987): 587–611.

6. George C. Homans, *The Human Group* (New York: Harcourt, Brace and World, 1950), 321.

7. George C. Homans, *Social Behavior: Its Elementary Forms* (New York: Harcourt, Brace and World, 1961), 12. Here, Homans says his basic propositions arise from "behavioral psychology and elementary economics." In the revised edition of *Social Behavior* (New York: Harcourt Brace Jovanovich, 1974), Homans formalizes his propositions into exact statements.

8. George C. Homans, "Bringing Men Back In," in *Certainties and Doubts: Collected Papers, 1962–1985* (New Brunswick, NJ: Transaction, 1989), 8, 12–13.

9. For the UFO story, see Rodney Stark, *Exploring the Religious Life* (Baltimore: Johns Hopkins University Press, 2004), 165–67. For the Italian church story, see Rodney Stark, "Catholic Contexts: Competition, Commitment and Innovation," *Review of Religious Research* 39 (March 1998): 206.

10. John Lofland, *Doomsday Cult: A Study of Conversion, Proselytization, and Maintenance of Faith*, enlarged ed. (New York: Irvington, 1977), 344.

11. Rodney Stark, "Bringing Theory Back In," in *Rational Choice Theories of Religion: Summary and Assessment*, ed. Lawrence A. Young (New York: Routledge, 1997), 10.

12. Rodney Stark and William Sims Bainbridge, "Toward a Theory of Religion: Religious Commitment," *Journal for the Scientific Study of Religion* 19 (1980): 114–28 (axiom 2, 115; axiom 5, 118).

13. Charles Y. Glock and Rodney Stark, *Religion and Society in Tension* (Chicago: Rand McNally, 1965), 9–11; Rodney Stark and Roger Finke, *Acts of Faith: Explaining the Human Side of Religion* (Berkeley: University of California Press, 2000), 89, 91.

14. Milton Friedman "The Methodology of Positive Economics," in Milton Friedman, *Essays in Positive Economics* (Chicago: University of Chicago Press, 1953).

15. Douglas Clement, "Interview with Gary Becker," *The Region* 16 (June 2002): 16–25 (also at http://www.minneapolisfed.org/publications_papers/pub_display.cfm?id=3407).

16. Gary S. Becker, *The Economic Approach to Human Behavior* (Chicago: University of Chicago Press, 1976), 8.

17. Ibid., 14.

18. Interview with Roger Finke, January 24, 2008.

19. Stark, "Bringing Theory Back In," 19.

20. Interview with Finke, January 24, 2008; Stark, "Bringing Theory Back In," 19.

21. Martin Marty, "The Churching of America: Winners and Losers in Our Religious Economy," *Christian Century* 110 (January 27, 1993): 88.

22. Interview with Laurence R. Iannaccone, May 5, 2008.

23. E-mail interview with Ronald Ehrenberg, May 19, 2008.

24. Interview with Timur Kuran, January 26, 2009. For an overview of Kuran's argument, see Timur Kuran, "The Islamic Commercial Crisis: Institutional Roots of Economic Underdevelopment in the Middle East," *Journal of Economic History* 63 (2003): 414–46. His earliest work is Timur Kuran, "Behavioral Norms in the Islamic Doctrine of Economics: A Critique," *Journal of Economic Behavior and Organization* 44 (December 1983): 353–79.

25. Interview with Iannaccone, May 5, 2008.

26. Interview with Finke, January 24, 2008.

27. Interview with Iannaccone, May 5, 2008.

28. Laurence R. Iannaccone, "Introduction to the Economics of Religion," *Journal of Economic Literature* 36 (September 1998): 1491–2.

29. Stephen R. Warner, "Work in Progress Toward a New Paradigm for the Sociological Study of Religion in the United States," *American Journal of Sociology* 98 (1993): 1044–93. See also Andrew M. Greeley, *Religious Change in America* (Cambridge, MA: Harvard University Press, 1989), 121–23.

30. Stark, "Bringing Theory Back In," 21.

31. Deepak Lal, *Cultural Stability and Economic Stagnation: India, c. 1500* bc–ad *1980* (New York: Oxford University Press, 1988). See Martin Marty et al., eds., *Fundamentalisms and the State: Remaking Polities, Economies, and Militance*, vol. 3: *The Fundamentalism Project* (University of Chicago Press, 1993). The four essayists were Lal (Hinduism), Iannaccone (Christianity), Kuran (Islam) and Charles Keyes (Buddhism).

32. Interview with Anthony Gill, December 15, 2008; see Anthony Gill, *Rendering unto Caesar: The Catholic Church and the State in Lain America* (Chicago: University of Chicago Press, 1998); quoted in Anthony Gill, *The Political Origins of Religious Liberty* (Cambridge: Cambridge University Press, 2008), 8; Timothy Samuel Shah, "The Accumulation of Many Laws," book review, *Review of Politics* 71 (2009): 330.

33. Brian J. Grim, "Triangulating the World's Most Dynamic Religious Market: Africa Using a Quanti-Qualitative Method (QQM)," paper presented at the annual meeting of the Association for the Study of Religion, Economics, and Culture, November 2, 2007; Rebecca Samuel Shah, "How Spiritual Capital Promotes Economic Betterment: The Case of Dalit Conversions to Christianity in India," paper presented at the annual meeting of the Association for the Study of Religion, Economics, and Culture, April 3, 2009. The Finke project is the Association of Religion Data Archives: www.TheARDA.com. For the Islamic archive, see Timur Kuran, Duke University. The survey of Buddhism is being conducted by J. Gordon Melton, Institute for the Study of American Religion, and editor of *Melton's Encyclopedia of American Religion*.

34. Charles Y. Glock and Phillip E. Hammond, *Beyond the Classics?* (New York: Harper and Row, 1973); Phillip E. Hammond, ed., *The Sacred in a Secular Age* (Berkeley: University of California Press, 1985), 2.

Chapter 7

1. Henry Ford, *Today and Tomorrow* (Garden City, NY: Doubleday, 1926), 21.

2. "Religious economy" was coined by Stark in 1983, although the idea has been around for a few centuries. "Religious marketplace" and "religious economy" are virtual synonyms. Stark and Finke define the latter: "A religious economy consists of all of the religious activity going on in any society: a 'market' of current and potential adherents, a set of one or more organizations seeking to attract or maintain adherents, and the religious culture offered by the organizations(s)." See Rodney Stark and Roger Finke, *Acts of Faith: Explaining the Human Side of Religion* (Berkeley: University of California Press, 2000), 193.

3. Robert J. Barro and Rachel M. McCleary, "Which Countries Have a State Religion," *Quarterly Journal of Economics* 120 (November 2005): 1331–70.

4. Brooks B. Hull and Gerald Moran, "A Preliminary Time Series Analysis of Church Activity in Colonial Woodbury, Connecticut," *Journal for the Scientific Study of Religion* 28 (1989): 478–92.

5. For a complete marketplace interpretation of Whitefield's career, see Frank Lambert, *"Pedlar in Divinity": George Whitefield and the Transatlantic Revivals* (Princeton, NJ: Princeton University Press, 1994).

6. The idea of sociodemographic niches was developed in Peter M. Blau, "A Macrosociological Theory of Social Structure," *American Journal of Sociology* 83 (1977): 26–54. He called these segments "structural parameters." Sociologist Roger Finke calls them "preference dimensions" so as to focus not on demographic traits but on elements of religion: beliefs, styles, and rules.

7. Adam Smith, *The Wealth of Nations, Books IV–V* (London: Penguin Books, 1999 [1776]), 381–82.

8. Gary Becker, *The Economic Approach to Human Behavior* (Chicago: University of Chicago Press, 1976), 5.

9. Stark and Finke, *Acts of Faith*, 195–98.

10. H. Richard Niebuhr, *The Social Sources of Denominationalism* (New York: Meridian Books, 1957), 232, 201.

11. Ibid., 221.

12. Benton Johnson, "On Church and Sect," *American Sociological Review* 28 (1963): 539–49.

13. Rodney Stark and William Sims Bainbridge, *The Future of Religion: Secularization, Revival, and Cult Formation* (Berkeley: University of California Press, 1985), 25–26.

14. For an economic model of how the preferences or loyalties of individuals can shift entire denominations between strict and liberal niches, see James D. Montgomery, "Dynamics of the Religious Economy: Exit, Voice and Denominational Secularization," *Rationality and Society* 8 (1996): 81–110.

15. Dean M. Kelley, *Why Conservative Churches Are Growing: A Study in the Sociology of Religion* (New York: Harper and Row), 1972. Kelley clarified the book's point in Kelley, *Why Conservative Churches Are Growing* (Macon, GA: Mercer University Press, 1986), xvii; see also Stark and Finke, *Acts of Faith*, 194.

16. For a critical history of Sōka Gakkai, see H. Neill McFarland, *The Rush Hour of the Gods: A Study of the New Religious Movements in Japan* (New York; Harper and Row, 1967), 194–20; the membership figure comes from "Sōka Gakkai," in *The Perennial Dictionary of World Religions*, ed. Keith Crim (San Francisco: Harper and Row, 1981), 697.

17. For data on sects and cults in the western United States and Canada, see Stark and Bainbridge, *The Future of Religion*, 429–56, 457–74.

18. On the numbers in Europe, see Rodney Stark, "Europe's Receptivity to Cults and Sects," in *The Future of Religion*, 475–505.

19. Smith, *The Wealth of Nations, Books IV–V*, 375–76.

20. Wesley quoted in Robert Southey, *The Life of John Wesley and the Rise and Progress of Methodism* (New York: Harper and Brothers, 1847), 2:308. Wesley is quoted in full by Weber in *The Protestant Ethic* (175), where Weber puts in his own italics to emphasize Wesley's capitalist spirit: "We ought not to prevent people from being diligent and frugal; *we must exhort all Christians to gain all they can, and save all they can; that is, in effect, to grow rich.*"

21. Christopher P. Scheitle and Roger Finke, "Pluralism as Outcome: Resource Distributions and Organizational Diversity," working paper provided to the author, June 2009.

22. On specialized groups and niches, see Michael T. Hannan and John Freeman, "The Population Ecology of Organizations," *American Journal of Sociology* 82 (1977): 929–64. On the rarity and challenge of heterogeneous groups, see Brad Christerson and Michael Emerson, "The Costs of Diversity in Religious Organizations," *Sociology of Religion* 64 (2003): 163–81.

23. J. Gordon Melton, ed., *Melton's Encyclopedia of American Religion*, 8th ed. (Detroit: Gale, Cengage Learning, 2009).

24. Niebuhr, *The Social Sources*, 230.

25. Ibid., 230, 234.

26. For the debate on pluralism, see Daniel V. A. Olson, "Religious Pluralism and U.S. Church Membership: A Reassessment," *Sociology of Religion* 60 (1999): 149–73; Mark Chaves and Philip S. Gorski, "Religious Pluralism and Religious Participation," *Annual Review of Sociology* 27 (2001): 261–81; David Voas, Daniel V. A. Olson, and Alasdair Crockett, "Religious Pluralism and Participation: Why Previous Research is Wrong," *American Sociological Review* 67 (2002): 212–30.

27. R. Phillips, "Religious Market Share and Mormon Church Activity," *Sociology of Religion* 59 (1998): 117–30. On the Mormon exception, sociologist Darren Sherkat says: "The religious monopoly enjoyed by the Mormons in Utah should not lead to low levels of religious activity if most in Utah prefer the religious goods provided by the Church of Latter-Day Saints, or if substitutes for religious participation are unavailable." See Darren E. Sherkat, "Preferences, Constraints, and Choices in Religious Markets: An Examination of Religious Switching and Apostasy," *Social Forces* 73 (March 1995): 1017.

28. Massimo Introvigne, "Niches in the Islamic Religious Market and Fundamentalism: Examples from Turkey and Other Countries," *Interdisciplinary Journal of Research on Religion* (online), 1 (January 2005), article no. 3, 2 (at http://www.bepress.com/ijrr/vol1/iss1/art3).

29. Ibid., 6.

30. Ibid., 16.

31. Between 2000 and 2004, the number of "religion surfers" rose from 20 million to 82 million. Most of them said the Internet "supplements their ties to traditional institutions" rather than offering an alternative. See Pew Internet and American Life Project, "64% of Online Americans Have Used the Internet for Religious or Spiritual Purposes," press release for the "Faith Online" study, Washington, D.C., April 7, 2004 (at http://www.pewinternet.org).

32. Robert B. Ekelund Jr., Robert F. Hebert, and Robert D. Tollison, *The Marketplace of Christianity* (Cambridge, MA: MIT Press, 2006), 74–79.

33. Anthony Gill, *The Political Origins of Religious Liberty* (Cambridge: Cambridge University Press, 2008).

34. Anthony Gill, *Rendering unto Caesar: The Catholic Church and the State in Lain America* (Chicago: University of Chicago Press, 1998), 85.

35. Ibid., 106.

36. Fenggang Yang, "The Red, Black, and Gray Markets of Religion in China," *Sociological Quarterly* 47 (2006): 99, 94.

37. Ibid., 99.

38. Ibid., 114.

Chapter 8

1. Robert S. Lynd and Helen Merrell Lynd, *Middletown: A Study in American Culture* (New York: Harcourt Brace, 1956 [1929]); Robert S. Lynd and Helen Merrell Lynd, *Middletown in Transition: A Study in Cultural Conflicts* (New York: Harcourt Brace, 1965 [1937]), 306–7.

2. Theodore Caplow et al., *All Faithful People: Change and Continuity in Middletown's Religion* (Minneapolis: University of Minnesota Press, 1983).

3. Jeffrey K. Hadden, "Toward Desacralizing Secularization Theory," *Social Forces* 65 (1987): 598.

4. Rodney Stark and William Sims Bainbridge, *The Future of Religion: Secularization, Revival, and Cult Formation* (Berkeley: University of California Press, 1985), 1–2.

5. Bryan R. Wilson, *Religion in Sociological Perspective* (Oxford: Oxford University Press, 1982), 154; Bryan R. Wilson, "The Debate over 'Secularization,'" *Encounter* 14 (1975): 80.

6. Peter L. Berger, *The Sacred Canopy: Elements of a Sociological Theory of Religion* (Garden City, NY: Doubleday, 1967), 107–8.

7. Peter L. Berger, *The Heretical Imperative: Contemporary Possibilities of Religious Affirmation* (Garden City, NY: Anchor Press, 1979).

8. Berger, *The Sacred Canopy*, 129.

9. Baylor Institute for Studies of Religion, "Paranormal America," in *American Piety in the 21st Century*, September 2006, 45–50 (at www.baylor.edu/content/services/document.php/33304.pdf).

10. Harvey Cox, *The Secular City* (New York: Macmillan, 1965), 1.

11. Wilson, "The Debate over 'Secularization,'" 77.

12. Lynd, *Middletown: A Study in American Culture*, 407, 406.

13. Caplow, *All Faithful People*, 37, 35, 38.

14. Hadden, "Toward Desacralizing Secularization Theory," 588.

15. Roger Finke and Rodney Stark, "Religious Economies and Sacred Canopies: Religious Mobilization in American Cities, 1906," *American Sociological Review* 53 (1988): 44.

16. Ibid., 44, 47.

17. Roger Finke and Rodney Stark, *The Churching of America, 1776–1900: Winners and Losers in Our Religious Economy* (New Brunswick, NJ: Rutgers University Press, 1992); Finke and Stark, "Religious Economies and Sacred Canopies," 47.

18. Rodney Stark and Laurence R. Iannaccone, "A Supply-Side Reinterpretation of the 'Secularization' of Europe," *Journal for the Scientific Study of Religion* 33 (1994): 231.

19. Wilson, "The Debate over 'Secularization,'" 80.

20. David Yamane, "Secularization on Trial: In Defense of the Neosecularization Paradigm," *Journal for the Scientific Study of Religion* 36 (1997): 109–22. See also Mark Chaves, "Secularization as Declining Religious Authority," *Social Forces* 72 (1994): 749–74.

21. David Martin, *A General Theory of Secularization* (New York: Harper and Row, 1978), 4–7, 18.

22. Peter Berger, Grace Davie, and Effie Fokas, *Religious America, Secular Europe? A Theme and Variations* (Aldershot: Ashgate, 2008), 2.

23. Stephen R. Warner, "Work in Progress Toward a New Paradigm for the Sociological Study of Religion in the United States," *American Journal of Sociology* 98 (1993): 1044–93.

24. Albert O. Hirschman, "The Paternity of an Index," *American Economic Review* 54 (September 1964): 761.

25. Laurence R. Iannaccone, "The Consequences of Religious Market Structure," *Rationality and Society* 3 (1991): 156–77; Rodney Stark, "Do Catholic Societies Really Exist," *Rationality and Society* 4 (1992): 261–71; James T. Duke, Barry L. Johnson, and James B. Duke, "Rates of Religious Conversion: A Macrosociological Study," *Research in the Sociology of Religion* (Greenwich, CT: JAI Press, 1993), 5:89–121.

26. Mark Chaves and David E. Cann, "Regulation, Pluralism, and Religious Market Structure," *Rationality and Society* 4 (1992): 272–90.

27. Wilson, *Religion in Sociological Perspective*, 150.

28. R. Martin Goodridge, "The Ages of Faith: Romance or Reality?" *Sociological Review* 23 (1975): 394.

29. Stark and Iannaccone, "A Supply-Side Reinterpretation of the 'Secularization' of Europe," 235.

30. Grace Davie, *Religion in Britain Since 1945: Believing Without Belonging* (Oxford: Basil Blackwell, 1994), 84; Grace Davie, *Europe, the Exceptional Case: Parameters of Faith in the Modern World* (London: Darton, Longman and Todd, 2002).

31. David Voas and Alasdair Crockett, "Religion in Britain: Neither Believing nor Belonging," *Sociology* 39 (February 2005): 25.

32. William H. Swatos Jr., "The Relevance of Religion: Iceland and Secularization Theory," *Journal for the Scientific Study of Religion* 23 (1984): 32–43.

33. Rodney Stark, Eva Hamberg, and Alan S. Miller, "Spirituality and Unchurched Religion in America, Sweden, and Japan," in Rodney Stark, *Exploring the Religious Life* (Baltimore: John Hopkins University Press, 2004), 114–35.

34. Steve Bruce, *Religion in the Modern World: From Cathedrals to Cults* (Oxford: Oxford University Press, 1996), 34, 58.

35. William H. Swatos Jr. and Kevin J. Christiano, "Secularization Theory: The Course of a Concept," *Sociology of Religion* 60 (1999): 222.

36. Dimitry Pospielovsky, *The Russian Church Under the Soviet Regime 1917–1982*, 2 vols. (Crestwood, NY: St. Vladimir's Seminary Press, 1984).

37. Paul Froese, *The Plot to Kill God: Findings from the Soviet Experiment in Secularization* (Berkeley: University of California Press, 2008).

38. Ibid., 184.

Chapter 9

1. Fischer quoted in David J. Chalcraft, "Introduction," in *The Protestant Ethic Debate: Max Weber's Replies to His Critics, 1907–1910* (Liverpool: Liverpool University Press, 2001), 32.

2. Max Weber, *The Protestant Ethic and the Spirit of Capitalism*, trans. Talcott Parsons (New York: Routledge, 1992 [1930]), 117, 124.

3. Ibid., 27.

4. Weber quoted in Chalcraft, "Introduction," 32; Weber, *The Protestant Ethic*, 38.

5. Michael Novak, *The Catholic Ethic and the Spirit of Capitalism* (New York: Free Press, 1993); Michael Novak, "Max Weber Goes Global," *First Things*, April 2005, 269. The classic criticism of Weber (for overlooking medieval Catholic developments, among other things) is Kurt Samuelsson, *Religion and Economic Action: A Critique of Max Weber*, trans. E. Geoffrey French (New York: Harper Touchstone, 1964 [1957]).

6. Arthur Lewis, *The Theory of Economic Growth* (London: George Allen and Unwin, 1955), 105.

7. Robert J. Barro, "Spirit of Capitalism: Religion and Economic Development," *Harvard International Review* 25 (2004): 67.

8. Alexis de Tocqueville, *Democracy in America* (New York: Vintage Books, 1990), 2:123.

9. Gary Becker, *Accounting for Tastes* (Cambridge, MA: Harvard University Press, 1996), 18.

10. On the quality needs of a workforce, see Anne Krueger, "Factor Endowments and Per Capita Income Differences Among Countries," *Economic Journal* 78 (1978): 641–59. See also Jan S. Hogendorn, *Economic Development* (New York: Harper and Row, 1987).

11. Alfred Marshall, *Principles of Economics*, 3rd ed. (London: Macmillan, 1895), 1:643.

12. Adam Smith, *The Wealth of Nations, Books IV–V* (London: Penguin Books, 1999 [1776]), 381–82.

13. Rebecca Samuel Shah, "How Spiritual Capital Promotes Economic Betterment: The Case of Dalit Conversions to Christianity in India," paper presented at the annual meeting of the Association for the Study of Religion, Economics, and Culture, April 3, 2009.

14. Joseph Potter and Robert D. Woodberry, "The Growth of Protestantism in Brazil and Its Impact on Income, 1970–2000," paper presented at the annual meeting of the Association for the Study of Religion, Economics, and Culture, April 3, 2009; Robert D. Woodberry, "Pentecostalism and Economic Development," in *Markets, Morals, and Religion*, ed. Jonathan B. Imber (New Brunswick, NJ: Transaction, 2008). See also David Martin, *Tongues of Fire: The Explosion of Protestantism in Latin America* (Oxford: Basil Blackwell, 1990).

15. James Q. Wilson, "Religion and Public Life," *Brookings Review* 17 (Spring 1999): 38–39; Donald Browning, "Human Development, Attachment, and Love," paper presented at the conference Empathy, Altruism and Agape, Boston, October 12, 1999.

16. Barro, "Spirit of Capitalism," 64.

17. Adam Smith, *The Wealth of Nations, Books I–III* (London: Penguin Books, 1999 [1776]), 119; Adam Smith, *The Theory of Moral Sentiments* (Amherst, NY: Prometheus Books, 2000 [1759]), 3.

18. Friedrich von Hayek, "Economics and Knowledge," in *Individualism and Economic Order* (Chicago: University of Chicago Press, 1949), 54.

19. Friedrich von Hayek, *The Fatal Conceit: The Errors of Socialism* (Chicago: University of Chicago Press, 1988), 18.

20. Vernon Smith, "Constructivist and Ecological Rationality in Economics," Nobel Memorial Lecture, December 8, 2002, 553 (at http://nobelprize.org/nobel_prizes/economics/laureates/2002/smith-lecture.pdf).

21. Weber quoted in Bryan S. Turner, *Max Weber: From History to Modernity* (London: Routledge, 1993), 47.

22. Nelly Hanna, *Making Big Money in 1600: The Life and Times of Isma'il Abu Taqiyya, Egyptian Merchant* (Syracuse, NY: Syracuse University Press, 1998).

23. Ibid., 41.

24. Timur Kuran, "The Logic of Financial Westernization in the Middle East," *Journal of Economic Behavior and Organization* 56 (April 2005): 593–615. For the success of religious minorities in the Middle East, see Timur Kuran, "The Economic Ascent of the Middle East's Religious Minorities: The Role of Islamic Legal Pluralism," *Journal of Legal Studies* 33 (June 2004): 475–515.

25. Interview with Timur Kuran, January 26, 2009.

26. Timur Kuran, *Islam and Mammon: The Economic Predicaments of Islamism* (Princeton, NJ: Princeton University Press, 2004), 26.

27. Ibid., 58, 55, 136.

28. World Bank, *World Development Report* (1985): 29.

29. Hanifan quoted in Robert D. Putnam and Kristin A. Goss, "Introduction," in *Democracies in Flux: The Evolution of Social Capital in Contemporary Society*, ed. Robert D. Putnam (New York: Oxford University Press, 2004), 4.

30. Laurence R. Iannaccone, "Religious Practice: A Human Capital Approach," *Journal for the Scientific Study of Religion* 29 (1990): 299; Peter L. Berger and Robert W. Hefner, "Spiritual Capital in Comparative Perspective," October 2003, 3 (at www. spiritualcapitalresearchprogram.com/pdf/Berger.pdf). On social capital applied to religion, see also Corwin Smidt, ed., *Religion as Social Capital: Producing the Common Good* (Waco, TX: Baylor University Press, 2003).

31. Rachel M. McCleary, "Religion and Economic Development," *Policy Review* 148 (2008): 50, 48, 50.

32. Ibid., 57.

33. Luigi Guiso, Paola Sapienzad, and Luigi Zingales, "People's Opium? Religion and Economic Attitudes," *Journal of Monetary Economics* 50 (January 2003): 225–82.

34. David B. Audretsch, Werner Boente, and Jagannadha Pawan Tamvada, "Religion and Entrepreneurship," Jena Economic Research Paper no. 2007-075, June 2007, 5–6, 13, 14 (at http://zs.thulb.uni-jena.de/receive/jportal_jparticle_00081757).

35. Joshua J. Lewer and Hendrik Van Den Berg, "Religion and International Trade: Does the Sharing of a Religious Culture Facilitate the Formation of Trade Networks?" *American Journal of Economics and Sociology* 66 (2007): 782.

36. Ibid., 782.

37. Philip Jenkins, *The New Christendom: The Coming of Global Christianity* (New York: Oxford University Press, 2002).

38. Kuran, *Islam and Mammon*, 70.

39. Putnam and Goss, "Introduction," *Democracies in Flux*, 8–9.

40. Mark Granovetter, "The Strength of Weak Ties: A Network Theory Revisited," *Sociological Theory* 1 (1983): 209. See also Mark Granovetter, "The Strength of Weak Ties," *American Journal of Sociology* 78 (1973): 1360–80.

41. Putnam and Goss, "Introduction," *Democracies in Flux*, 11–12.

42. Alan Krueger, *What Makes a Terrorist: Economics and the Roots of Terrorism* (Princeton, NJ: Princeton University Press, 2007).

43. Eli Berman, "Hamas, Taliban and the Jewish Underground: An Economist's View of Radical Religious Militias," NBER Working Paper 10004, National Bureau of Economic Research, September 2003. See also Eli Berman and Laurence R. Iannaccone, "Religious Extremism: The Good, the Bad, and the Deadly," NBER Working Paper 11663, September 2005; Eli Berman, Jacob N. Shapiro, and Joseph H. Felter, "Can Hearts and Minds Be Bought? The Economics of Counterinsurgency in Iraq," NBER Working Paper 14606, December 2008.

44. Eli Berman, *Radical, Religious, and Violent: The New Economics of Terrorism* (Cambridge, MA: MIT Press, 2009).

45. Eli Berman and David D. Laitin, "Religion, Terrorism and Public Goods: Testing the Club Model," NBER Working Paper 13725, National Bureau of Economic Research, January 2008.

46. Brian J. Grim and Roger Finke, "Religious Persecution in Cross-National Context: Clashing Civilizations or Regulated Religious Economies?" *American Sociological Review* 72 (August 2007): 633–58.

Chapter 10

1. Harvey Cox, "The Market as God: Living in the New Dispensation," *Atlantic Monthly* 283 (March 1999): 20.

2. Robert N. Nelson, *Economics as Religion: From Samuelson to Chicago and Beyond* (University Park: Pennsylvania State University Press, 2001), xv.

3. David Sloan Wilson, *Darwin's Cathedral: Evolution, Religion, and the Nature of Society* (Chicago: University of Chicago Press, 2002), 82, 85.

4. Gary Becker, "Altruism, Egoism, and Genetic Fitness: Economics and Sociobiology," in Gary Becker, *The Economic Approach to Human Behavior* (Chicago: University of Chicago Press, 1976), 282–94.

5. Brooks B. Hull and Frederick Bold, "Towards an Economic Theory of the Church," *International Journal of Social Economics* 16 (1989): 5–14.

6. John Brockman, ed., *What We Believe but Cannot Prove: Today's Leading Thinkers on Science in the Age of Certainty* (New York: Free Press, 2005).

7. For a defense of the supply side approach in history of religion, see Roger Finke, "Religious Deregulation: Origins and Consequences," *Journal of Church and State* 32 (Summer 1990): 609–26; Roger Finke and Laurence R. Iannaccone, "Supply-side Explanations for Religious Change," *Annals of the American Academy of Political and Social Science* 527 (May 1993): 27–39; Roger Finke, "The Illusion of Shifting Demand: Supply-Side Interpretations of American Religious History," in *Retelling U.S. Religious History*, ed. Thomas Tweed (Berkeley: University of California Press, 1997).

8. William G. McLoughlin, *Revivals, Awakenings, and Reform* (Chicago: University of Chicago Press, 1978), 2.

9. H. Neill McFarland, *The Rush Hour of the Gods: A Study of the New Religious Movements in Japan* (New York: Harper and Row, 1967), 12, 82.

10. Ibid., 224, 211.

11. Brian J. Grim and Roger Finke, "Religious Persecution in Cross-National Context: Clashing Civilizations or Regulated Religious Economies?" *American Sociological Review* 72 (August 2007): 633–58.

INDEX

Printed in the USA/Agawam, MA
August 9, 2016

638835.025